J.P.MORGAN

BY THE SAME AUTHOR

Guy de Maupassant
A Short Walk from the Temple
The Savoy
The Sassoons
The Great Barnato
Caruso
Monsieur Butterfly
Inside Monte Carlo
The Old Bailey

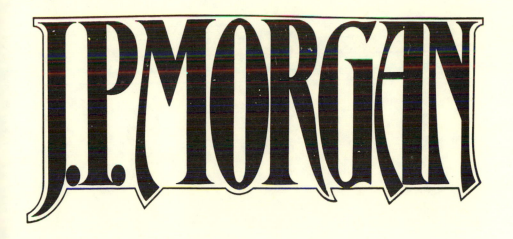

J. P. MORGAN

A BIOGRAPHY BY
STANLEY JACKSON

STEIN AND DAY/*Publishers*/New York

First published in 1983
Copyright © 1983 by Stanley Jackson
All rights reserved, Stein and Day, Incorporated
Designed by Louis A. Ditizio
Printed in the United States of America
STEIN AND DAY/*Publishers*
Scarborough House
Briarcliff Manor, N.Y. 10510

Library of Congress Cataloging in Publication Data

Jackson, Stanley.
  J. P. Morgan, a biography.

  Bibliography: p.
  Includes index.
  1. Morgan, John Pierpont, 1837–1913. 2. Bankers—
United States—Biography. 3. Capitalists and financiers—
United States—Biography. I. Title.
HG2463.M6J32   1983   332.1'092'4 [B]   81-40333
ISBN 0-8128-2824-0

For
My Daughter
Tisha Browne

"He was a great and good man."

—Pope Pius X

"A beefy thick-necked financial bully,
drunk with wealth and power, who bawls
his orders to stock markets, directors,
courts, governments and nations."

—Boston Commercial Bulletin

CONTENTS

Preface: The Riddle of J. P. Morgan 11
Part One. THE SOWING 19
Part Two. THE HARVEST 79
Part Three. THE STUBBLE 243
Postscript 313
Bibliography 325
Index 329

Illustrations

Morgan in 1903
Amelia Sturges, Morgan's first wife
Loan contract made during Franco-Prussian War
Junius Spencer Morgan
J. Pierpont Morgan, 1881
The Morgan Library
West Room of the Library
East Room of the Library
Morgan watching the Yale-Harvard race, 1910
J. P. Morgan, Jr.

PREFACE

THE RIDDLE OF
J. P. MORGAN

The New York banker arrived in Washington late on a chilly, windswept afternoon. No less a person than the Secretary for War had been dragooned for messenger duty and sent to the station to inform him that the president would not consent to receive him. The financial magnate responded, "I have come down to see the president, and I am going to stay here until I see him," and then calmly proceeded to his hotel suite at the Arlington.

It was the winter of 1895, and the U.S. Treasury would soon be unable to meet the demands for gold that were being made against it. It was on the verge of collapse. The government had offered a public issue of gold bonds in the previous year and had met with a poor response. President Cleveland, hampered by an unsympathetic congress, had no remaining methods by which to forestall a suspension of payment in gold. Such a suspension could hardly take place without destroying U.S. credit in the markets and on the stock exchanges of the world. By statute, the U.S. Treasury was required to hold a minimum of $100 million in gold bullion. Its actual holdings were now well below half that amount.

It was left to J. P. Morgan to convince Grover Cleveland that only through a private bond sale, organized and sold by a syndicate he would head, could collapse be averted. On February 8,

Morgan was brought to the White House, and before the morning was over the arrangements were made. The government's gold reserves stood at less than $10 million. A check that would withdraw that amount was expected to be presented at the sub-Treasury in New York by the end of the day. The U.S. Government had come within twenty-four hours of default.

It was neither the first nor the last occasion on which Morgan would crucially alter the history of American finance. One of the members of a senate investigating committee would later ask him, "If you were actuated by the desire to prevent a panic, why were you not willing that other people should do it, if they wanted to?" Morgan replied, "They *could* not do it." That reply may have reflected Morgan's arrogance; it was also no more than the simple truth.

Yet twenty-five years before, Morgan had written to his father expressing a desire to retire and evincing a profound sense of disillusionment. The urge to retreat, at the age of thirty-three, into a haven of rural placidity soon passed off, but the disillusion was real. Morgan had not adjusted to, nor would he ever fully adjust to, the traumatic conclusion of his first, and probably only, deep romantic love.

The young lady came from his own level of society—she was a well-bred, upper class Episcopalian girl. They were married on October 7, 1861, in a brief and somber ceremony. Four months later she was dead of the tuberculosis from which Morgan had sought to save her. It was the one blow the dexterous and adaptable young banker was never to recover from.

That fact, however, was little appreciated in Morgan's own lifetime and has been little noted since. The omission is not necessarily surprising. J. Pierpont Morgan was one of the major figures of his age, and the *influence* he had upon great affairs attracted a close scrutiny that was not extended to an investigation of the causes of his uniquely formidable and, to some extent, forbidding personality. This book may, in part, redress the balance.

Morgan's career gave him such remarkable money power that not even European giants like the Rothschilds, Hambros, and Barings could match it. The mystique of his name and reputation, his friendship with three kings, his presidency of the Metropolitan Museum of Art, and commodoreship of the New York Yacht Club, have inevitably attracted biographers. All owe an obvious debt to Herbert L. Satterlee, his son-in-law and official historian. Satterlee had the unrivaled advantage of intimacy with his subject and a close-up view of historic occasions, but he was wholly uncritical and recorded the "great man's" activities in tones of hushed reverence.

This book, conceived seven years ago as a study in banking power, soon emerged as something other than a clear-cut success story. Morgan's motives and tactics needed to be considered in the light of accounts by many people including his opponents—Theodore Roosevelt, Andrew Carnegie, Jacob Schiff, and E. H. Harriman.

The widely accepted view of J. P. Morgan as an all-conquering financial genius looked flawed upon close examination. His pride and prejudice led him into certain gross errors of judgment. He once rejected the opportunity to buy General Motors for only half a million dollars. He allowed an executive wizard like Charles Schwab to leave United States Steel and found the rival Bethlehem Trust. He underrated the talents of Bernard Baruch and would long despise E. H. Harriman, the greatest railroad man of his time, as "only a two-dollar broker." His dream of establishing an Atlantic shipping monopoly would founder with the collapse of International Mercantile Marine.

Outside of business he revealed many paradoxes. He considered himself a good Christian but was guilty of all but one of the Seven Deadly Sins (not even his harshest critics could accuse him of Sloth!). He was an affectionate family man but also a notorious womanizer. He shared the upper crust Yankee bias against Jews but unhesitatingly signed a check for over a million dollars to save Henry Duveen from going to prison.

His run of success lasted so long and influenced so much that it has an epic quality to it. The cautious, solid, respectable folk who were his ancestors had shown nothing in their history to hint they might produce a man of destiny. Prosperous and conservative, they provoked neither scandal nor controversy. Perhaps the only exception was his maternal grandfather, the Reverend John Pierpont, who baptized him in the old Hollis Street Church, Boston.

Soon after that baptism, the Reverend shocked his congregation by inviting them to forsake their "service to Mammon."

This book examines how his grandson responded to that challenge. ,

THE HOUSE OF MORGAN (in condensed form)

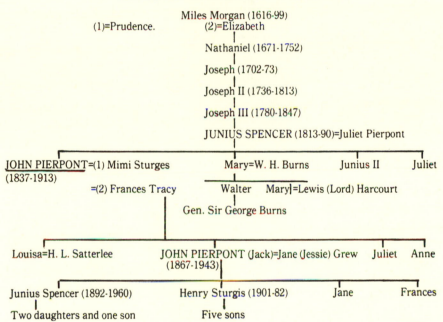

Miles Morgan (1616-99)
(1)=Prudence.   (2)=Elizabeth

Nathaniel (1671-1752)

Joseph (1702-73)

Joseph II (1736-1813)

Joseph III (1780-1847)

JUNIUS SPENCER (1813-90)=Juliet Pierpont

JOHN PIERPONT=(1) Mimi Sturges   Mary=W. H. Burns   Junius II   Juliet
(1837-1913)
        =(2) Frances Tracy   Walter   Mary=Lewis (Lord) Harcourt
                    Gen. Sir George Burns

Louisa=H. L. Satterlee   JOHN PIERPONT (Jack)=Jane (Jessie) Grew   Juliet   Anne
                (1867-1943)

Junius Spencer (1892-1960)   Henry Sturgis (1901-82)   Jane   Frances

Two daughters and one son   Five sons

15

J.P.MORGAN

Part One

THE SOWING

CHAPTER ONE

The Morgans set foot in America in January 1636, sixteen years after the *Mayflower* had beached on the barren coast of Massachusetts. The little colony at Plymouth, which still numbered only three hundred after its first precarious decade, might have remained an insignificant trading post and fishing station, but its survival had stimulated others in England to propose further settlements that offered freedom of worship from the autocratic high Anglicanism of King Charles I and the intolerant Archbishop Laud. Before long a body of liberal-minded but shrewd merchants, headed by many from Boston in Lincolnshire, were canvassing support for a prospectus that promised a lavish return, both spiritual and material, for the cash and cloth to underwrite another voyage.

The new emigrants, led by John Winthrop, a prominent lawyer and Suffolk squire, were very different, except in religious fervor and determination, from the Pilgrim Fathers, mainly simple artisans who had cast themselves across the Atlantic relying upon the mercy of God. Winthrop's puritanism had lost him the post of attorney to the Court of Wards and Liveries, and he had been about to emigrate to Ireland with his family when the king, eager to rid himself of a troublesome sect, signed a charter incorporating the Massachusetts Bay Company but reserving to himself the power to revoke it if they failed to prosper.

In March 1630, Winthrop sailed from Cowes with a small flotilla carrying five hundred souls on a storm-tossed voyage of nine weeks. Among his passengers were landed gentry, dissident clergymen, lawyers, and Oxford scholars, as well as unemployed craftsmen anxious to use their skills in the new settlements, and several yeomen desperate for the land denied them altogether in England or leased at exorbitant rents.

The flagship *Arbella* landed at the old Indian settlement of Naumkeag that a temporary governor had renamed Salem. Wearing his sword of state, John Winthrop looked down his long aristocratic nose at the huddle of bark huts and sod-roofed dugouts, as a servant hoisted a padlocked chest containing the charter. It authorized the administration to make "all Manner of wholesome and reasonable Orders, Lawes, Statutes and Ordinances, Direccons and Instruccons . . . not contrairie to the Lawes of our Realme of England." Within three months almost one-third of his company, including several titled ladies unused to hardship, had succumbed to smallpox or childbed fever. Many suffered the miseries of scurvy. The survivors, driven by Winthrop's fanatical energy and his constant exhortation, "Sow the good seed and the Lord will furnish the good harvest in His season," raised their crops, fished for cod, and began trading in furs.

More emigrants soon followed from Europe. Most of the British accepted the chill challenge of Massachusetts in preference to Virginia or the balmy West Indies. The canny Hollanders preferred the rich soil and deep-water harbor of fortified Manhattan Island. Among them was Jan Aertsen, an illiterate peasant from Bilt in Utrecht, who served as an indentured servant to a Dutch landowner before buying his own small holding on Long Island. His descendant, Cornelius Vanderbilt, would become America's richest railroad and shipping magnate. Another compatriot, Claes Van Roosenvelt, landed soon afterward at New Amsterdam. He was the ancestor of Theodore and Franklin Delano Roosevelt, both destined to rock the House of Morgan.

In 1636 little Boston was already thriving on overseas trade when a new influx of settlers included Miles Morgan, a sturdy twenty year old, and his two brothers, John and James. The family annals are sketchily documented, but the Morgans of Llandaff in Glamorgan could be traced back to the eleventh century, with probably some subsequent history as minor landowners, since the three brothers were literate and spoke English, as well as their native Welsh. Following the example of a Llandaff merchant, Thomas Howell, and others who had fallen on hard times, William Morgan departed for Bristol to set up as a saddler and harness maker. His sons were raised as God-fearing Protestants, but economic pressure rather than any fierce religious conviction had driven them across the Atlantic. They faced the New World with only a few sovereigns and the clothes of humble but respectable artisans; leather jerkins, breeches, and a change of linen. Among their fellow-passengers were the Gilberts, whose daughter Prudence later became Miles's first wife.

Boston offered little scope to the vigorous young Morgans, who lacked the capital to buy land, the one way to a vote or any part in civic affairs. It was soon obvious that they had exchanged a royal tyrant for a bigoted puritan who equated Episcopalians and other "heretics" with the sons and daughters of Beelzebub. The bodies of men and women convicted of adultery dangled from rough scaffolds. Whipping posts and the pillory were automatic for those guilty of fornication or the faintest taint of blasphemy. Men slunk by with a red D for Drunkard sewn on their doublets. In the meetinghouse, none dared to protest after one rash colonist had both his ears chopped off and was shipped back to England for rashly plotting against Winthrop.

Winthrop sternly disapproved of all indulgence in spirits and tobacco and even condemned the wearing of wedding rings as popish vanities. He repressed local sin, but his dream of Zion was threatened from every side; New France to the north, papist Maryland to the south, and across the sea a hostile monarch all too eager to revoke his charter. Winthrop detected treachery in any whisper of dissent, and from the high-backed chair in his mansion he issued orders like a monarch. His subjects were regularly reminded that "A Democratie is, amongst nations, accounted the meanest and worst of all forms of government."

Many sailed for Barbados to escape his harsh edicts. Others like John Morgan, the least devout of the brothers, decided to quit joyless Boston for the plantations of Virginia. James was next. Spending his all on a nag, he rode over a hundred miles of rough track to the tiny river cantonment that grew into New London.

Soon afterward, Miles joined a few families heading for Agawam, an Indian settlement in the valley of the Connecticut River where it flows through Massachusetts. The party leader, Colonel William Pynchon, paid the Pequots thirty sovereigns for a fertile tract that he named Springfield in memory of his old home in Essex. He parceled it out fairly and lent the purchase price for two dozen acres on the west bank to young Morgan, who did not disclose that he was still a minor.

Miles Morgan built a cabin for himself and Prudence, who presented him with four sons and four daughters. He farmed industriously and in time repaid Pynchon, but animals were scarce and often stunted. Miles was one of the few with a countryman's background; he cleared more and more land, going for quick crops. In the short spring he and his sons dug potatoes, fattened their hogs, repaired the cabin, and toiled at sowing, fencing, and plowing. Most of their neighbors followed primitive Indian methods. Few New Englanders had either the specialized skills or the splendid draft horses of the German immigrant farmers who transformed Pennsylvania and the Ohio Valley into a golden land of towering barns, lush meadows, and orchards.

With the arrival of more families Springfield had slowly expanded, but there was no doctor and the local apothecary stocked only makeshift drugs. During one smallpox epidemic the settlers survived on toast, watery gruel, warmed milk, and boiled apples. Sufferers from dysentery, induced by the brackish well water, were advised by Boston's physicians to swallow lead bullets. The Morgan children learned to read and write from the *New England Primer,* and were taught the rudiments of arithmetic and geography. They paid fees to attend the Common School, locally built and maintained as in all Massachusetts townships with more than fifty families. The girls sewed, darned, baked, and peeled rush for candlewicks. Their brothers worked the land until they married, when Miles rented them small neighboring holdings at a nominal £6 a year in advance of their inheritance, when each acquired a full title.

Miles prospered from careful husbandry and the shrewd marketing of his surplus crops and beef. He also had the invaluable asset of four robust sons. But the family had to endure oven-hot summers and cold, foggy winters, with wolves howling close by and muskets always loaded to repel the famished Indians, who never hesitated to scalp their captives or roast them alive. The Morgans had known long months when game was scarce, corn bins scraped, and the clan, soon including daughters and daughters-in-law continuously swollen with pregnancy, subsisted on powdered beef, mussels, wild berries, and a communal bowl of cornmeal mush. Their faith and physical stamina pulled them through illnesses and disease, but there were worse terrors.

Miles had soon put up a blockhouse on his homestead and served in the militia, which initially wore no uniforms. Officers were elected more for their civic standing and acreage than any military talents. When threatened by Indian attacks they would gather in the local garrison house. Following the example of Hadley and Northampton, they quickly built themselves a stockade, drilled, and had regular arms inspections. It was accepted as routine for men, women, and even small boys to attend church meetings with muskets or axes at the ready.

The attacks could be alarming, though not altogether unwelcome. Large tracts were seized from the Pequots after an unsuccessful raid or accepted as "fines" for some trumped-up border dispute. Miles Morgan and his neighbors were on the whole less pious than the Bostonians or Salem's puritanical elders but just as rapacious. They fully merited the cynical gibe, "The Pilgrim Fathers fell first on their knees and then on the aborigines." In Springfield, as in the other settlements of Massachusetts and Connecticut, captive braves and their squaws were herded into an enclosure and auctioned off like cattle for transportation to the Indies or, at best, they were taken into household drudgery.

There is no evidence that Miles joined in this slave trade, but his efficiency with hatchet and gun won him a sergeant's stripes. By 1649, when the fearsome Winthrop at last died, Miles Morgan had already become a man of substance with fine herds and pastures much enlarged by "confiscations." That year he was elected a member of the influential Committee to Grant Land, soon followed by his appointment as Constable or "Fence Viewer" to supervise byways and boundaries. This naturally helped him to buy lots cheaply.

He raised his family strictly on solid Christian principles but without the narrow puritanism that ruled most other New England settlements. They gave thanks to the Lord twice on Sundays, and the womenfolk had charcoal foot warmers in the pew reserved for them as leading citizens. The sons all sired large families with a predominance of males, all of whom miraculously survived infancy. Prudence, weakened by overwork and almost nonstop childbearing, died in 1660. Nine years later Miles, then in his early fifties, married Elizabeth Bliss, a comely young woman from Hartford, who gave him their only child, Nathaniel.

This comfortable era of full granaries and pedigreed cattle was interrupted in October 1675 when Indian warriors, enraged by the ruthless pillage of their lands and hunting grounds, stormed several other settlements before advancing on Springfield. Pynchon's militia mounted the barricades but failed to halt the braves, who went on a rampage of killing and looting after setting fire to many barns. They were finally repelled after a heroic stand in Sergeant Morgan's blockhouse. His leadership was rewarded by a captaincy.

That winter he organized a plan to rebuild the township. Two centuries later a statue to him was put up in Court Square by "one of his descendants of the fifth generation"—J. P. Morgan. Miles was described simply as "an early settler," but during his lifetime he won fame as a relentless Indian hunter. His own property was among the very few to escape damage in the attack of 1675, but, nonetheless, he suffered a bitter loss when leading a force of militia to round up and massacre the last of the marauders. One of his sons was tomahawked.

A huge territory was taken from the Pequots in retribution. Miles was granted a fourth share in "all the Swamp against their meddow over Agawam River," which made him one of the largest landowners in the area. He resented paying the harsh taxes but was careful not to air his views on politics or on the inflexible moral disciplines prescribed by the church elders of Boston and Salem. The first of the American line, he would not be the last Morgan to nail his colors firmly to the fence.

He had remained silent when Colonel Pynchon, too outspoken in his criticism of Winthrop's theocratic system of government, was maneuvered out of his magistracy and sailed back to England. Miles, saddened but philosophical, continued to add to his holdings until his death at the turn of the century. By then his sons and grandsons were all fairly considerable landowners, some of them in outlying Northampton, where property was cheaper than in fast-growing Springfield.

The dynasty moved on smoothly tilling its fertile acres and giving worthy service to church and community. Whiggish in outlook but cautiously neutral under pressure, they seemed permanently tethered to their farms, untouched by the opening of the West or the growth of towns like New York that glittered with temptations for merchants and industrialists.

The first to crack this solid mold was Miles's great-great-grandson and J. P. Morgan's grandfather, Joseph, who unobtrusively bought up small holdings that he rented out or resold at a profit. He regarded real estate as no more than an investment and a possible escape route to a more exciting city life, and he was backed by a money-conscious wife, the former Sally Spencer of Middletown, Connecticut. She grew bored with rustic West Springfield after the arrival of their children, Mary, Lucy, and Junius.

Joseph inherited $10,000 and this finally stimulated him to branch out into the business world. The 1812 War with England scarcely touched Springfield. Very few had responded to the president's national appeal for 100,000 militiamen, and Joseph Morgan was not among them. He joined in patriotic rallies after Washington was captured and the White House burned down, but he seemed far more distressed by the catastrophic fall in farm values. Fortunately, he had invested in a Northampton firm of moneylenders that discounted the bills of his needier neighbors.

His war pickings were welcome but insignificant beside the huge profits hauled in by speculators on the blockaded eastern seaboard. John Jacob Astor, a German butcher's son who had first arrived in Baltimore with a stock of seven flutes, soon turned to peddling furs and to other enterprises. He had siphoned his trading profits from Canada, England, and China into mortgages on small farms, mostly seized by ruthless foreclosures. He also put up hundreds of miserable jerry-built dwellings in the overcrowded city, renting them out at extortionate rates. A graceless man, scarcely able to read or write, he funded a desperate government's war loan, subscribed at 83 cents on the dollar. His patriotism cleared him a cool half-million.

Another semi-illiterate, Cornelius Vanderbilt, had far less capital, but his two-fisted opportunism was ideal for wartime buccaneering. A $100 loan from his mother enabled him to buy a boat for running the blockade between the upstate farms and starving New York with cargoes of meat, milk, vegetables, and precious firewood (at $3 a bundle). By the end of the war he could easily afford $9,000 for a schooner. It was the first of a fleet that he multiplied by undercutting freight and passenger charges. This Staten Island pirate's background and values were remote from those of the cautious ultrarespectable landowner from West Springfield, yet their descendants would one day join forces in the multimillion dollar deal that first launched J. P. Morgan as a railroad baron.

Coincidence led both Joseph Morgan and Vanderbilt to buy coaching taverns after the 1812 War. The Dutchman took over a ramshackle hotel in the slum area of New Brunswick, New Jersey, near the pier. It was convenient for passengers changing coaches to and from Philadelphia, and it was obviously useful for a freebooter to establish an operating base beyond the New York State line. In the early days, his wife cooked the meals and scrubbed the floors, while the two small children helped to carry the guests' baggage. Vanderbilt, when not concocting shady deals, relaxed with whores and waterfront gamblers.

Joseph Morgan's life-style was quite different. After years of driving a wagon over bad roads to sell his farm produce or buy machinery, he began to use stage coaches. He sometimes had occasion to stay overnight in a comfortable inn at Westfield that was used by Hartford merchants to break their cross-country trips. In the winter of 1815, the establishment came on the market, and Joseph decided to buy it together with the stage line. He found it possible to operate both ventures without giving up the home farm that his brothers kept going under his wife Sally's watchful eye.

The tavern quickly paid for itself. At times his guests needed cash in a hurry, and he was more than ready to make short-term loans at good interest. He was a sociable man who discovered that an innkeeper's life was far more congenial—and lucrative—than postwar farming. Within two years he had sold the tavern and stage line to a cousin and was able to finance a more ambitious venture.

He bought the spacious Exchange Coffee House on Hartford's State Street. Modeled on Edward Lloyd's celebrated establishment in the City of London, it had become a rendezvous for merchants and insurance brokers who would meet to talk business, often rounded off by private banquets. Joseph soon added amenities like a concert hall, a reading room, and a restaurant, which transformed what had been a businessman's club into Hartford's most popular social center.

He had retained the Springfield property, a future retreat for Sally and the children during their school holidays. Meantime he was buying good farms and prime locations in and around Hartford, including a site on Asylum Street where he planned to build a house for his family. The coffee house developed into a useful springboard for his investment portfolio, thanks to his reputation as a discreet confidant and go-between. Within a couple of years he had quietly picked up good shares in both a local bank and the Connecticut Steamboat Company, but his first real coup was to secure a directorship in the new Aetna Insurance Company, which had been launched at Morgan's. His low-priced stock earned him bumper profits over the coming years.

Joseph read his Bible, worshipped God and Henry Clay, and had a pew in the Congregational Church. He chose the right moment to dispose of the Coffee House and bought a fifty-room hotel on Main Street at an inviting price, after it had been closed for some months. He spent freely on redecoration and new furnishings, mostly from New York, an outlay soon justified by the healthy turnover.

The family occupied a large suite but the children spent little time there. They were educated at boarding schools and passed their vacations either with relatives in Saratoga Springs or on the Springfield estate, where Junius, the son, was expected to plow fields and herd cattle. This was wholly characteristic of Joseph Morgan, whose only extravagance was a barouche.

Confident that Hartford would continue to prosper, Joseph took a lively interest in the Erie Canal, the first link between the West

and the Eastern seaboard. Three years later, in 1828, he subscribed to the Baltimore and Ohio Railroad, which had been
promoted with a capital of $5 million. He was also one of the first
stockholders in the New Haven and Hartford line but invested
mainly in canals, land, and fire insurance. He and Sally lived
modestly at the hotel and seemed socially unambitious. Both
their daughters had married young. Lucy chose a Congregational
minister with a living in New Hampshire; soon afterward her
sister became the wife of James Goodwin, an energetic Hartford
business man.

Although heir to a considerable fortune, Junius Spencer Morgan was discouraged from expecting a life of ease and security. At
16, after being educated at private academies in Middletown and
East Windsor, he started his business career as a clerk in the
counting house of Alfred Welles, a respected Boston merchant.
He served a five-year apprenticeship, working hard and proving a
capacity to assimilate detail, but showing no other indications of
his future eminence in Anglo-American banking. He was a tall,
rather solemn young man with the good manners and dignity
normal in an affluent New England family of sound breeding. He
regularly attended the Congregational Church in Hollis Street
whose pastor often asked him to Sunday supper and poetry
readings. A keen student of phrenology, John Pierpont used to
"read" his guests' heads and seemed most impressed by young
Morgan's bumps.

The Rev. John Pierpont's lineage dated back to the Norman
Conquest. Like the Morgans, his ancestors had farmed in Massachusetts but on a far larger scale. He graduated from Yale (one of
his forbears was a cofounder) and he had entered the ministry
only after a career as schoolmaster, lawyer, and bankrupt merchant. He soon antagonized the starchly orthodox elders of Hollis
Street by his "heretical" support of Unitarianism and his genuine
love for the lower classes who were kept firmly in their places by
their psalm-singing masters. He lashed his flock in sermons
denouncing slavery and inveighed against intemperance with all
the fervor of the early Puritans. At moments of overexcitement,
his very large nose became alarmingly inflamed. All in all he was
the very antithesis of the acquisitive, circumspect, and wholly
conventional Morgans, but Junius was much taken with the

minister's daughter, Juliet Pierpont, a quiet and sensitive girl who had inherited her mother's charm. At the end of his five-year term he was already planning to propose after being invited to buy a junior partnership in the counting house. However, Joseph suspected that this "promotion" owed something to Mr. Welles's sudden need of cash. He quickly rejected the offer to invest. Instead, he sent the young man to New York City to join the private banking house of Morris Ketchum, a one-time patron of the Hartford Coffee House.

For an unobtrusive and cautious man, Joseph Morgan was surprisingly impressed by Ketchum, who had made a quick fortune from his financial dealings. Still a provincial at heart, he seemed dazzled by Ketchum's city mansion, his elegant summer home at Westport, Connecticut, and his retinue of servants. Ketchum's offices were among the busiest in New York, with a dozen or more clerks scurrying like mice to nibble at the endless supplies of mouth-watering prospectuses.

Overrapid industrialization and an insatiable demand for manufactured goods, distributed by the new railroads and canals, had made it easy for banks, with the help of investment brokers like the Ketchums, to promote undercapitalized companies. They relied on paper currency frenziedly printed, often without adequate specie cover, by many private state-chartered banks with the connivance of corrupt state legislatures. By this method enormous parcels of bonds were sold in London for every kind of wildcat enterprise.

This artificial bonanza favored such operators as "Commodore" Vanderbilt, now busily linking his steamboat empire with a railroad network, and the notorious Daniel Drew, whose long run of stock watering would only end when J. P. Morgan put him out of business. Junius was uncomfortable visiting the Wall Street office where Drew chewed tobacco, spat toward his cuspidor, and hatched the schemes that ruined thousands of gullible investors. The lanky scarecrow figure, inseparable from a shabby umbrella, professed the Episcopalian faith and prayed fervently before each stock issue, sometimes inviting clients to join him in psalm singing. He would also remind nervous officials that "if a cat would eat fish, he must be willing to wet his feet!"

There were many others like Drew in the Wall Street of the

mid-thirties. Mr. Ketchum had more style and the cosmopolitan gloss of a financier who made frequent trips to Europe, but Junius never felt at home in the firm's feverish atmosphere. After slow-moving, gracious Hartford and stiffly proper Boston, he was depressed by New York's slums and by a drainage system foully inadequate to the needs of 200,000 citizens. He could not even accustom himself to its horse-drawn rail cars hurtling through the inferno-like summer streets and whenever possible he escaped to Boston for a rest and the chance of seeing his Juliet. On these home visits he often hinted to his father that a banking career had quite lost its appeal, if it needed to be pursued in New York City.

Joseph was sympathetic but preoccupied. He had sold the hotel, built a fine house at 26 Asylum Street, and was applying himself to numerous enterprises, but most energetically to those of the Aetna Insurance Company, for whom he traveled back and forth to New York and other cities, selling fat policies. Business thrived until a disastrous fire in December 1835 destroyed the Merchants Exchange and other badly constructed buildings in the Wall Street district. Aetna faced ruin. Several directors panicked and wished to plead contributory negligence or invoke the fine print of escape clauses, but Joseph Morgan insisted on meeting all legitimate claims, whatever the cost, to save the company's good name. His action, well publicized, brought in so many applications for new policies that Aetna was soon able to charge higher premiums. At the end of that year's boom his share of the profits was said to exceed $150,000.

Junius had put in almost two years in the Wall Street office and now pleaded to be allowed home to start work with a less volatile house. Joseph agreed provisionally. After careful investigation, he bought him a partnership for $10,000 in the Hartford firm of general merchants, Howe, Mather & Co., who did a flourishing cotton trade with the South. With the warm approval of both families, Junius at once proposed to Juliet, at twenty his junior by three years. They were married at the Hollis Street Church in Boston. A deputy performed the ceremony instead of the bride's father, who had been suspended by an irate vestry for attacking greedy factory-owners and advocating the abolition of imprisonment for debt. He had departed angrily for a tour of Europe and the Levant, which, his parishioners hoped, without too much conviction, might restore his physical and mental health.

The newlyweds moved into part of the house on Asylum Street. Within a short time Junius was voted into a directorship of the Hartford Fire Insurance Co. His income from Howe, Mather was also increased by a further investment of $25,000 on his behalf. He seemed set for the prosperous and uneventful life of a provincial merchant, who would be able in due time to pass on his position to his own son.

CHAPTER TWO

The baby was safely delivered in Asylum Street on April 17, 1837. He had the large Pierpont nose and dark deep-set eyes but seemed likely to inherit the Morgans' sturdier physique. The fire-eating pastor performed the baptism, flattered by Juliet's insistence that her son should be christened John Pierpont. He had returned from his travels refreshed but even more aggressive. In one of his first sermons J. P. Morgan's grandfather had fiercely invited the congregation to examine "the relative amount of our service to God, and to Mammon."

The question was topical as well as direct. His grandson had entered a world of crisis, the result not merely of crop failures, but of the greed of state legislatures who exploited shipping lines and of the reckless overspeculation encouraged by Andrew Jackson's administration. The economy slithered into a near-panic loss of confidence when banks in the city of New York, soon followed by those in Hartford and other towns, suspended specie payments. Inflated securities became as suspect as the government's paper currency. American banking credit had all but collapsed in London when Maryland and Pennsylvania repudiated liability on their bonds and promissory notes. Massachusetts was rather less vulnerable, although merchants like Howe, Mather had their anxieties when the southern farmers began to insist on cash or negotiable securities for their cotton.

The situation overseas had become even more desperate, as George Peabody, a native of Danvers, Massachusetts, soon discovered when he sailed for England in 1837 with two other businessmen. They were hopeful of selling $8 million in bonds to finance the new Chesapeake and Ohio Canal, but received only evasive and discouraging replies. Peabody kept his nerve when his colleagues hastily packed their bags.

It was not his first visit. Ten years earlier he had arrived in London with little more than a passport signed by Henry Clay and a personality of engaging charm. He had enjoyed only four years of formal schooling but had emerged with superb penmanship and an exceptional memory for figures, names, and places. He had seen naval service in the War of 1812, followed by some years of hawking his uncle's dry goods from door to door. An imposing man of six foot one with twinkling light blue eyes and prematurely silver sideburns, he was a born salesman. Careful with his money, he had opened small stores of his own in Baltimore, Philadelphia, and New York, and then became restless to try his luck in England.

During that first trip he lived in cheap lodgings, ate in a modest chophouse, and counted his pennies. En route to Lancashire to reconnoitre the cotton market he was overcharged by a railway booking clerk and had him dismissed. "Not that I could not afford the shilling," he wrote to the directors, "but the man was cheating many travelers to whom the swindle would be oppressive." The episode typified both his persistence and deep sense of justice.

During his second visit he decided to start a small import-export business in Old Broad Street and soon discovered that some shippers needed credit or wished to place spare funds at tempting rates of interest. He also began to discount notes and even compete modestly with the American house of William and James Brown, who for some time had accommodated their countrymen with letters of credit.

He was horrified that a prestigious banking house like Baring Brothers, which had helped to finance the historic Louisiana Purchase at four cents an acre, now hesitated to invest further in an American economy shaken by the failure of Middle West grain crops and under the cloud of Wall Street's growing disrepute. But he had meantime noted that shrewd N. M. Rothschild of New Court, St. Swithin's Lane, "a sovereign's throw from the Bank of England," still thought it worthwhile to send a representative to New York; one August Belmont, an elegant, portly young fellow of German-Jewish origin, who had changed his name from Schönberg and expediently embraced the Episcopalian faith.

Peabody carried on a one-man crusade to restore faith in his country's probity. When the panic at last started to subside, he called time and again on the big City barons to assure them that Maryland and other states would honor their bonds. He also continued backing American securities with his personal funds. Buying at almost giveaway levels, he later reaped a rich harvest. He unloaded most of the Chesapeake and Ohio Canal bonds and won acclaim back home for returning his $60,000 commission intact to Maryland's meager treasury.

His successful bond sales in London stimulated the American stock market to reinvest in railroads, canals, and export merchandise. Joseph Morgan was among the prudent minority who resisted the bogus prospectuses, with unrealistically high dividends, touted by Drew and other shark promoters. Instead, he shrewdly invested in sounder, low-priced securities and set aside part of his profits to increase his son's holding in Howe, Mather & Co. He then bought a house for him on the Farmington Road, where two more babies, Sarah and Mary, were born, followed by the birth of a second son, Junius Spencer Morgan, Jr. Another sister, Juliet, arrived in 1847 shortly after Joseph's death.

Henry Thoreau's wooden box, containing forty-seven of his manuscript notebooks, would one day occupy a place of honor in the Morgan Library, but Pierpont found it difficult to echo his view of a puffing steam engine as "wickedness going faster." His own happiest early memory was of a train ride, at the age of seven, from Hartford to Boston on his grandfather's knee. It had been sheer bliss after several months in bed with convulsions and scarlet fever.

When Joseph Morgan died in 1847, he was rumored to have left several million dollars, but his trustees declared only a nominal $102,000 for probate, ignoring details of real estate and an extensive hoard of stocks and shares. Junius was now a very rich man, still on the sunny side of forty, and anxious to spread himself. Sobriety and a strong physique were assets in his travels to explore new outlets for his firm, but he also had a courtesy rare among businessmen outside New England and the leisurely South. He did not neglect his personal affairs. He had soon disposed of his father's farms and the building plots that absorbed too much time and cash. He chose instead to pump his surplus capital into railroads or any insurance concern that would offer him a seat on the board.

He joined the Episcopal Christ Church and was elected to the vestry. He also supported the Wadsworth Atheneum, Hartford's cultural center. The greatest change from his parents' way of life was social. He and his wife developed a streak of snobbery and became prominent in a circle of affluent friends with a similar pride of ancestry. They were an exceptionally handsome couple. Their son's thick eyebrows and blunt features recalled deep roots in Welsh peasant stock, but Junius had been favored with looks of almost magisterial distinction. Juliet had her father's aristocratic, rather gaunt bone structure. Always tastefully gowned, she remained slender even after childbearing. They seemed almost primly conventional and maintained the tradition of churchgoing twice on Sundays, Thanksgiving at Grandmother Morgan's, and a lavish Christmas dinner for the family at Farmington Avenue.

The girls were sent off to fashionable academies but Pierpont's ill health made his education more erratic. For a few months in 1846 he attended the Middle District School near his home, soon followed by a short spell at the Connecticut Episcopal Academy in Cheshire. He left to go to the Pavilion Family School in Hartford, first as a day boy, and then as a boarder early in January 1848. Eighteen months later he was sent to the city's Public High School on Linden Place. Here, from all accounts, he was high-spirited and exceled at sports. He swam and rode bareback but most of all enjoyed fishing with his cousin, Jim Goodwin, a good-natured lad who cheerfully followed his lead.

If crossed he could be sulky and self-willed, once insisting that he was right when the arithmetic primer differed. He had the satisfaction of proving a misprint. He showed an aptitude for languages, both ancient and modern, and wrote a fluent hand.

His schoolmates called him Pip, a nickname he discouraged as vulgar, and he took to formally signing all his letters *J. Pierpont Morgan*.

He had the average schoolboy's passion for stamp collecting and also cherished an autograph album with the signatures of Oliver Wendell Holmes and Charles Dickens, whom Junius had met in Hartford during one of the novelist's tours. Although a rich man's son, his weekly allowance was only twenty-five cents. He entered every item in a cash book, including his outlay on postage stamps, candy, and numerous oranges. From an early age he exhibited an abnormal determination to win at all costs, even in friendly games of chess, and he would sleigh at reckless speeds to prove his superiority.

After spells of illness which sometimes left traces of eczema on the large nose he had inherited from Grandfather Pierpont, he would grow morose and refuse to talk to anyone but his sympathetic cousin. He was always happiest out of school and often visited Grandmother Morgan in Asylum Street to scrounge homemade cookies. He liked to spend part of his holidays in Boston with bearded, white-thatched Rev. Pierpont, who could so magically recall the fabled wonders of Constantinople and the treasures of the Uffizi in Florence. He loved the old man deeply and was shocked when he departed for another parish in Troy, New York, after the church elders had forced him to resign. Junius, however, was none too upset. Although by now a senior partner, he was secretly planning to leave the firm and move on to Boston where his prickly father-in-law could only have caused him embarrassment. Meantime, in February 1851, Pierpont was readmitted to the Cheshire Academy and boarded in the home of the principal, the Rev. Dr. Paddock. He won some celebrity by climbing the belfry at midnight, carving his initials on the bell.

While the rest of the country seemed to be bursting with trade, Hartford was dwindling into a placid backwater. Florida had been bought from Spain, and Mexico ceded Texas, which won statehood in '46 with Sam Houston as governor. Above all, the discovery of gold in California was making fortunes for the steamship companies and a host of grasping storekeepers. Almost overnight the village of San Francisco had mushroomed into a polyglot rumbustious city of 25,000.

39

Close on a thousand ships left New York in a single year for California. Most went around Cape Horn. The more reckless forty-niners risked cholera or yellow fever by taking the short cut across the isthmus of Panama. Undercutting all competitors, Commodore Vanderbilt had made enough from his leaky, seldom insured boats to buy himself a mansion in Washington Place with ample stabling for a string of trotters. Among many others to cash in on the bonanza was the bearded giant Collis P. Huntington, who opened a Sacramento store in partnership with Charles Crocker, a former sawmill laborer and blacksmith. Their profits would help them build the Central Pacific Railroad with former attorney Leland Stanford, who had also cornered goods in short supply during the boom years.

Far more significant than the gold rush was the advancing frontier. Thousands of settlers followed the tracks of earlier pioneers in their feverish hunger for rich farm and pasture land. Inevitably, factories would be required to supply farm machinery and manufactured goods, with railroads linking the fast-growing townships to the cities of the Midwest and the eastern seaboard. Shady promoters, encouraged by corrupt state officials, began to float companies, often with bogus share certificates, but the whole future hinged on two vital elements; foreign capital and an influx of manpower.

The rapid expansion of the West would have been impossible without immigrant labor.

Survivors of Ireland's earlier potato famines had now been joined by a host of refugees from Europe's revolutionary upheavals. Most of the Irish, Germans, Austrians, Poles, and Swedes trekked westward to plow the land or take underpaid jobs in the new factories and mills. Jews from the ghettoes of Russia and Germany swarmed into New York, where the Jewish community had numbered barely 2,000 in 1837, the year of Pierpont Morgan's birth. They scratched a livelihood as street peddlers or worked a sixteen-hour day in the sweatshops on the Lower East Side. Families were crammed into flea-ridden ratholes owned by the heirs of John Jacob Astor, who had died recently in doddering, spoonfed senility. He had left $20 million—without a cent for his employees but a grudged $400,000 for a library to sanctify his memory.

Jews with a little capital and more initiative moved on. The

40

future banking magnate, Joseph Seligman, had sailed steerage from Bremen with one hundred American dollars sewn into his pants. For a while he hawked dry goods among the farmers of Pennsylvania but soon headed for the mining camps of California, where he and his brother carefully piled up their dollars and cents. They opened the first brick-built store in San Francisco, the only one to remain standing after the fire of '51.

Meyer Guggenheim, a Swiss-German immigrant, was equally enterprising. In Philadelphia he made and successfully marketed a stainless stove polish. His dynasty founded a gigantic smelting and refining empire in the United States and Latin America, with offshoots in every corner of the industrial world. In Cincinnati, Abraham Kuhn and Solomon Loeb opened a clothing store and amassed enough capital to start the brokerage house which would eventually provide the Morgans with their toughest competition on Wall Street.

Already restless in Hartford, Junius Morgan became distinctly more impatient after sailing to England in the summer of 1850 on his first overseas business trip. He was dazzled by the imposing mansions of the nobility, whose coaches were manned by retainers in livery and cockaded hats, but just as impressed by the City of London—the name by which the British capital's financial district was, and still is, referred to. He paused outside the Royal Exchange to admire Chantrey's equestrian bronze of the Duke of Wellington. Risking life and limb to avoid the hansoms, four-wheeled growlers, and heavy drays, he made his way on foot to the paneled offices of the houses who represented his firm. In St. Swithin's Lane he stared up at the windows behind which the mighty Rothschilds settled the world's financial destiny.

During that three-month visit he was tempted to call at 22 Old Broad Street, but without any business to transact with Peabody & Co. he considered a smalltown Yankee merchant like himself of too little consequence even to leave a card. He was constantly reminded of the prestige enjoyed by George Peabody, now accepted in the highest banking circles as his country's ambassador of goodwill. Peabody commanded the respect and friendship of Thomson Hankey, governor of the Bank of England, who had made his fortune in the East India Company and married a delightful American girl. The Hankeys never missed his lavish

41

Fourth of July dinners, graced at times by royalty, with the United States ambassador and England's leading statesmen invariably among his guests. The newspapers often mentioned that he was supervising arrangements to have America's industrial renaissance suitably represented at the Great Exhibition due to be staged in Hyde Park the following year.

Back home, galvanized by all he had seen and heard in the City of London, Junius was actively preparing to switch from Hartford. He still had no taste for New York and soon decided in favor of Boston, where he had established a number of useful contacts, among them one with James M. Beebe, with whom Mather, Morgan & Co. had traded profitably for some years. Beebe had built up a flourishing business in dry goods and hoped to expand abroad, probably through George Peabody & Co. and other reputable London houses. Junius chose the right moment to make a tactful approach.

He joined Beebe as a partner on New Year's Day, 1851, and settled in smoothly, but at first only saw Juliet and the children on occasional weekends. However, 37 Kilby Street was congenial. He liked his colleagues, notably Levi J. Morton, an engaging young fellow who had advanced rapidly from his first years as a dollar-a-week clerk in a Vermont store. He would one day become vice-president of the United States, but so far had set his sights on starting up as a broker on Wall Street. He handled most of the firm's business with Baring Brothers and other leading London houses.

Junius soon settled in with his family. Juliet was overjoyed to return to her native Boston. No doubt she also saw useful matrimonial prospects for her two elder daughters who would soon be leaving their school in New Haven. She was kept busy furnishing the comfortable though unpretentious house they had rented at 15 Pemberton Square.

Pierpont entered the English High School founded by Juliet's father and others thirty years earlier. He was peeved at leaving Hartford and above all he missed his favorite cousin, Jim Goodwin, now far closer to him than his own brother, a sickly boy and so withdrawn that he could almost have sat as a model for doomed little Paul Dombey, whose tragic fate in the Dicken's novel, *Dombey and Son,* was breaking readers' hearts on both sides of the Atlantic. Junius was of course far kindlier than stony

Mr. Dombey, but it was left to Juliet to fuss over "The Doctor," as her younger son was known to the family.

Junius's dedication to business made it difficult for him to give much attention to his children. When he was not visiting the cotton plantations in the south, he shuttled back and forth among Boston, New York, Philadelphia, and Chicago. But somehow he found time to study every photograph and scrap of gossip about the Great Exhibition that had opened in London in May 1851 and drew six million visitors to Joseph Paxton's fairylike Crystal Palace. Queen Victoria considered the American offerings "inventive though not entertaining," but graciously approved of the Bowie knives manufactured in Sheffield, while the Iron Duke admired the craftsmanship of the Springfield rifle and had even nodded to Samuel Colt.

The display, though limited, was a personal triumph for George Peabody, who had arranged for several of his country's leading inventors and industrialists to come over at his expense when a skinflint Congress refused to vote a dime. It had cost him $10,000 for a stand displaying Colt's revolver, Hobbs's unpickable lock, Hoe's printing press, and Cyrus McCormick's mechanical reaper. He also contributed to building the New York Yacht Club's 170-ton schooner, *America,* which defeated fourteen British rivals in a race around the Isle of Wight for a silver ewer put up by the Royal Yacht Squadron.

At the English High School, Pierpont loftily passed around his father's copies of the London *Times* and the *Illustrated London News,* which did not endear him to his classmates, who regarded him as standoffish and too dandified. He once wrote to Paris in fluent French to order a $9 pair of handmade boots. He also liked to toy with a rather showy watchfob when playing—and almost always winning—whist, chess, and backgammon.

Early in 1852, his school attendance was interrupted by a severe attack of rheumatic fever. It left him with a slight but permanent limp. High temperatures persisted for so many months that the family doctor prescribed dry warmth and sunshine. By chance a merchant banker friend of his father's, C. W. Dabney, mentioned that he would shortly be sailing for the island of Fayal in the Azores, where he acted as honorary U.S. consul. He invited the boy to accompany his family.

They left in November and landed twelve days later at the port

43

of Horta. Pierpont hobbled off the barque, but he had benefited from the voyage and was one of the lucky few to escape seasickness. When walking became rather too painful he would ride across the island by donkey. As soon as he regained his strength he started a vigorous regime of sailing, fishing, and swimming, but most of all enjoyed chatting in French or pidgin Portuguese with the seamen who put into port.

The Dabneys always asked him to Sunday supper after services in their private chapel, but he had politely declined their kind invitation to stay at the villa and moved instead into a small hotel. His room cost six Spanish dollars a week, with laundry at four cents an item, but his collars were seldom ironed to his satisfaction. Next to hill climbing and picnicking with the Dabneys' daughter and her friends he loved shopping—mostly on his own—for silk stockings, trinkets, boxes of fruit, and local wine, which he packed carefully and sent home to his parents, sisters, The Doctor, and Grandmother Morgan. He was not extravagant, however, and already seemed obsessed with prices, currency, and fluctuating rates of exchange. "I made a great mistake in bringing quarters here," he complained to his father. "I find they are worth only 24 cents . . . Sovereigns are worth from $5.40 to $5.60 according to the wants of the Jews here to send money to England. . . ."

During that four-month holiday he had put on weight and started bursting out of his pantaloons and vests. Too vain and fastidious to go to a local outfitter, he insisted on having new Boston-cut clothes shipped out to him before joining his parents in England. He sailed to Southampton in April 1853 and spent a week alone in the capital, excited by his first view of Buckingham Palace, Westminster Abbey, and the Bank. He then traveled up to Manchester where Junius was meeting various millowners and cotton merchants. Back in London they stayed at a hotel in St. James's Street and Pierpont again toured the Bank of England, this time with his father. An official showed them around and— an appropriate memory for one who would one day be America's greatest banker—he would often recall the excitement of actually touching bullion worth a million in sterling.

In mid-May his parents received an invitation to dine with George Peabody at his house in Richmond. Peabody twinkled with good nature and insisted on giving Junius introductions to several of his well-placed City friends. Juliet came away utterly charmed, though grieved that a man so prosperous and well-liked should be condemned to face old age as a childless bachelor. She was unaware that Peabody had secretly opened his heart and purse to relieve some of the misery which even in the poorest districts of Hartford or Boston would not have been tolerated. One Sunday Pierpont went twice to St. Paul's to hear the Archbishop of Canterbury preach at morning services, followed by another visit in the late afternoon when the Bishop of Oxford delivered an eloquent sermon. There was no mention, however, of London's foul slums, the rouged child prostitutes, or the hordes of verminous beggars whose importunities the Morgans had found so distasteful.

They sailed home in July after a whirlwind shopping and sightseeing tour of Germany and France. After eight heady months abroad, Pierpont very naturally found Boston flat and provincial. He dreaded the tedium of his last year at school and often drifted over to the waterfront to hear old salts reliving their exploits against Chinese bandits. He tingled with hero worship when, that July, Commodore Matthew Perry stormed into Yokohama Bay with four warships and "requested" that the Shogun sign a commercial treaty. Like so many restless and introspective boys of his own age, he had contemplated running off to sea but was talked out of it by his calmer cousin, Jim Goodwin, with whom he often went fishing in Hartford throughout that hot summer. They mapped out an exciting future and planned to go into partnership together, possibly in marine insurance.

Pierpont had reported in September for his new term at the English High School. He seemed even more abrupt and aloof, studying hard for his examinations. He graduated not far behind the Head Boy, which was a more than creditable performance after almost a year's absence. For the graduation essay read out on Exhibition Day, most of his classmates chose to speak on such figures as George Washington or the Pilgrim Fathers. Morgan without hesitation chose Napoleon Bonaparte.

Over in England Mr. Peabody had arrived at a momentous decision. Now nearing sixty and planning to ease himself into retirement, he urgently needed to train a successor so he could

45

devote more of his time to philanthropy. He thought Junius Morgan might be his man. Since that dinner party in Richmond he had made discreet but exhaustive inquiries, ranging from Lancashire to New England. Everyone spoke well of Morgan's judgment and his sound experience of the growing Anglo-American market in securities and commodities. Equally important to George Peabody, long familiar with English snobbery, was the fact that he had breeding and dignity.

Peabody would not easily forget the fiasco of Commodore Vanderbilt's visit earlier that summer. The shipping magnate, who once boasted that he could pick any lock ever made, found London's mansions impregnable. Instead of being received at Buckingham Palace, as he expected, he had to glimpse the Queen and her consort from Mr. Peabody's box at Covent Garden. Peabody pulled wires frantically to persuade the Lord Mayor to receive the Vanderbilts at the Mansion House. He was mightily relieved to see the brash commercial freebooter depart with his entourage for St. Petersburg and Constantinople.

He had no doubt that Junius Morgan would be far more acceptable to the City of London. He tactfully approached Beebe, who confirmed that his partner was "the best business man in Boston" and generously agreed not to stand in his way, though reluctant to lose him after three booming years. Peabody no longer hesitated. He was confident of Junius Morgan's entire suitability and also saw Juliet as a valuable social asset. After so many years of playing host to his City friends and important American visitors in clubs or at his house in Richmond, he looked forward to passing on the burden to this attractive and still youthful couple.

Junius needed little persuasion to accept a partnership in London's leading Anglo-American business house, plus a handsome allowance of $25,000 a year for entertaining. He would join the firm October 1, 1854. Neither he nor George Peabody had any reason to expect that within three years they would be facing financial ruin.

CHAPTER THREE

Miles Morgan and his brothers had anchored in Boston with little more than a few sovereigns between them. Barely two centuries later Junius steamed back to England by first-class passage and with several hundred thousand dollars in capital. He had every prospect of swelling his assets in the handsome offices at 22 Old Broad Street where Peabody & Co. was enjoying an unprecedented turnover. The Crimean War had boosted imports of high-priced wheat, cotton, and manufactured goods, while British investors rushed to buy into American shipping lines and new railroads. Even the City's most conservative bankers were tempted by prospectuses that promised high returns on foreign capital. August Belmont kept the Rothschilds informed about Wall Street's sounder promotions, and several of Peabody's agents continued to send over massive blocks of bonds and securities for sale on a continually rising market.

Young Junius Morgan II (The Doctor) and his seven-year-old sister, Juliet, had sailed with their parents. The two older girls stayed to complete their schooling in New England but would come to London for holidays. Pierpont was sent to Vevey on Lake Geneva, where a Swiss couple, the Silligs, ran an institute specializing in languages and other subjects required for university entrance. Among its attractions was a good indoor gymnasium, and the locale offered opportunities for boating, hill climbing, and winter sports. Several pupils hailed from Boston, among them the Payson brothers, William G. Tiffany, and Willy Riggs, all of whom became Pierpont's lifelong friends.

He soon improved his French and settled down to learn German, but his one outstanding talent was for mental arithmetic. Taller and more muscular than most of his classmates, he excelled at sport. At picnics and tea parties he impressed the Silligs with his good manners, but they disapproved of his cigarette smoking and a weakness for gambling at *petits chevaux* in the Kursaal instead of dutifully dancing with the daughters of the local gentry. He was not miserly and always started the subscription list for secret dormitory feasts of beer and sausages. As in Hartford, however, he continued to keep careful accounts of anything he paid for—items from cravats and ice cream to alms for beggars. He informed Jim Goodwin that a ticket to a ball had cost him $5.75; "dog cheap" for so much enjoyment.

He spent the holidays with his family in their new five-story Georgian house at 13 Prince's Gate. Situated on the south side of Hyde Park, it was adjacent to Rotten Row where Junius rode his horse and took the children to watch the fashionable Sunday parade. He already exuded the confidence of a prosperous banker. He wore a modish London-cut frockcoat over lighter drainpipe trousers as he left by carriage for the City every morning. At night he and his wife ritually changed into evening clothes for dinner served by a well-trained domestic staff supervised by Mortlock, their stately butler. Smoking a fine Havana afterward in his library, Junius seemed delighted with the change of scene, although Juliet had not relished her first taste of London's chilly fogs. She particularly missed her lovable old father who had settled in Medford, Massachusetts, after affronting his Troy congregation. But for the time being she was too preoccupied with furnishing their house and shopping for new clothes and jewelry to brood on Boston.

London's population had grown to over a million, with 130,000 in the City alone. The summer heat and stinking sewage had soon induced Junius to purchase Dover House at Roehampton, which offered pleasing glimpses of the Thames beyond his acres of good arable land and lush pastures. It was by no means a baronial mansion; more a smallish country house with a gilded salon, spacious dining room, a leather-scented paneled library, and several chintz-curtained bedrooms. After exhausting days in Old Broad Street or on the Exchange, Junius liked to sit back in a favorite wicker chair to watch his family and visitors playing the newly popular game of croquet.

Dover House and 13 Prince's Gate were both equipped to reciprocate the extensive hospitality of an endless London season. The Morgans could afford an excellent table and employed a front-rank French cook to prepare banquets or after-opera suppers. Junius prided himself on his cigars and a cellar of vintage clarets and burgundies, with even a few cases of rare Tokay for connoisseurs. Several of his guests arrived in carriages adorned by ancient crests or coronets. Aware of the English gentry's traditional abomination of "trade," George Peabody was gratified but not taken in by the number of invitations Junius received to shoot pheasant in the Shires. He knew that most of the titled hosts had benefited from the high-dividend issues handled by the firm, which consistently justified its claim to do "only first-class business, and that in a first-class way."

The shrewd old Yankee could congratulate himself on his choice of a partner whose manner perfectly suited the house's varied clientele, a cross-section of old nobility and a new-rich merchant breed. Though a confirmed Whig, Junius discreetly avoided taking sides on foreign policy or sensitive domestic politics. His dinner parties often included Members of Parliament, a Privy Councillor or two, and City moguls such as Thomson Hankey or a Baring. American businessmen liked to savor their port and cigars with East India Company directors and blunt-spoken industrialists from Lancashire or Yorkshire.

The Morgans were among privileged spectators at the Horse Guards when Queen Victoria, wearing a lilac dress with her bonnet and mantilla, dipped into a basket to hand out the first medals to Crimean heroes, some of whom hobbled on crutches or were brought forth in wheelchairs, while a band played stirring military airs. It was sweet music to Junius, who would often recapture the scene for his mother and some of his Boston cronies.

Juliet was less enchanted with the capital and now openly

49

yearned for New England. She was still a handsome woman, if slightly obese, and had to be squeezed by her maid into the elegant hooped skirts and tight bodices worn under short fur jackets, then the rage. She bought costly bibelots in Bond Street but still cherished the very ordinary china figurines collected in her schooldays. She arranged vast guest lists or worked on her needlepoint samplers when she was not writing long letters to her parents and her much-missed daughters. The whirl of entertainment always left her exhausted by the end of the season. At times she wept from homesickness and self-pity after friends had departed for America. The nervous strain would start rashes that made her seek refuge in her bedroom for weeks on end.

Pierpont was also becoming alarmed by blotches of eczema. Madame Sillig assured him sympathetically that they would clear with the coming warmth of spring, but he would often cut classes and spend long hours at solitaire. He also took to wandering by himself around the countryside, picking up broken fragments of stained glass outside ruined churches.

Junius had now decided that the Royal University of Göttingen would be more useful than Oxford or Harvard for his son's future career in international finance, then dominated by the cosmopolitan houses of Rothschild, Baring, and Hambro. Founded in the last century by England's King George II, when Elector of Hanover, Göttingen not only had an established academic reputation but prided itself on lectures delivered in the very best German, both in accent and phraseology. Otto von Bismarck, Emerson, and Longfellow figured among its eminent alumni.

Pierpont, who would concentrate on languages and mathematics, was delighted at being joined by Frank Payson, one of the brothers from Boston who had been with him at Vevey. En route for Germany they spent a few carefree days in Paris, visiting the theaters and tippling in boulevard cafés. But Pierpont surprised his friend by an unsuspected interest in paintings and antiquities. He was intoxicated by the wonders of Versailles and went twice to the Beaux-Arts Exposition, making detailed notes on the pictures that had most impressed him.

He soon discovered that Göttingen, whose hundreds of students included several from Britain, Scandinavia, and the United

States, was very different from the Sillig Institute where he had lorded it with no trouble. He received his first shock on being curtly enrolled as "John Morgan" after inscribing his two Christian names in full. Like Payson he needed private tuition in German to keep up with the lectures, but made good progress in that language as well as in French, chemistry, and mathematics. For several hours a day he buried himself away from temptation in the magnificent library of nearly half a million volumes.

Morgan was too high-spirited for that to last. In his second term he joined in a very full program of student parties and was quickly accepted. His bearing proclaimed good blood and old money. Even the most critical dandies could not fault his well-cut coats, the brocaded waistcoats, and obviously handmade boots. He wore his clothes with all the confidence of a tall strongly built figure; but for his too prominent nose that tended to redness, he was a handsome youth, full-lipped and with dark brown hair always carefully groomed.

His classmates were mostly of proud birth; the sons of generals, titled court functionaries, and rich landowners. Almost without exception they were intended for exclusive army regiments or careers in government service or the diplomatic corps. He liked best those from Saxony with flaxen hair and hard blue eyes. They typified a tradition of heel-clicking arrogance, rowdy horseplay, and bouts of heavy drinking.

Pierpont liked to air his loud bullfrog voice in songs around the piano at the local beer cellars. He had a remarkably good head for drink and could down huge steins like a true Bavarian. He cultivated a brief taste for strong Virginia tobacco but soon replaced his meerschaum with cigars. He had not smoked a cigarette since Vevey. He took up fencing and was elected to an exclusive club that permitted him to wear a saber but, although a fairly good swordsman, he did not care to risk having his face scarred on the University's *pank-boden* (dueling-ground).

After his first term, he was joined in London by his sisters, Sarah and Mary, whom he escorted around the sights with an undergraduate's air of cynical boredom. They were less amused by the Junker arrogance he had picked up. He took riding lessons and hacked every morning in the Row for an hour before driving off to Old Broad Street with his father. He had a desk in the counting room where he learned about the foreign securities market and sorted out correspondence for Mr. Peabody, who was about to leave for America. "He is a very agreeable gentleman and very full of wit, but a regular old bachelor," he reported to Jim Goodwin. Junius had confided with amusement that his generous partner, who could not resist a begging letter, was quirky about petty office economies. It seemed that he loved apples and would often send out a young clerk with tuppence to buy a penny ha'penny bag. The youth sometimes came back drenched or shivering with cold, but he was never allowed to keep the change.

After Sunday Church, Pierpont often strolled in the grounds of Dover House at Roehampton, which Junius had now extended by several acres and where he planned to start a model dairy farm with pedigreed Jersey cows. Juliet seldom emerged even for meals. Flaccid and listless, she languished in bed, propped up by pillows and with a bell at hand to summon the weary housemaids. That September she had pleaded so pathetically to be allowed to go home that her husband, perhaps with relief, arranged for her to stay first with Grandmother Morgan in Hartford and then spend Christmas at Medford with her parents. Pierpont and his father saw her off from Liverpool. On the train back to London Junius mentioned—not for the first time—that a year or two in Old Broad Street might prove beneficial, but Pierpont argued that a spell in some German or Dutch business house with American connections would suit him better.

In Göttingen, he was horrified to learn that his trunkful of letters and photographs, including a precious one of his mother, had vanished. Most of all he mourned the loss of his prized autograph album ("worth at least $100," he informed cousin Jim). The police arrested two youths and recovered the trunk but without the contents. In court Pierpont gave evidence clearly and in his much-improved German. He shed no tears when the culprits were jailed for seven years.

In April 1857, he celebrated his twentieth birthday with his American and German friends, followed some weeks later by a sentimental farewell party. He was sorry that the pleasant year had ended but consoled by a holiday tour with Jim Goodwin. They met in Berlin and ate a huge Fourth of July dinner. Over bumper-sized brandies they once again revived the dream of starting up in business together, preferably in Boston. Young and superoptimistic, with rolls of crisp banknotes padding their wallets, they now set off for Cologne, Brussels, and Paris, where Pierpont impressed his cousin with his fluent French and sophisticated ease. His euphoria cracked in Venice where a letter from his father awaited him. He was ordered to return to London at once to meet a Mr. Alexander Duncan, who might have a place for him in his offices at 11 Pine Street, New York City.

Arrangements were swiftly made for him to serve a two-year apprenticeship with Duncan, Sherman & Co., who acted as agents for Peabody's and other American houses in London. That September Morgan sailed for New York and moved into rooms at 45 West Seventeenth Street as the paying guest of Mr. Peabody's amiable nephew, Joe, who was older than himself and employed by a shipping firm.

He started in Pine Street as a very junior clerk under the friendly eye of one of the partners, Charles Dabney, a cousin of his former host in the Azores. The post was unpaid, but he had a satisfactory allowance from his father and an ample English-style wardrobe. Though not flush, he could afford a cab to downtown Manhattan when it was too wet for walking. Sometimes he hired a horse and rode there and back for the exercise. He continued to keep careful accounts of his expenditures, which normally ran to thirty cents for luncheons, thirty-seven cents for supper, and an occasional Saturday night dollar dinner. On impulse he once sent a five-dollar check to the Five Points Mission but later decided to serve the derelicts personally with hot soup and coffee.

He often stayed weekends in Hartford with his grandmother and, of course, met Jim Goodwin to compare notes and exchange gossip. He seemed exhilarated by New York, where he had been warmly received by several families with whom his father had social or business links. At the Dabneys' home he was reunited with his old friend, Frank Payson, whom he had met at Vevey in Switzerland and who would later marry Mary Dabney. Joe Peabody introduced him to the Grinnells, and it was at their house that he met George S. Bowdoin, who was courting their daughter, Julia, and would one day become his partner. After church the Grinnells would welcome him to Sunday supper, usually followed by hymn singing in which he joined with more gusto than tunefulness. He was also entertained by his father's one-time employer, Morris Ketchum, in New York and on his estate at Westport. He could not help envying the poise and self-assurance of young Edward, who had married recently and was already a partner in the firm of Ketchum, Son & Company.

With so much hospitality offered, he was out most evenings except Tuesdays and Fridays when he dutifully wrote to his father, reporting at length on market trends and anything else of mutual interest. He was attracted most of all to the Sturgeses of 5 East Fourteenth Street. He had first met the family at a weekend party in Newport and came to know them better through attending St. George's Episcopal Church in Stuyvesant Square, where Jonathan Sturges was a vestryman. His wife and two daughters, Virginia (Mrs. William Osborn) and Amelia, always known as Mimi, often performed duets on a grand piano, said to be the first in New York City.

In their home Pierpont met artists, poets, and accomplished musicians, recapturing a cosmopolitan ambience he had missed since leaving Europe. At twenty, however, he was still rather gauche under his veneer of Göttingen culture. At times he felt overawed and would have been at sea if he had not quickly established a relationship with Mimi, who drew him out when the others talked so fluently about books he had not read or debated the finer points of painting or music.

Two years older than himself, she was a petite, attractive brunette with a porcelain skin and sparkling white teeth. She laughed often but was less frivolous at heart than her sister and two brothers. She sensed the shyness behind Pierpont's curt overformal manner. She soon encouraged him to recall his escapades at Vevey and Göttingen, which he described with an amusing dash of irony. He often mentioned Junius Morgan's growing prestige in the City of London, but with pride rather than a son's warmth, and though he gave no signs of self-pity, Mimi may have guessed that his mother was more emotionally involved with her her daughters and the semi-invalid younger boy.

When the talk at 5 East Fourteenth grew too heavy or esoteric they would find a quiet corner and settle down to chess. He had quickly taken to Mimi's brothers, Frederick and Henry, who shared his taste for sports. She noticed how much more relaxed he seemed at the family's country retreat in Fairfield. He swam vigorously and always led the others at hill climbing and camping. Once or twice he was asked by Mimi's sister, Virginia, and her husband, Bill Osborn, to their Hudson Valley cottage near West Point, but he usually excused himself unless Mimi was going.

These weekends offered a welcome relief from his stuffy, airless office. He often suffered from headaches after long hours under the hissing gasjets, but he worked diligently at cost accountancy and bookkeeping under Charles Dabney, who approved his quick grasp of figures. Occasionally he broke the monotony of routine by taking messages or documents to Wall Street. He was fascinated by the busy Merchants Exchange in the Lord's Court Building, which straddled William and Hanover Streets and would later become the site of the National City Bank. Here baggy-eyed, paunchy brokers, who had paid $1,000 each for membership, lounged about in their chimney pot hats and brocaded vests, wearing silk pantaloons on hot summer days. The air was rich with cigar smoke and a buoyant market. For the past three years, month after month, six days a week including Saturdays, the members had fattened on profits from railroads, insurance, mills, factories, and almost anything else that could be transformed from prospectuses into quick-selling bonds on Wall Street or across the Atlantic in the City of London and on the Paris Bourse.

Pierpont Morgan had been in New York only a few short weeks before the panic started. At 11 Pine Street he began to notice that Mr. Dabney, normally so urbane, looked strained whenever he emerged from lengthy conferences in the partners' room. The end of the Crimean War had abruptly cut the demand for American wheat and Midwest farmers became impoverished. It was only the first of several blows to an overheated economy. Many small Western banks, which had recklessly backed speculative ventures, suddenly found it difficult to recover their huge loans or unload their debtor's notes on Wall Street even at heavy discounts. All over the country hundreds of undercapitalized factories and stores crumbled into bankruptcy. The Ohio Life and Trust was only one of a thousand companies that ruined their hapless investors. Mismanaged railroads buckled in the heat like their hastily laid tracks. Even those with large resources had to take punishing losses. Erie stock slipped from $64 to $18, and New York Central diminished by half. By mid-October the most reputable New York banks began to suspend payment in specie.

The slump was catastrophic for Peabody & Co. It suddenly found itself committed to acceptances of £2 million and with no hope of discharging even part of a stockpile of depreciating bonds on New York brokers and bankers, themselves now desperately short of ready funds. The firm was soon paying out thousands of pounds a day. Without raising a large temporary loan the partners would be forced to suspend business altogether. Both had agreed to supplement the firm's reserves from their own private capital. and Junius now faced the unpleasant prospect of having to sell or mortgage his two houses. Their only hope of salvation was a breathing space until the market recovered its balance.

Junius called on City bankers, large and small, to request temporary credits. He was received courteously but several houses hedged with half-promises of support. One or two hinted that credits might be available if Peabody's, so long a powerful competitor in the American market, would agree to go out of business with its good name intact. It was cynical opportunism and well timed. George Peabody had often announced his intention to retire, while Junius, still a relative newcomer, might be disposed to join some other banking house or even cut his losses and return home.

The partners saw through the maneuver and continued to put out feelers in reputable quarters. Thomson Hankey, governor of the Bank of England, earnestly reminded his fellow directors in Threadneedle Street of Peabody's invaluable contribution to Anglo-American relations throughout the past two decades. Wall Street meantime seethed with rumors that his firm had little hope of survival.

During those anxious weeks of crisis, Junius Morgan spent nerve-racked days and often sleepless nights searching for a solution. In late November he wrote to his son, gloomily predicting that he was about to lose everything he had made in his career. Pierpont reacted with a tenderness that only his two closest intimates, Mimi Sturges and Jim Goodwin, might have suspected. In one of the very few letters to be preserved, he wrote to his father on December 4, 1857, assuring him of his warmest sympathy and support. "It certainly is rather mortifying to call for aid although it is brought about by the conduct of others," he commented gravely. He announced his solemn intention to move to less costly rooms and possibly to persuade his employers to pay him *"some* salary" as from the first of January. It was a heartfelt though pathetic gesture, as Duncan, Sherman & Co. would certainly crash if their most important London client had to suspend.

The clouds lifted dramatically when the Bank of England announced a loan to Peabody's of £800,000, at very reasonable interest, with the promise of further funds up to a million sterling if and when required. It was a remarkable vote of confidence as Thomson Hankey had already rejected similar appeals from various American firms who did not measure up to his standards. A number of the City's most important houses soon followed his lead and also offered to assist. Several Wall Street brokers promptly renewed their orders to 22 Old Broad Street. Peabody & Co. recovered almost overnight and indeed hoisted its turnover above pre-slump levels.

This relief was soured for the Morgans by a cruel family tragedy in March 1858. Juliet was staying with friends in New York, recovering from a severe attack of jaundice, when a letter from Junius broke the news that their beloved younger son had died suddenly, probably from undiagnosed meningitis, then incurable. Pierpont tried to comfort his mother, but she would never forgive herself for not having been at her dying son's bedside. It was several weeks before she felt strong enough to sail for England. At Dover House she lay prostrate throughout a summer of appalling heat and drought, which so exposed the Thames sewage that the Queen and Prince Albert had to abandon a cruise from Windsor after only a few minutes, and Parliament adjourned when the stench became intolerable.

During the past months of crisis Pierpont Morgan had found a new respect and lasting affection for his father, but the totally unexpected prospect of poverty had made him determined to seek independence. His allowance had continued and the need to leave his comfortable lodgings with Joseph Peabody had passed, but he nevertheless approached his employers and was promoted to the post of junior cashier at a modest salary.

In his letters home he still conveyed his intention to branch out, preferably with Cousin Jim, once he had served his time in Pine Street. Junius counseled caution, but his son was plainly determined to rely more on his own efforts. His shelves now included several volumes on banking, currency, and shipping, which he often studied doggedly until past midnight. Most evenings he ate alone in a cheap neighborhood restaurant and gave up patronizing the Broadway billiard halls or dining at Delmonico's with Payson, Bowdoin, and other old comrades. He also declined invitations to sup with the hospitable Babcocks and Grinnells, usually returning to his rooms straight after Sunday evening services at St. George's.

But with the coming of spring he started to reappear at the Sturges soirées and drew even closer to Mimi. It was soon plain that they were becoming romantically attached. Her sister, Virginia, helped to steer them together with the discreet approval of Mr. and Mrs. Sturges, and Pierpont had noted that his mother took to Mimi from their very first meeting. Marriage, however, seemed remote unless he could make some money for himself. Duncan, Sherman & Co. offered little scope and he was restlessly aware that both Edward Ketchum and George Bowdoin, already established brokers, were growing more affluent by the hour.

The previous winter's slump had been like a New England frost, severe but short. The sudden thaw released a flood of new securities as bankers and company promoters, ignoring all recent experience, indulged in an orgy of plunging. From his office at 9 Battery Place, Vanderbilt was expanding his shipping empire and seeking to destroy the rival Cunard and Collins Lines by offering passage to Europe for only £50. He was also said to be planning control of the eastern railroad system by buying into small lines that might be extended to the Great Lakes and possibly the rich West. In New York he and other operators were blatantly aided and abetted by Tammany Hall and Mayor Fernando Wood, who doled out franchises for the fattest bribes.

A new breed of brash promoters, even more unscrupulous than the Commodore, had appeared on Wall Street. Among them was

Jim Fisk, a former circus barker turned theatrical impresario, who grabbed the undervalued Fall River Steamboat Line and strutted around in an admiral's gold-braided uniform. He talked too much, but his flashy bonhomie went down so well in Tammany Hall that "Uncle" Daniel Drew, who preferred to slink in the shadows, began to use him as a front for the floating of companies that offered extravagant dividends on insignificant, often quite imaginary, assets.

Another newcomer, Jay Gould, was subtler and more dangerous than Drew, Fisk, or even the Commodore himself. A year older than Pierpont Morgan, he had inherited none of his advantages and always cursed the cruel destiny that denied him a college education. He had survived a barefooted childhood, become a country store clerk, and followed this with grim toil in a tannery where he weakened his lungs. By cheating his employer he was able to set up as a leather merchant in Spruce Street, New York City.

In his teens he mastered geometry and developed into a passably good surveyor. He shared Vanderbilt's vision of one day building a railway clear across to California, but in temperament and appearance he was the complete antithesis of the flamboyant buccaneer, who would one day become his associate and pay dearly for the experience. He spoke and trod softly, his straggling black beard helping to give him the look of a half-starved traveling preacher. He ingratiated himself into the confidence of his father-in-law, a prosperous grocer who had enterprisingly acquired a small 62-mile railroad between Troy, New York, and Rutland, Vermont. Gould tricked him out of the deeds and soon sold out for $130,000. With the proceeds he bought up mortgage bonds in the Rutland and Washington line, then slipping into bankruptcy.

In a small office off Wall Street, where he had set up as a broker, he revealed the appetite of a voracious young jackal for tender guinea pigs. While Pierpont was still pondering his future, Jay Gould had already enriched himself by selling his clients short. Within a couple of years he was operating alone after driving one of his two partners to suicide and ruining the other.

Early in 1859 Junius joined his wife in New York, where he had meetings with bankers, insurance presidents, and various finan-

59

ciers, including Vanderbilt. He approved of Mimi Sturges and cordially invited her to accompany Juliet back to England. She would stay as their house guest until her parents arrived in London that April for a visit. He had several talks with Pierpont, who seemed more impatient than ever to quit his desk in Pine Street. Junius soon hinted to Dabney that his son might perhaps familiarize himself with the cotton business. Duncan, Sherman & Co., which had been rescued by Peabody's when so many other New York firms had crashed, could hardly ignore this "request." Pierpont traveled south soon after Mimi and his mother had sailed for England.

He passed a few days in Cuba visiting agencies. He also bought cigars for himself and various friends, including Jonathan Sturges, who had shown him so much kindness. He then settled down in the firm's New Orleans office, where he soon assimilated the essential facts and figures of the cotton trade. His good manners and fluent French helped to charm the plantation owners.

Although he missed Mimi Sturges and wrote her long letters, he reveled in the city's semitropical warmth and, when in funds, sampled the exquisite cuisine of the best restaurants. Most of all he enjoyed wandering around the wharves to watch ships loading and unloading sugar, cotton, and tobacco. Quite by chance he met a sea captain who mentioned that he had a cargo of Brazilian coffee that his consignee was unable to pay for. Pierpont expressed sympathy, asked him to quote a price, and extracted a few sample bags, intimating that his own firm could well be interested. He promptly made the rounds of the leading coffee importers and large stores, taking orders that would guarantee disposing of the entire cargo at a healthy profit. He then gave the captain a draft drawn on Duncan, Sherman's, which he casually informed of the deal. They wired back instructions to withdraw from the transaction immediately, as they had never previously bought or sold coffee and had no means of knowing whether his customers' drafts would be honored. By then he had already shifted his entire stock and cleared several thousand dollars.

Back in Pine Street his initiative was rewarded with a generous commission but also a little finger-wagging from Charles Dabney for so high-handedly pledging the firm's credit. The other directors were possibly none too sorry to see him depart for England that summer for a few months of unpaid leave.

He was overjoyed at being reunited with Mimi, who was staying with her parents at a rented apartment in Hanover Square. They dined often in Prince's Gate and admired the model dairy farm and well-stocked conservatories on the Dover House estate. Pierpont grandly spent part of his New Orleans commission at his father's tailor, Poole's of Savile Row. Elegantly turned out, he appointed himself guide to the Sturgeses for sightseeing. They joined the Hyde Park parade on Sundays in Junius's handsome barouche and paused to admire John Nash's Marble Arch, which had been removed from Buckingham Palace as it was found to be too narrow to accommodate King George IV's equestrian statue. That rainbow summer was only briefly clouded by Grandmother Morgan's death in Hartford.

Pierpont was too absorbed by his enchanting Mimi to attend 22 Old Broad Street for more than a few hours a week. He hardly ever saw George Peabody, now in his mid-sixties and absorbed in his plans to build homes for London's wretched slum dwellers and endow schools for American blacks. Junius humored the senior partner's philanthrophic tendencies but, like the English aristocracy, preferred to take his cue from the new "Ladies Newspaper and Court Circular," *The Queen*. Its first proprietor, Mrs. Beeton's husband, pontificated in an early editorial, "What the poor like is a simple soup as they will not digest anything very different from their usual fare. I think they may be taught to like lentil soup made without meal, thickened with good dripping and flavoured with a little onion or salt. Poverty or misery, be it remembered, are more generally the results of vice, laziness, and improvidence than of misfortune."

The Sturgeses were not called upon to judge the merits of Samuel Beeton's recommended lentil soup, with or without good dripping. At the Morgans' they sampled the best English fare, prepared by an admirable chef and supplemented by fresh milk, cream, and eggs from Junius's dairy. When they sailed home with Pierpont in December, their staterooms on the Cunard steamship bulged with several additional trunks for the ladies' newly bought gowns, furs, and trinkets, and space had to be found for

61

baskets of flowers and fruit from the hothouses at Dover House. Juliet's spirits had revived during their visit but she quickly subsided into her usual self-pity and she wept as she read and reread Pierpont's letter describing his jolly Christmas with Mimi and her family at the house on East Fourteenth Street.

Junius had proposed buying Pierpont a junior partnership in Duncan, Sherman and was nettled when the directors, apart from Charles Dabney, showed little enthusiasm for absorbing the banker's headstrong scion. Their reluctance would prove costly to them, but was welcomed by Pierpont, still exhilarated by his New Orleans coup, which had made him even more eager to set up for himself and marry.

With his father's approval and the promise of handling part of Peabody's American business, he rented a second-floor office at 54 Exchange Place and engaged a youth to keep his files in order. He would also be useful when Pierpont was incapacitated by his headaches or the alarming fainting spells that so often coincided with outbreaks of eczema. These troubles, often followed by a curious lethargy, vanished when he joined the Sturgeses for weekends at Fairfield or went back to Hartford to go fishing with Jim Goodwin.

That first year young Morgan was far too busy to worry overmuch about the anti-Abolitonist clamor from the southerners after Lincoln's nomination by the new Republican Party. Peabody & Co. commissioned him to buy securities on their behalf and Duncan, Sherman soon noticed that several other important clients were being discreetly steered to Exchange Place. Influential friends like the Ketchums, George Bowdoin, Bill Osborn, and Levi P. Morton, together with a number of Junius's important contacts in Boston and Philadelphia, were invaluable in getting the new firm started, but its rapid growth owed most to Pierpont's own efforts. Tall, erect, always immaculate in both dress and manner, he made an excellent impression whenever he appeared at the nearby Stock Exchange. He remained cool in crisis and showed a surprising grasp of foreign exchange in his twice-weekly letters to his father, who also learned with satisfaction that he had arranged to be confirmed at St. George's on March 29, 1861, by Bishop Horatio Potter.

That month Lincoln was inaugurated and several southern

states seceded. Soon Fort Sumter was bombarded and the Civil War began. One weekend in July, while Pierpont was staying with the Sturgeses at Fairfield, the company was stunned to hear of the Union Army's crushing defeat at Bull Run. It came at a time when the family was deeply concerned about Mimi, who that spring had developed a troublesome cough and high fevers.

Many had rushed to join the colors but volunteers became thinner on the ground after the first reports of horrific slaughter. Pierpont's uncertain health perhaps justified his avoiding the draft. At any rate, it is certain he paid the standard rate of $300 for a substitute. It requires an admiring official biographer like Herbert Satterlee to record with unblushing enthusiasm the fact that "he kept in touch with the man and helped him for years after the war."

The Rev. John Pierpont was less charitable toward his relations and felt more keenly the stimulus of a personal call to duty. At the age of 76 he enlisted as a chaplain with the 22nd Massachusetts but had to resign because of ill health. Secretary Salmon P. Chase gave him a desk in the Treasury where he copied out records of casualties in meticulous copperplate. From his eyrie he grieved for the thousands of boys on both sides who bled to death or rotted in stinking prison pens while others, including the prominent Morgans, father and son, were cosily insulated from anything more hazardous than peddling war bonds and inflated commodity stocks.

CHAPTER FOUR

The Civil War boosted profiteering in weapons, uniforms, provisions, and anything else that was needed quickly or was in short supply. A golden era of speculation—and peculation—had dawned. Contractors, often in league with venal politicians, bureaucrats, and customs men, disgorged leaky tents, hay, flour, and maggotty pork at extortionate prices. In the first months the Union government bought five million pairs of substandard shoes from suppliers who pocketed over $3 million in profit. Through his open line to Tammany Hall, Jim Fisk sold shoddy blankets by the tens of thousands.

Commodore Vanderbilt, by now the second richest man in the United States after William B. Astor, trumpeted his patriotism by presenting Lincoln with his favorite steamer for which action he was later awarded a gold medal by Congress. When shipping became essential to blockade the southern ports and carry merchandise across the Atlantic, he offered his fleet of sixty vessels for as much as $2,500 a day, while his eastern railroads carried soldiers and freight to and from the battle zones.

The Union's million-dollar-a-day expenditure could not be met by taxation alone and depended largely on bond sales to the public. A pushy young Philadelphian named Jay Cooke soon broke all records in this field. He made his debut in June 1861 by promoting a $3 million loan for Pennsylvania. Its success led to an invitation from Washington to spearhead a nationwide campaign. In a barnstorming drive he used brass bands, extensive newspaper advertising, and an army of salesmen to dispose of almost 60 percent of the Union's bond issues, sometimes raising as much as $2 million in a single day. From his headquarters in South Third Street, Philadelphia, he undercut old-established local houses like Drexel & Co. by charging a commission of only 0.5 percent. In four years he showed a profit of over $7 million on an immense turnover. His near-monopoly was resented by many bankers in New York, like Ketchum's, who had to satisfy their greed by gobbling up Treasury notes at well below par. Smaller operators, such as Pierpont Morgan, continued to deal profitably in foreign exchange and acceptances, though always vulnerable to an unsettled London market.

George Peabody had, under wartime pressure of business, reluctantly postponed his retirement, but most of the firm's turnover in securities was handled by Junius. Both partners needed all their finesse to maintain a diplomatic stance in the environment of London. The majority of liberals favored the Union cause, supported even by Lancashire's millhands facing unemployment through reduced cotton imports. The City bankers piously denounced slavery but regarded the Confederates as a gallant gentleman's army heroically defending its traditions, though outgunned and outnumbered rather like the immortal Light Brigade at Balaclava.

While Peabody & Co. nervously trod water, Pierpont tried to concentrate on his duties, though he was much concerned over Mimi, with whom he spent every weekend at Fairfield. Her eyes had lost their old sparkle and he would often hold her in his arms until her terrible spasms of coughing had passed.

Pierpont was absorbed in routine, but his long office hours and Mimi's distressing condition may have combined to impair his normally cool judgment in one unfortunate deal. With ample funds from his father to start up in Exchange Place and with his own mounting income, he presented an inviting target to operators in need of ready capital and, above all, a reputable front. Pierpont Morgan had both, but he still lacked the caution and experience that would have put him on his guard when a business proposition that appeared to guarantee easy money with a minimum of risk came his way.

Early in August 1861, when the Union Army was short of weapons after Bull Run, he was approached by a smalltime political lobbyist and entrepreneur, one Simon Stevens, whose very respectable sister had been a teacher at the Public High School in Hartford. Stevens glibly explained that he required financing to purchase 5,000 Hall carbines at $12.50 each. They were on offer from a dealer named Arthur M. Eastman at $11.50, and an extra dollar would be needed to rifle the barrels for army use. General John C. Frémont (a former presidential candidate) had unhesitatingly agreed to pay $22 for each satisfactorily serviced weapon.

With the carbines as collateral and assured of being reimbursed from the first proceeds, Pierpont advanced Stevens $20,000, with an extra dollar for every weapon delivered, plus his expenses for insurance and carriage. It seemed a routine transaction, but the J. P. Morgan of future years would have first checked out Arthur Eastman's distinctly shady record. And he might have investigated the provenance of those Hall carbines, which had previously been declared obsolete by the Chief of Ordnance and placed on the market, more or less as scrap.

Eastman had bought them at $3.50 each, but still lacked the cash to take delivery when he agreed to dispose of them for $11.50 to Simon Stevens. The latter, also wholly without means, now had to raise enough to complete his deal with Eastman and then have the carbines rifled for resale to his good friend, General Frémont. Morgan's loan would therefore open the way for the Army to hand over $110,000 for the very weapons, slightly adapted, which Eastman had so recently picked up for a paltry $17,500.

The old carbines were duly released to Eastman by the Ordnance Department, but the rifling took far longer than Stevens had anticipated. After almost six weeks, when only half the adapted weapons had been delivered to Frémont's headquarters, Pierpont Morgan impatiently demanded the $26,345.54 due to him. He deducted this sum from the Army's first draft, but refused to advance Stevens the further cash he urgently needed to pay Arthur Eastman for the second batch of 2,500 carbines.

By now Pierpont was far too alarmed by Mimi's illness to continue with a troublesome deal and he had grown suspicious of both Stevens and his shadowy partner. He may also have heard

67

whispers that the House of Representatives was appointing a select committee to look into fraudulent war contracts which could well include the Hall carbine affair. Ketchum's, however, pooh-poohed any serious threat from the antiprofiteering lobby in Washington. They had no hesitation in loaning Stevens $50,000 at 7 percent, plus commission.*

Edward Ketchum was more than grateful to pick up this profitable piece of business. A cynical opportunist, he imagined that his rather straitlaced, churchgoing friend had either lost his nerve or suffered a last-minute tweak of New England conscience. He was still more astonished to find Pierpont turning his back on Wall Street to play the quixotic role of lovesick nurse.

At the end of the summer Mimi was brought home to New York for better medical and nursing care. The doctors had diagnosed advanced tuberculosis. Pierpont visited her every evening and could feel the dry burning skin when he stooped to kiss her flushed cheek. Her condition rapidly worsened. She was sinking so fast that a leading consultant announced her only slender hope to be a prolonged stay in a warm climate. Pierpont at once made a proposal of marriage that Mimi sobbingly rejected. Mr. and Mrs. Sturges, who were making hasty arrangements to take her abroad, also implored him to think again, but he brushed all arguments aside so impulsively that Mimi at last accepted him. He had decided that only his devotion could save his beloved.

Jim Goodwin came to New York and agreed without hesitation to take a leave of absence from his father's business in Hartford and stand in at Exchange Place. Pierpont had hoped to be married at St. George's, but Mimi's doctors thought a short simple ceremony in the bride's home would be wiser and they were married there by the rector of St. George's on October 7, 1861. There had not been sufficient time for Junius Morgan and his wife to arrange passage from London.

---

*The Ketchums would have to wait almost four years for their money. They refused to settle for a lesser amount proposed by the Secretary of War's Commission after the tawdry background came to light. The courts reluctantly decided to uphold Stevens's claim, but only after a congressional committee had severely censured him, Eastman, Frémont, and the Ketchums. Pierpont Morgan was not called to testify or even named.

The guests who were assembled in the front room could just glimpse the ceremony performed in the back parlor. Mimi was so near collapse that, immediately afterward, the folding doors were closed to spare her the strain of joining her relatives and friends for the wedding breakfast. Most of them were in tears when she waved a spindly hand in farewell as her husband carried her out to a waiting carriage. They drove to the West Fourteenth Street pier and embarked on a steamship for Liverpool.

Anxious to lose no time, they stayed only briefly in Prince's Gate and left for the warm sunshine of Algiers where Pierpont had reserved a capacious hotel suite. He lavished large sums on doctors and a relay of nurses, who could do little to ease her sufferings. Her stertorous breathing and pathetic moans gave them sleepless nights while most days she drifted into a slurred drowsiness only broken by the coughing up of blood-flecked sputum. After a joyless, tearful Christmas, endured in a bedroom sickly with disinfectant and medicaments, he arranged to take his wife to Nice to consult a specialist in pulmonary diseases. The doctor held out no prospect of recovery. They were joined in Nice by Mrs. Sturges, who comforted him when her daughter's long suffering was mercifully ended on February 17.

Pierpont stayed for a while at Prince's Gate while arrangements were being made to sail back to America with the coffin. He wore stiff mourning black and had grown a straggly moustache. A widower at twenty-four, after only four agonizing months of marriage to a wraith, he looked gaunt and crumpled. HIs father attempted to rally him, but he had withdrawn into a numb desolation. He ate little but endlessly smoked the cigars that he had naturally put aside during the last months with Mimi. He had to be persuaded to take even a short daily walk in Hyde Park and preferred to sit quietly in his mother's room, now fully understanding her sense of loss after his brother's death. He found it almost impossible to make polite conversation with the few visitors who called during that bleak winter. London itself lay under a pall of mourning for the Prince Consort, a recent victim of typhoid.

Mimi was laid to rest in Fairfield, in a cemetery heavy with the fragrance of May blossom. For the rest of his life Pierpont Morgan would visit her grave either on their wedding anniversary or on February 17, when he had knelt with Mrs. Sturges beside her deathbed. He sobbed as the coffin was lowered. With it he buried his own youth, and for the first time in his life, he wept in public; he would do so only once again—when he learned of his father's death.

Soon after the funeral he appeared to have regained his normal self-control. He persuaded Jim Goodwin to stay on with him, and they rented a house together at 42 West Twenty-first, with a capable Irish cook and a man-of-all-work who acted as a valet and waited on them at table. Pierpont remained in somber mourning for an entire year, refusing all social invitations except from Mimi's parents. He had retained his moustache but kept it neatly trimmed. Although dressed in black, he was always perfectly attired and betrayed no hint, except to Jim Goodwin, of his inner suffering. When his mother arrived in the fall, she moved in and persuaded them to give a few quiet dinner parties for close friends like Mimi's two brothers, Edward Ketchum and his wife, Joe Peabody, and Charles Dabney, his old mentor at Duncan, Sherman's.

Business flourished during the Civil War. Speculation rode tandem with a frantic development of transport. On July 1, 1862, President Lincoln had signed the Pacific Railroad Act sponsoring the building of a line linking the 100th meridian with the West Coast. It would be seven hard, slogging years, with much skullduggery, before the two rivals, Union Pacific, building its track across the prairies from the East, and Central Pacific, driving over the Sierras from California, finally met at Promontory Point in Utah.

The rewards were enormous. Between them the two companies would be handed twenty million acres of free land and over $50 million in government subsidies. Over difficult locations that was as much as $48,000 per mile of track laid. The vast rights of way, extending to ten miles on either side of each mile of track, were split up and sold in sections to an army of real estate operators, not too finicky in their dealings with the officials who, for a share of the loot, promoted bond issues. The speculators sold many sites at high prices to new settlers but retained areas confirmed by surveyors as potentially rich in coal, oil, and minerals.

Commodore Vanderbilt, though aware of the handsome fringe benefits enjoyed by the heavily subsidized contractors in the West, was not interested in laying new track. He preferred to direct the bulk of his wartime shipping revenues into strategic eastern railroads like the Erie, of which he became a director in 1862, and New York Central, a small line connecting Albany and Buffalo. He then decided to invest heavily in the almost insolvent New York and Harlem, paying only $9 for its nominal $100 stock. By April 1863 it touched $75. He made another killing by buying control of the Hudson River line.

Meantime, in New York and other cities the sale of war bonds and corporation stock, notably in railroads, netted rich hauls for brokers. Pierpont Morgan had enterprisingly installed a private telegraph wire in his office to stay abreast of the fast-changing war news. He made good use of it in his coded messages to the London office.

Junius was now in almost full charge of the City office as George Peabody had virtually retired to devote himself to philanthropy. He had donated a million dollars to build model dwellings for 650 London artisans at only five shillings a week for two rooms, and six shillings for three. The tenement blocks would have playgrounds for the children, and each apartment was to be equipped with fireplace, oven, boiler, and cupboard space. Tenants would also enjoy unfamiliar luxuries like baths and a laundry. The original site chosen was the East End's worst black spot, Spitalfields, where at first very few could afford even this low rent for what was a patch of relative paradise. Peabody persevered and soon found other suitable locations in Chelsea, Shadwell, Bermondsey, and Islington. He would invest another two million dollars before "Peabody Buildings" were at last ready for occupation in 1865. He also earmarked $3 million to endow an educational fund for emancipated blacks once the war he was confident the Union would win was over.

Like Junius he staunchly backed the Union, but the firm's status as official representatives of the Lincoln administration was viewed with suspicion by Southern sympathizers in the City of London. They placed huge blocks of American securities, but it was a high-risk business while the war situation remained uncertain. Often they had to sell at well below par and had to buy in unsold stock on their own account. This finally yielded large profits when the market turned bullish with the news of Union victories by the summer of 1863.

Their huge turnover inevitably attracted venomous sniping from some Wall Street brokers who had either stayed on the sidelines or overcautiously hedged their bets. The London partners, both strongly anglophile, also had some uncomfortable months when Lincoln's supporters violently denounced Britain following the Confederate *Alabama*'s devastating raids on Union shipping. Built by Laird's of Birkenhead and armed by British seamen off the Azores—a clear breach of neutrality—her prey included Vanderbilt's *Ariel,* which was intercepted and boarded off the coast of Cuba. The victim was surprisingly allowed to proceed after her skipper had signed a bond pledging the owner to pay $250,000 within thirty days of Southern independence!

Pierpont had emerged from his year's mourning with a romantic aura for the young ladies in his circle. He behaved with the grave decorum expected of a devout churchgoer. It was all the more praiseworthy in those free-and-easy wartime years when New York boasted several hundred brothels and houses of assignation. Some mornings he would ride in Central Park. He was readily identified by his stiff Prussian-like seat and the familiar cigar jutting from his mouth. At the office he worked all hours and relaxed most evenings by visiting dear friends like the Sturgeses, Babcocks, and the younger Ketchums. He had also made the acquaintance of Charles Tracy, a vestryman at St. George's and a prominent lawyer, who occasionally invited him home for Sunday supper at his home on Seventeenth Street.

The six Tracy girls ranked high among New York's beauties. Like many others Pierpont was smitten by twenty-year-old Frances, who disliked his rather abrupt manner but made allowances for what she assumed were the effects of his tragic bereavement. "Fanny" was a tallish, vivacious brunette with a deliciously slim waist admirably suited to the contemporary hooped skirts. She could afford to dress in the height of fashion, and Pierpont approved of her elegant suede gloves in her favorite color, lavender, and the long jet earrings she usually wore at night. She was not coquettish, but on Sunday evenings she liked to sit beside him and did not join in the teasing when he sang hymns off key.

During the summer of 1863 when he first joined the Tracy circle, he also met William Henry ("Billy") Vanderbilt, from whom he extracted a liberal donation to the Y.M.C.A. Despised by his father as a slow-thinking weakling, Billy had been packed off to work on one of the family farms after a modest grammar school education. He started his business apprenticeship by clerking in Daniel Drew's Wall Street office for three dollars a week. Browbeaten, nervous, and painfully shy, he took to piety and married the daughter of a Brooklyn minister.

In his middle years his ruddy side-whiskered face suggested a plodding farmer, but he proved his ability as receiver of the derelict thirteen-mile Staten Island Railway, which he quietly restored to profitability. When the Commodore started to fight off Gould, Drew, and other enemies it was noticed that Billy appeared more often at conferences in Battery Place. His appointment as chief executive of the Hudson Line confirmed whispers that he was being groomed as the aging Commodore's successor, but most of Wall Street's insiders still ridiculed the prospect of the obese, clumsy-looking heir ever running the gigantic Vanderbilt empire.

Pierpont Morgan was among the very small minority who did not underrate his ability. Morgan's firm did a brisk turnover in railroad shares, but Pierpont avoided speculation on his own account even in such tempting Vanderbilt stocks as Harlem and Hudson River when they stood at very low levels. He preferred foreign exchange, a field which always fascinated him.

Edward Ketchum shared his view, but he had also noticed that, since Morgan's return from Europe, he seemed harder, less approachable, and at times almost neurotic in his dedication to business routine. Utterly amoral and rapacious himself, Ketchum suspected that his prim and outwardly punctilious young friend might be feeling restless and not altogether fulfilled by his role as agent for the powerful London office.

In the late summer of '63, he dropped a hint that the bullion market offered far more lucrative and safer returns than railroad shares. Pierpont agreed. He was aware that the federal government had been forced to issue millions of dollars' worth of paper bills for the soldiers' pay and other expenses. Only the interest was paid in specie. Soon three paper "Greenbacks" were needed to buy a single gold dollar. It was a clear signal to speculators, who began to meet in the so-called Gold Room on the corner of William Street and Exchange Place where they dabbled in bullion after the Stock Exchange had closed.

The price of gold zigzagged with the changing military situation, which could be profitably exploited by rumormongers buying and selling on a 10 percent margin. These pickings seemed negligible to Edward Ketchum, who saw a far bigger potential in cornering gold. Part of the hoard might be unobtrusively unloaded on the London market through some reputable house like Peabody & Co. Pierpont, already well established in foreign securities, provided perfect cover for Ketchum, whose open intervention would inevitably have alerted rival speculators. The telegraph wire at 53 Exchange Place might also be invaluable for prompt action on the latest war news.

That September the two partners, working through Pierpont's firm and a number of nominees, bought gold on margin to the tune of almost $5 million. The price rose steadily from 130 to 143 an ounce, with Edward Ketchum's participation still remaining a closely guarded secret. By mid-October *The New York Times* noted that over a million dollars in gold had been shipped to England by "a young House in Exchange Place, respectably connected on the other side," briefly commenting that this seemed higher than the firm's normal run of bullion trading. But it was more than enough to jolt other dealers whose activity sent gold up to 156 on Wall Street and 171 in the London market. By the time Ketchum judged the moment ripe to sell, he and his partner shared a tidy profit of $160,000.

The bullish market quickly subsided, burning the fingers of those who had dared to sell short. On October 21, *The New York Times* hit out at "a knot of unscrupulous gamblers who care nothing for the credit of the country." Again Pierpont's name was unmentioned, no doubt due to his association with the esteemed firm of Peabody, Morgan & Co. (Satterlee's official biography omits all mention of his hero's part in the dubious adventure.)

In June 1864 Congress passed an act making it a criminal

offense to trade in gold futures but left too many loopholes open. The notorious Gold Room was temporarily shut down but speculators like the Ketchums merely transferred their operations to a nearby venue known as The Coal Hole, and a Wall Street banking lobby, which included Pierpont Morgan, angrily denounced Congress for its "utter lawlessness in seeking to paralyze legitimate business." The repeal of the act soon followed.

This time, however, young Morgan did not join in the charge of the bulls. Although Junius valued his penetrating market analyses, he was disquieted by his impetuosity and the undue influence of smooth-talking hustlers like Ketchum. It seemed to him that the busy office in Exchange Place might benefit from the appointment of another director, preferably some experienced old hand like Charles Dabney. Pierpont welcomed the idea. He persuaded Jim Goodwin to stay on for a further spell and together they rented a well-appointed brownstone house at 227 Madison Avenue. It was not large but suitable for entertaining friends and important clients.

The new firm of Dabney, Morgan & Co. came into being in the fall of 1863 and flourished from the start. Pierpont continued to deal with bonds and other securities, but he was relieved of tedious routine by Mr. Dabney, who united accountancy skills with a strong New England conscience. He disapproved of all wildcat speculation, especially in bullion. Pierpont had prudently kept clear of the Coal Hole, which seethed with profit-crazed gamblers, including his former partner.

The *Alabama* had at last been sunk, but various Confederate successes again tempted Edward Ketchum to buy gold on margin. Calamities for the Union of course depressed the value of its currency thus making gold more valuable and increasing the number of dollars that would have to be paid for every ounce. The price of gold shot up but declined when reports pointed to an inevitable Union victory. Morris Ketchum advised his son to cut his losses, but he preferred to gamble on a rise and continued to stockpile. He soon ran out of funds and stole $2 million in cash and securities from the family firm, forging checks for an extra $1 million that he needed as collateral for still more loans.

Pierpont Morgan parted with $85,000 on the strength of seventeen of these forged checks. This not only wiped out his entire profit from their earlier venture, but actually left him $5,000 out of pocket. The gesture, which invoked no sympathy from either Junius or Charles Dabney, was costly, but he never regretted answering Ketchum's desperate cry for help. He sent a clerk to testify at the eventual trial and thus avoided seeing his friend condemned to four and a half years in jail.

As the Civil War entered its last stages, seventy-year-old George Peabody finally left his firm. It would now trade as J. S. Morgan & Company. As the Union government's chief fiscal agents, the partnership had profited by its initiative while conservative houses like Rothschild and Baring cautiously awaited the outcome of the war suspicious of the paper currency pumping out of Washington. They disapproved of Wall Street's feverish speculation in gold and received reports from reliable agents like August Belmont confirming widespread civic corruption over land grants and franchises.

Junius Morgan was far more sanguine. Even before Peabody's retirement he had already mapped out the firm's future business scenario. With much of America's merchant fleet destroyed, it seemed obvious to him that links between the Midwest and the Atlantic and Pacific coasts must quickly expand to carry grain, cattle, coal, and iron. A reservoir of war profits would clearly become available for investment, and not only in railroads like the Union Pacific. Pierpont's detailed reports hinted that Vanderbilt, Collis Huntington, and other railroad operators might extend their empires to include monopolies in public utilities, sugar, tobacco, and a whole range of consumer goods. The competition would be fierce, with dozens of private corporate industries, which had previously relied on small local banks, thirsting for more capital.

A victorious federal government, preferably led by the Republican Party, would need to float massive bond issues for reconstruction. And Junius could not doubt that England, anxious to sell her piled-up surpluses of manufactured goods and hungry for American raw materials, would recruit an army of investors attracted by high yields on stocks and bonds.

Everything pointed to a boom for the firm of J. S. Morgan & Co., with smaller but significant benefits for its offshoot in Exchange

Place, now enlarged to four roomy offices. Pierpont was comforted for his losses in the painful Ketchum affair by his first year's share of Dabney, Morgan's profits: a satisfactory $53,286. With the prospect of further expansion, if and when his father's postwar plans matured, he felt justified in proposing to Fanny Tracy in March 1865. Only seven weeks later they went to the altar in St. George's, with Joe Peabody acting as best man.

The marriage was no romantic love match but, at least for Morgan, a merger that would pay handsome dividends in comfort, without personal inconvenience. Morgan was a man with a powerful sexual appetite, as he would prove in the years ahead, but he was probably still a virgin when he married for the second time. Mimi's frail and infectious condition had almost certainly ensured that their brief union had not been consummated.

Sensible, practical Fanny would dutifully accept her role as wife, mother, and chatelaine. At the time of their marriage she was still too young to fathom the depths of his lasting grief or suspect that no other woman could ever challenge the etherealized image of his doomed first bride. During his anguished year of mourning he had bought a painting by George A. Baker for $1,500 at an auction. It was a portrait of a fragile-looking girl who reminded him of Mimi, and he gave it pride of place over the mantelpiece in the living room at West Twenty-first Street. Later he removed it to his library where he spent his solitary hours.

On June 14 the bride and groom sailed to Europe for a ten-week honeymoon, staying for a while at Prince's Gate where Fanny charmed Pierpont's parents and sisters. Flattered at being interviewed for once instead of his father, he broke off a morning's sightseeing to air his views about the possible effects of Lincoln's assassination. "We are going some day to show ourselves to be the richest country in the world in natural resources," he solemnly predicted. "It will be necessary to go to work, and to work hard, to turn our resources into money to pay the cost of the war just as soon as it is ended." The newlyweds went on to Paris and then Vevey to visit the warm-hearted Silligs.

They moved into 227 Madison Avenue where Louisa, the first of their three daughters, was born within a year. Pierpont's son and heir arrived on September 7, 1867, in the house they had rented for the summer at Irvington-on-Hudson. Other marriages

77

had meanwhile expanded the clan. Pierpont's sister, Sarah, became the bride of George Hamilton Morgan, who traced his ancestry back to Miles Morgan's first marriage. He was soon taken into partnership in Exchange Place. Pierpont's younger sister, Mary, married a Wall Street broker, Walter Hayes Burns, whom Junius persuaded to leave Morton, Bliss & Co. and join his London office.

The Rev. John Pierpont ignored these celebrations. Since the early days of the war he had distanced himself from his self-absorbed daughter and her millionaire husband. He died at eighty-three, almost penniless, but rich in pride and principle, rejoicing over the liberation of the black man and the healing of his country's wounds.

To the grandson he had baptized, he bequeathed not only his name but a nose that, like the foul instrument of some witch's curse, would swell into a monstrous obscenity even as its owner's wealth and power grew.

Part Two

THE HARVEST

CHAPTER FIVE

Pierpont Morgan's unfortunate venture into bullion dealing was only partly due to Ketchum's guile. It was also the result of greed and an urge to assert himself exemplified by his earlier cotton coup in New Orleans. Even at school he had shown his itch for leadership by taking charge of weekend climbs and informal picnics. During his bachelor days with Joe Peabody and Jim Goodwin, he organized small dinner parties with the same mathematical precision he applied to his office duties and the meticulous reports to his father.

His friends good-naturedly tolerated an eagerness, bordering on eccentricity, to supervise christenings, weddings, and even funerals outside his own family circle. He could be difficult and pedantically critical of inefficiency, but they regarded his autocratic manner as evidence of perfectionism rather than ostentation. They had to admit that arrangements went well in his hands, and that he spared neither time nor personal expense to ensure success.

This managerial thrust, backed by an old family name and his close links with a powerful London house, automatically drew him to committee work. Soon after the Civil War he had become a member of the St. Luke's Hospital board of management, followed by his election to the vestry at St. George's Church in Stuyvesant Square, and the post of honorary financial adviser to the Y.M.C.A. Often chairing committee meetings, he would pry open the most complex balance sheet and extract a very practical plan of action without time-wasting civilities. His efforts were appreciated, though some found him too curt and uncompromising for a man of barely thirty.

His wife soon became aware of his passion for regimentation. He not only dictated her choice of clothes, including color, style, and cut, but had the last word on menus once they began to entertain more lavishly. After the birth of their first child he insisted on having the crib at his bedside. Fanny and the nurse had to yield to his views on baby Louisa's diet and what she should wear for outings. He took still firmer control of the upbringing of his son, John Pierpont Morgan, Jr., whom he called Jack, a familiarity that was restricted to the closest relatives and friends.

Morgan's snobbish reserve, soon to become as familiar as his nose, was very much in evidence during the hot summer months when he traveled every day by train from Irvington-on-Hudson to New York. He hid behind his cigar smoke and a bulky wad of office papers so as to discourage smalltalk. However, with two regular fellow commuters, Samuel Sloan and Chauncey Depew, both in the railroad business but obviously "gentlemen," he would occasionally unbend.

Sloan, president of the small Delaware, Lackawanna, and Western line, was openly contemptuous of upstart new promoters, but in his conversation he did not spare more powerful entrepreneurs like Vanderbilt, whose undercutting threatened to put him out of business. Pierpont kept his ears open but remained neutral when Sloan argued with Depew, who had recently joined the Commodore's staff. When tempers became overheated, he would tactfully propose a game of three-handed whist. Within a very few years this same trio would be playing for million dollar stakes. Sloan first paved the way into railroad finance for Pierpont Morgan, who would in turn assist Chauncey Depew's spectacular rise to the presidency of New York Central.

Yale-educated Depew had been on the point of accepting the post of Minister to Japan in 1866 when Vanderbilt, sensing his potential as a lobbyist in Washington and Albany, invited him to become attorney for the Harlem line. He had briskly overcome his reluctance. "Don't be a damned fool! There is nothing for you in politics or Japan. Railroads are the career for a young man."

For once he had not exaggerated. Congress had continued Lincoln's policy of land grants and subsidies that would double the nation's railroad mileage in eight frenzied postwar years. While Vanderbilt and Gould still concentrated on the smaller eastern networks, the two great transcontinental lines, Central Pacific and Union Pacific, were moving rapidly to completion.

Such developments, demanding enormous investment, had transformed the financial scene from the heady war years when shady companies, quite often proclaiming paper assets of $500,000 with no more than 50 cents in hard cash behind them, had mushroomed with the connivance of the small state banks whose reserves would seldom have stood up to proper auditing. Financial power had switched to the big-city financiers and bankers who were equipped to handle a phenomenal industrial boom generated by the inventive genius which, before the end of the century, would result in the grant of half a million new patents. The names of Graham Bell and Thomas Alva Edison would soon ring around the world. Meantime, in addition to the thousands of high-interest prospectuses issued by promoters of mining, real estate, machinery, and commodity companies, a vast reservoir of investment capital would be tapped by industrialists like Andrew Carnegie and John Davison Rockefeller to create their monopolies in steel and oil.

The opportunities for plunder were obvious in this new age of feverish enterprise. Tammany Hall's "Boss" Tweed, who ruled New York City for three freebooting years from 1868, had a private army of political wheeler-dealers and judicial doormats on his payroll. He amassed a large private fortune from turning a blind eye to the issue of fraudulent municipal bonds and granting franchises like that for building New York's Viaduct Railroad. Few dared to withhold contributions to his slush fund. When Vanderbilt rebelled at his gross extortion, Tweed and his chief accomplice, Mayor Oakey Hall, at once switched their allegiance to Jay Gould, Daniel Drew, and diamond-studded Jim Fisk, who together set out to rob Vanderbilt of his majority holding in the Erie line.

They managed to get on the board and started buying more

shares. When this proved too costly, they engineered the flotation of more stock, printing so many new certificates, which were snapped up by an unsuspecting public, that even Vanderbilt's resources failed to block the trio's short-selling, a technique that he had himself used so profitably in the past. After the market had enjoyed an artificial boost from so much heavy investment, the Gould trio swiftly depressed Erie stock by unloading their holdings, which they then bought back at the lowest figure.

By this maneuver Vanderbilt not only lost control of the railroad but his attempt to maintain its stock at realistic price levels cost him the better part of $7 million, most of which went into the pockets of the conspirators. Boss Tweed was rewarded with a seat on the board, plus a substantial block of shares and over a million dollars as "legal expenses" for persuading judges and political lackeys in Albany to condone the fraud.

Gould, an evil genius with an infinite capacity for raking in gains, had this time underrated his opponent. Early in 1868 Vanderbilt secured an injunction preventing him from printing further blocks of Erie bonds, which could be converted into stock and dumped on the market. With the likelihood of arrest also imminent, Gould and his friends thought it high time to depart from the jurisdiction of New York. They holed up at Taylor's Hotel in Jersey City with suitcases stuffed full of greenbacks. It was an uneasy sanctuary. Gould went to Albany where, with the help of a lobby of corrupt officials and a battery of lawyers, he succeeded in having Vanderbilt's injunction rejected. However, after a short but unpleasant time under arrest on a technicality, Gould decided to make his peace with the Commodore by agreeing to buy back Erie stock at a figure that restored almost all of his victim's losses. "Never kick a skunk," declared Vanderbilt when taunted by a reporter for not putting his enemies behind bars.

But the sordid tale had shaken investor confidence, which was soon to reach rock bottom with the Crédit Mobilier scandal. Working through this dummy construction company, the Union Pacific promoters had originally contracted to build their line for $50 million in federal bonds. Thanks to falsified accounts, the bill soared to $94 million and its stockholders were being paid a 100 percent dividend by the end of '67. By the time the railroad was

84

completed the Crédit Mobilier stock was valued at a cool $260 million.

However, the ugly rumors relating to Crédit Mobilier were temporarily dissipated in the euphoria of the celebrations on May 10, 1869, when the tracks of Central Pacific and Union Pacific at last met at Promontory Point, west of Ogden, Utah. Flanked by frock-coated dignitaries, who ignored the casualties among Chinese and Irish laborers working off old scores with pickhandles and revolvers, Governor Leland Stanford of California, the Central Pacific chief, lifted a sledgehammer to drive a ceremonial gold spike into the last cross tie. He lost his footing and sprawled in the mud, but the historic moment, recorded coast to coast by telegraph, was cheered in Wall Street and echoed in the thunder of a hundred-gun salute.

The shenanigans failed to allay public suspicion of railroad shares. On Exchange Street where Pierpont now occupied the largest of four offices on the first floor, he found it easier to launch a $2 million loan for the Peruvian government than to float Kansas Pacific's 7 percent mortgage bonds, a sound enough issue under more normal market conditions. He finally shifted them, thanks to support from the London house.

Although the firm had kept well clear of the unsavory Erie battles, it benefited when Commodore Vanderbilt suddenly needed to import vast quantities of iron rails for New York Central. The deal was smoothly handled in London by Junius Morgan, but Pierpont's quiet efficiency at the New York end had impressed Vanderbilt, his son Billy, and Depew. Not long afterward he took a minor but useful part in another important deal initiated by his father. This time the rising young ironmaster, Andrew Carnegie, who had already piled up his first million and commanded an income of $50,000 a year, made a special visit to London to engage the services of J. S. Morgan & Co.

He had secured an option to buy $4 million of first mortgage bonds to build a bridge across the Mississippi at St. Louis. With the New York Exchange too volatile and top-heavy with railroad shares, he wisely turned to the City of London where Junius managed to dispose of the bonds. It did Pierpont no harm when Carnegie enthused on his return about Junius's efficiency and the immense prestige enjoyed by George Peabody, a Freeman of the City.

In that summer of 1869 Pierpont's future looked enviably secure. He was still only thirty-two and, although making $75,000 a year, lived modestly at 243 Madison Avenue in the house rented from Levi P. Morton. Now, with a growing family, he decided to buy a larger brownstone at 6 East Fortieth. His conservative outlook would express itself in the décor and solid appointments that Fanny, docile as ever, approved. The furniture would be in traditional mid-Victorian mahogany, with each of the high-ceilinged rooms crammed with heavy carpets or rugs, much bric-à-brac, and several undistinguished, gilt-framed landscapes. Only the paneled library, in which he would install shelves with the vague intention of collecting first editions, hinted at any individuality of taste. He had bought several showcases, but his coins and stamp albums would so far fill only one or two of them.

While the new house was being furnished and extended with a spacious nursery, he spent more time at the elitist Union Club, a refuge from the hurly-burly of Wall Street now being invaded by the likes of Abraham Kuhn and Solomon Loeb, the Cincinnati clothiers who had set up as brokers with a capital of $500,000. They had quickly established links in Europe with German-Jewish finance houses rumored to hold close to a billion dollars in U.S. bonds from the Civil War. Pierpont had at first scorned them as pushy small-time financiers with little hope of breaking into the top echelons of the Stock Exchange. He was rather more irritated by the arrival from San Francisco of the Seligmans, whose profits from Union Army uniforms had been channeled into a flourishing New York banking firm with outlets in London, Paris, and Frankfurt. The Club's enclave of Boston Brahmins had been bitterly critical of Grant for appointing Joseph Seligman as his fiscal adviser and almost apoplectic when the upstart Jew had waltzed with the president's wife at the Inaugural Ball.

Pierpont's health and temper suffered under office pressure, now that Charles Dabney had grown less active. Disturbed by reports of his insomnia and fainting attacks, Junius urged him to take regular exercise and stop bolting his food. Even his friends at the Club, though used to his gruffness, felt the edge of his tongue. One evening he turned on Depew for glossing over Vanderbilt's own dubious record in Erie in an interview in which he had outlined the Vanderbilts' ambitious plans to develop New York Central. Pierpont considered such publicity-mongering unseemly for a member of the Union Club. "I find you never get into trouble for what you don't say," he grunted sourly. Depew charitably dismissed the rudeness as due more to his young friend's snobbish reticence and ill health than any real animosity toward Vanderbilt.

His long office hours and an anxiety to handle the smallest detail of the move to East Fortieth Street had brought on severe headaches and another nasal eruption of *acne rosacea*. His doctor prescribed a holiday. In July, accompanied by Fanny, a sister-in-law, and Jim Goodwin's sister Mary, he set out for a tour of the West. It would afford both a change of scene and a chance to meet several clients whom so far he knew only by name or through correspondence.

They visited the Chicago stockyards, then proceeded by Pullman to Utah and took a stage coach to California by way of Salt Lake City, where Brigham Young received them. In the Yosemite Valley he already felt vigorous enough to ride many miles a day on horseback, with a black cigar between his teeth, while the ladies endured endless hours in the swaying coach, exhausted by an itinerary that he imposed like a pioneering wagon boss. In San Francisco several banker friends offered civilized hospitality, all the more welcome after so many nights in rough log cabins. During the trip only Sundays had broken the harsh trail routine, for on them he dismounted to take morning and evening services and lead the party in hymn singing.

Pierpont made careful notes of his impressions, distilled into letters to the London office. Junius Morgan was already aware of Carnegie's expanding Pittsburgh empire, but Pierpont also reported the spectacular progress of a tall, rawboned Baptist, one John Davison Rockefeller, who was taking control of Ohio's oil wells and refineries. He was the son of a small-time adventurer who had prospered from selling patent medicines, including a "cure" for cancer. Young Rockefeller had started as a store clerk, but a thousand-dollar loan from his father (at 10 percent interest!) bought him a junior partnership in a commodity commission firm in Cleveland. He quickly spotted the possibilities of the new deposits discovered along Oil Creek. With the demand for kerosene booming during the Civil War he continued to invest and, at the age of twenty-six, owned Cleveland's largest refinery. He was now running a group of petroleum concerns soon to be incorporated as the Standard Oil Company of Ohio. But he remained wholly dependent on eastern transport and resented paying high freight charges to the railroads for carrying his crude petroleum to Cleveland and then reshipping the refined product to New York. He was rumored to be negotiating secret rebates that would help to drive his smaller competitors out of business.

Ohio's oil, Pennsylvania's coal, and the grain from the prairie promised an obvious bonanza for promoters like Gould (still in control of Erie) and Commodore Vanderbilt, now rapidly extending New York Central. But both would need to absorb weaker, rundown lines to dominate the eastern network. During that summer of '69 Gould directed his fire at the Albany & Susquehanna road, a mere 142 miles in length but linked with the coalfields. Only recently incorporated and financed by various municipalities, it was vulnerable to attack from Gould. With Tweed's influence in Albany and his own notorious skill in working through tame nominees, Gould covertly bought more stock and infiltrated the board. Only one man blocked his bid for supreme control: Joseph H. Ramsey, the line's shrewd president, who recognized the threat and speedily issued several thousand new shares, pledging company bonds as security. Unfortunately for him, the board by now included several pro-Gould directors closely allied to Tweed who could guarantee judicial help.

By mid-August Gould scented victory. State Judge Barnard, one of Tweed's lackeys, suspended Ramsey from the presidency and declared the new stock issue null and void. Another court order temporarily appointed Jim Fisk as one of the two receivers to operate the railroad. Gould's men broke into the head office and seized the books, but Ramsey's attorneys persuaded Judge Rufus Peckham of Albany's Supreme Court to suspend four of Gould's dummy directors. In this impasse Fisk cheerfully and characteristically invited Ramsey to play a hand of seven-up for outright control of the railroad! Writs and injunctions flew between the two groups, soon followed by fisticuffs as Fisk's hired toughs started to pull up sections of track and threaten dissident employees. Ramsey then recruited muscle to repel the navvies diverted from the Erie line to keep A. & S. rolling. When fights broke out in the very tunnels, threatening the safety of trains and passengers, Governor Hoffman in Albany called in the militia. Two army officers were appointed as managers until the ownership of the line was legally settled.

As this very uncivil war reached a climax, several interested parties watched anxiously from the sidelines. A number of minor railroad presidents faced the prospect of being gobbled up by Gould, while industrialists like Carnegie and Rockefeller feared extortionate freight charges if he gained a transport monopoly. Seventy-five-year-old Commodore Vanderbilt, celebrating a boisterous honeymoon with his young bride in Saratoga, remained in touch with Billy and Chauncey Depew. Unless Gould was literally stopped in his tracks on Ramsey's railroad, the Vanderbilts might expect attacks on the Michigan Central and Lake Shore lines, and that would bring the enemy into spitting distance of Grand Central Station itself.

Samuel Sloan, Pierpont's fellow commuter on the summer runs from Irvington to New York City, now took a hand. As his own little railroad connected with the Albany & Susquehanna at Binghamton, he had no wish to see a Gould-Fisk victory. Quite apart from his precarious stake, he also happened to be a longtime friend of Ramsey. Toward the end of August he suggested to him that Pierpont Morgan's family connections and his sound grasp of corporation finance might be useful to their cause.

Ramsey called at Exchange Place and was impressed by Morgan's crisp manner and his searching questions about the issue of new stock, which he considered controversial and a possible flaw in the case against Gould. He rather sniffily deferred his decision to cooperate until he had studied a detailed memorandum on that matter and other points that were relevant. Two days later he again received Ramsey and informed him that, having consulted his father-in-law, he would only act if given full and absolute authority to lead the entire rescue operation. Although much startled, Ramsey agreed.

Pierpont moved fast. In the firm's name, he applied for 600

A & S shares, which would give him voting power at the annual stockholders' meeting scheduled for September 7. Gould at once signaled Judge Barnard, who obligingly issued an injunction to restrain Dabney, Morgan from receiving or disposing of the shares. A "nuisance" suit was also served on Ramsey and his senior officials demanding their arrest for impropriety. It was shrewdly timed to prevent their taking part in the all-important board meeting.

Pierpont left for Albany to discuss tactics with the brilliant up-and-coming lawyer, Samuel Hand, who obtained an injunction to ensure Ramsey's presence at the meeting. Pierpont had meantime learned that the A. & S. shareholders, already disturbed by ugly breaches of the peace and the prospect of costly litigation, were nervous about yielding control to Gould after his unsavory dealings over Erie. He therefore worked out a strategy to allay their fears and also promise safer dividends.

He discreetly sounded out LeGrand B. Cannon, president of the Delaware and Hudson Canal Company, who seemed receptive to taking a long lease on A. & S. But nothing could be done without the shareholders' vote of confidence in Ramsey. The enemy was in no mood to surrender. A few minutes before the meeting, Fisk and a tipsy gang of toughs, posing as proxy holders, tried to break into the building. They were repelled by a bodyguard escorting Ramsey and Morgan, who stood their ground at the top of the staircase. Ramsey punched Jim Fisk, who was escorted from the premises by a company man wearing the borrowed uniform of a police officer. Fisk's posse tried to regroup, but by then the meeting had already started behind locked doors.

Ramsey carried the vote. While Gould's attorneys were still clamoring for his arrest and contesting the validity of the election, Pierpont, who had been elected vice-president, hurriedly called a board meeting. He formally proposed that A. & S. should dispose of a ninety-nine-year lease to Cannon, president of the Delaware and Hudson, for a 7 percent rental on a very generous valuation of $7 million for the company's assets. The vote was carried unanimously. Gould's attempt to set up an opposing board was rejected by a State Supreme Court decision restraining him from bringing any further suits.

Morgan's tactics had resulted in a spectacular triumph, but

Gould was consoled by another operation that promised a far bigger killing than the acquisition of a small railroad, however strategic. Throughout that September, his ring of speculators, including President Grant's brother-in-law Abel R. Corbin, an attorney and veteran lobbyist, had sparked off a bull market in gold by buying great quantities of the precious metal on margin. The administration, pressured by Corbin and others in the presidential circle, made no move to check the rise in the price of cornered bullion. It shot up thirty points in a few days of frenzied buying. "While Grant eats clams and don't care two damns," protested a financial reporter, Corbin pocketed $25,000 a week without putting down a red cent on his purchase of $1.5 million on margin. Jay Gould, however, cautiously stopped buying and hoarded his stock until he could sell out at an inflated profit. Fisk was greedier and continued to plunge in the ever-rising market.

By the end of the month President Grant, dreading a scandal through Corbin's involvement, at last decided to unload enough gold to force the price down to a realistic level. Gould heard of the proposed move through his spies in Washington and sold short without imparting his advance information to Corbin and Fisk, who kept on buying even when gold reached a dizzy 164. With his diamond rings flashing confidence, Fisk still rushed about Wall Street offering bets of $50,000 that the price would hit 200. He found no takers.

The bubble burst on "Black Friday," September 24, 1869, when the Treasury Secretary stepped in and formally announced sales of federal gold. Within minutes the price dropped to 133, ruining many bankers and brokers. Corbin and Fisk were prominent among those who could not meet their margin calls. Gould was reviled by the press as "a hyena" but calmly took shelter behind his haul of over $10 million. He could now well afford to return $6 million of his Erie Railroad loot to Commodore Vanderbilt.

The crisis was a disaster for numerous investors, large and small, but it shed a little gold dust on two struggling young men who would soon become household names. Edward Henry Harriman, then twenty-one, had been one of the prudent few to sell short when the market looked suspiciously tempting. The son of a hard-up Episcopalian minister on Long Island, he had started as an office boy with a Wall Street broker. He was small, sallow, bespectacled, and bowlegged, but fast on his feet in every sense. For a flyweight boxer he packed quite a solid punch. In local billiard halls his nimble cue and a shrewd eye for suckers enabled him to supplement his pay of only five dollars a week.

He won promotion to the post of cashier. Reserved and secretive, he saved enough cash to buy gold and, even without Gould's inside information, shrewdly sold out before the crash. With his profit of $3,000 he bought himself a seat on the New York Stock Exchange, specializing in the busy market of railroad securities, but eager to handle anything for the minimum commission. In later years Morgan would still refer to him contemptuously as "only a two-dollar broker."

Thomas Alva Edison, born in Ohio of Canadian parentage, was also practically self-educated. He had a mechanical flair but totally lacked Harriman's market instinct. After working for Western Union in Boston, he arrived in New York penniless and took a job with a firm that operated a tape service for stockbrokers. In his spare time he invented a duplex telegraph system and an improved ticker tape machine.

On Black Friday, while the Gold Room on Wall Street was rocking, the machine used for indicating and transmitting prices broke down, adding to the general chaos. The engineers panicked but young Edison discovered a broken spring in the transmitter and within a few minutes had restored the apparatus to full working order. His salary was increased to $300 a month but he decided to return to Western Union where he soon perfected a more efficient stock ticker. After the birth of his two children— impishly nicknamed Dot and Dash—he moved on to Menlo Park, New Jersey, to set up his first laboratory.

Pierpont Morgan had learned enough in the days of his temporary association with Edward Ketchum to stay clear of the gold market. He was still reveling in his triumph over Gould, which had earned him considerable prestige on Wall Street. Morgan's firm had received 5,000 shares in commission for handling the transfer of the A. & S. stock, and he had the satisfaction of seeing it rise from only 18 to 120 points when the lease to Delaware & Hudson was finalized.

His name again came into prominence that November when he volunteered to arrange the funeral of George Peabody, who had left instructions for his burial in Danvers, Massachusetts. Queen Victoria had ordered his remains to lie in state for some days in Westminster Abbey so that Londoners could pay a final tribute to the great philanthropist. Rich and poor alike subscribed for a statue that would be unveiled by the Prince of Wales on a prominent site near the Royal Exchange, an unprecedented honor for an American merchant.

The coffin was put aboard England's newest and most powerful battleship and escorted across the Atlantic by the U.S.S. *Plymouth* to Portland, Maine, where a flotilla under Admiral Farragut took over. Pierpont supervised all the detailed formalities of the procession. At his suggestion a combined guard of honor was made up of British and American sailors.

Soon afterward he was invited to represent St. George's for the first time as its lay delegate to a Diocesan convention. He also took an active part early in 1871 in founding the Metropolitan Museum of Art, whose founding trustees included William Cullen Bryant, editor of the New York *Evening Post,* publisher George P. Putnam, and the rising young lawyer Joseph P. Choate. He was among the original fifty patrons to subscribe to a fund drive that raised a meagre $106,000, barely enough to stage a few modest exhibitions.

He had settled comfortably into the new house at 6 East Fortieth. Life seemed brimful of promise. He had social position, a most satisfactory income and was rated highly by the Wall Street hierarchy for so skillfully salvaging the Albany & Susquehanna. But he was nauseated by the putrefaction spread by scoundrels like Gould, Fisk, and Boss Tweed, who still presided over Tammany Hall and Albany's seedy legislature.

He ate and smoked to excess, which aggravated his insomnia, and he had become morbidly sensitive to a bulbous nose increasingly susceptible to eczema. In the spring months of 1871 he began to yearn for Highland Falls. From there he could see a vision of gently sloping hills, a smiling valley shimmering in summer glow, and the classical elegance of West Point rising over a dreamlike Rip Van Winkle landscape. To an overtired brain it seemed an enticing refuge from Henry James's "huge jagged city," whose noise, corruption, and polyglot squalor could only briefly be shut out by the paneled walls and deep carpets of the Union Club. His wife, now placidly swollen with a third pregnancy, offered little sexual comfort. For a sensual man in his early thirties the enforced abstinence could only add to a growing malaise.

In a moment of profound ennui and depression, Morgan startled his father by announcing that, with the partnership at Exchange Place drawing to a close, he contemplated retiring altogether from business. He had amassed enough capital to travel for a while and then settle down to live like an English squire among his books, with a picturesque church nearby and the company of a few well-bred friends. Remote from a world of German Jews, grasping speculators, and chattering tickertapes, he vaguely proposed to raise prize dogs and perhaps a herd of pedigreed cattle.

This idyllic fantasy was diagnosed by Junius as an attack of spring fever perhaps induced by an overdose of Thoreau or Emerson. He had noted with pride his son's brilliant execution of the A. & S. coup and guessed that Pierpont's first taste of real power would soon stimulate him to accept greater challenges. Instead of pooh-poohing his quixotic notion of retiring at thirty-three, he gently urged him to watch his health and recommended a trip to Europe with Fanny after the birth of their baby, due in July.

Pierpont's psychological crisis swiftly passed as dramatic news came to him from the London office after the crushing defeat of the French by the army of Bismarck's Prussia at Sédan. In besieged Paris the one-eyed lawyer, Léon Gambetta, held out briefly before escaping by balloon to the provinces, where he hoped to raise an army and continue the fight. The provincial Republican government then desperately appealed for outside help, but the Rothschilds and the other London bankers showed no eagerness to finance a lost cause. Junius Morgan, however, hurried to Tours where he met Gambetta, now Minister of War, and agreed to float a $50 million loan with 6 percent bonds purchased at twenty cents below par. He issued them in London, where anti-Prussian sentiment ran high. Many rushed to buy the bonds at 85, but Junius had some anxious moments when they slumped heavily after the French surrender at Metz, followed by the fall of Paris. He injected more of the firm's capital to maintain the price of the bonds during the bloody street fighting that led to Gambetta's forces overthrowing the revolutionary commune. That news helped Junius to dispose of the unsold bonds both in London and in New York, where Pierpont took charge of sales. The two firms and others brought into a hastily formed syndicate netted a combined profit of $5 million.

Junius took no part in the gigantic rescue operation mounted by the Rothschilds, who issued 5½ percent bonds at 82½, enabling the new French Republic to pay off a savage war indemnity, but 22 Old Broad Street had won enormous prestige by its initiative in the bleak early days of the war. The House of Morgan had entered the arena of international finance for the first time. The affair paid other useful dividends. The Morgans improved their friendly relationship with the important Philadelphia bankers, Drexel & Co., whose Paris office had cooperated in handling the bond issue on Gambetta's behalf.

During a short visit to America Junius saw Anthony J. Drexel, who hinted that he planned to extend his activities to New York and might welcome the support of the London office, with Pierpont acting as liaison. Behind the small talk and the clouds of Havana smoke Junius scented a new factor in the conservative Drexel's impatience to expand. The Philadelphia firm had resented taking a back seat in Jay Cooke's wartime drives and knew that Cooke planned to sell the new Treasury issues that the administration would have to float after refunding its Civil War bonds. They aimed to share in this profitable market but did not underrate either Cooke or his allies.

Drexel and Junius were both aware that Cooke needed additional revenue for his grandiose railroad schemes. He had emerged from the Civil War a multimillionaire and quickly acquired the 1,400-mile Northern Pacific running from Duluth through the Rockies and the Missouri headwaters to the west coast. But he knew nothing of the practical difficulties of building or managing a railroad. He also discovered that raising $100 million for Northern Pacific in a saturated market against seasoned competitors like Vanderbilt, Gould, and Huntington was very different from peddling war bonds to wildly patriotic crowds. However, he remained certain that Washington would once more entrust him with its entire new issue of loan stock. Hugh McCulloch, Lincoln's former treasury secretary, managed his London office and had established strong ties with the Rothschilds. Their New York representative, August Belmont, had been instructed to back Cooke's future bond operations in alliance with Pierpont's *bête noire,* the fast-rising Jewish firm of Kuhn, Loeb & Co. The Drexels, facing a dogged fight, needed reinforcements. Junius had skillfully read between the lines. Unlike his son, who relied more on instinct and sheer determination in trampling all opposition, he was a cautious strategist and long-term planner, seldom inclined to take exceptional risks as he had done in the Gambetta affair. He knew of Tony Drexel's close personal friendship with President Grant. The family also owned Philadelphia's influential *Public Ledger,* which would no doubt campaign fiercely against Cooke's bid for a government bond monopoly. As a seasoned diagnostician of the complexities of finance, he hit on a remedy simultaneously palatable to the three Drexel brothers and beneficial to his own firm. Moreover, it was likely to wean his whimsical heir from romantic dreams of rural retirement when his partnership with Dabney ended. He was aware that Tony Drexel had been impressed by Pierpont's successful tussle with Gould over A. & S. and guessed that the snobbish Philadelphia house, coincidentally founded in the year of his son's birth, would also have noted his devotion to church affairs, his service on important committees, and his membership in the Union Club. Junius prepared the ground, but knowing his son's uncertain temper, remained diplomatically offstage.

Anthony Drexel duly sent Pierpont a telegram inviting him to Philadelphia for "a business talk." Over dinner he outlined his plans for moving into New York where the firm hoped to become more active in both government bonds and railroad securities. He offered him a junior partnership with a fifty-fifty share of profits, subject to a corresponding infusion of Morgan capital. Pierpont was flattered but objected on the grounds of ill health. Briefed by Junius, Drexel was sympathetic and blandly suggested a prolonged vacation after the dissolution of Dabney, Morgan. Pierpont at once reported the offer to his father, who naturally recommended acceptance!

All the pieces fell tidily into place. Charles Dabney had made half-a-million dollars in the past four years and was anxious to depart without undue delay. Jim Goodwin, although eager to return to Hartford, agreed to stay on while Pierpont, on his doctor's advice, took a lengthy vacation. The new firm would formally start up on July 8, 1871, with a combined capital of $1.5 million, Junius having contributed the bulk of his son's half share. Business would be carried on at 53 Exchange Place with Tony Drexel's brother, Joseph, in overall control, while a new office building was built on the southeast corner of Wall Street and Broad, next to the United States Assay Office and adjacent to both the Subtreasury and the corinthian-pillared Stock Exchange. Located on a site bought for only $349 a square foot, the Drexel Building was to be of solid white marble, constructed according to the highest standards, and equipped with elevators, among the first in New York. One million dollars had been allocated to make it a symbol of power, dignity, and taste.

Shortly after celebrating the Fourth of July with a family dinner, Pierpont sailed to Europe on the Cunard liner *Scotia* with Fanny and their three children, including one-year-old Juliet. As always he enjoyed the crossing, but Fanny was seasick. They stayed in Prince's Gate before crossing the Channel. In Paris they occupied a large corner suite at the Hotel Bristol in the Place Vendôme, managed by Junius's former butler, Mortlock. Pierpont was in a generous mood when they went shopping, although he tried Fanny's patience by insisting on accompanying her to the Rue de la Paix where the Englishman, Charles Frederick Worth, presided over a fashionable salon patronized by ladies eager to follow in the elegant tradition of the Empress Eugénie. He not only imposed his own taste on Fanny's choice of clothes but liked to fondle the silks and velvets, an idiosyncracy which even M. Worth's worldly *vendeuses* may have thought somewhat decadent and incongruous in a solemn cigar-chomping American banker. He had a similar penchant for sensuously caressing the jade cameos and ivories in the Rue de Rivoli before making his final choice. He spent lavishly but had not lost his schoolboy habit of entering every item of expenditure in a leatherbound account book. One day he meticulously noted: "3 bouquets, 18 francs . . . postage, 1.40 . . . cab, 1.80 . . . oranges, 1.70 . . . mineral water, .80."

In Karlsbad he kept his promise to Dr. George Elliott by submitting to an austere regime of bitter waters and saline baths, but fretted over limiting his daily indulgence in alcohol and cigars. However, he was in roaring spirits by the time they reached Innsbruck. Fanny found it impossible to keep pace with his nonstop sightseeing and shopping tours, hill climbing, and marathon walks, rounded off with visits every night to concerts or fashionable restaurants. He seemed invigorated by moving from city to city, and was content to ignore the discomfort of his unfortunate family. Suddenly bored with Rome, he took off for Cairo where some American friends were persuaded to join them in a cruise up the Nile. As the boat proved too slow for his taste, he had the whole party, complete with baggage swollen by countless souvenirs, transferred to a Cook's steamer.

Back in Rome Fanny collapsed with gastric fever and had barely recovered when her husband, alarmed by an outbreak of his eczema, whisked her off for a return visit to Karlsbad. There he received a letter from Charles Tracy informing him that one of their neighbors at Highland Falls had died and his beautiful house, Cragston, perched over the Hudson, was now on the market. He and Fanny had long admired the rambling old three-story mansion, converted from a farmhouse, set in about two thousand rolling acres, with well-kept lawns, ample stabling, and superb views of the distant hills. With her eager approval, he promptly cabled his father's London office and urged them to secure the property. Junius at once wired Tony Drexel instructions to buy it, whatever the price.

As soon as the contract had been signed, Pierpont was impatient to return home. They had been away almost fifteen months. Aside from refurnishing Cragston and making the necessary extensions to suit his growing family, he was eager to settle into the new marble fortress at 23 Wall Street and tackle the complex problems of a much-changed business scene. Cooke had already taken a leading role in placing the government's refunded war bonds, but they had subscribed very slowly indeed in America and even more slowly in the City of London, which was still reeling from the scandalous stock watering of the Erie Railroad and Union Pacific's corrupt offshoot, Crédit Mobilier.

In New York, certain familiar faces had passed from the scene. Boss Tweed had gone to prison and on January 6, 1872, Jay Gould's former henchman, Jim Fisk, was shot to death by a pimp in the Grand Central Hotel on Lower Broadway while bedding his latest favorite from the chorus. He was given a full military funeral in his home town of Brattleboro, Vermont, whose mourning citizens subscribed $25,000 for a marble monument.

Cooke's recent venture into railroad finance was also proving disastrous. He plunged deeper into Northern Pacific, but even its optimistically high dividends failed to attract investors. To stay solvent he was forced to raise short-term loans at crippling rates of interest. It soon became clear that his one hope of paying off a massive bank overdraft was to secure exclusive rights to handle the government's new bond issue. With support from the Rothschilds, working through their New York agent, August Belmont, and with the expert marketing skills of Kuhn, Loeb & Co., he was sanguine of repeating his Civil War triumphs.

Once before he had soundly defeated the proud Philadelphia Drexels, who would be bidding against him. This time, however, he would also be taking on Pierpont Morgan, who would be facing the first serious challenge to the newly established "Corner" at Wall Street and Broad. He had not only the Drexels supporting him but the full weight of his father's City of London resources.

CHAPTER SIX

In the spring of 1873 the Cooke-Rothschild combine first became aware of the opposition stacked against them. The Drexels were mounting a hostile press campaign with implied support from Washington. Reelected for a second term, Grant was anxious to recover popularity lost through his brother-in-law's unlucky gamble in bullion and the disclosures of railroad graft involving Speaker James Blaine and others in the presidential inner circle. He presented a "neutral" stance when Cooke turned to him but would obviously lean toward his old friend, Tony Drexel, in the crunch. In London Junius Morgan was enlisting the Barings and other leading City houses by offering them a stake in any federal bonds that came his way if Congress rejected Cooke's monopoly bid.

But success hinged upon Pierpont Morgan's skill in organizing a banking syndicate based on the strategy he had worked out with his father's old friend and former colleague, Levi P. Morton. Together they went up Capitol Hill to put their case to Treasury Secretary George S. Boutwell. Morton, smooth-tongued and persuasive, did the talking but Pierpont had prepared the strong brief. It stressed that Morton's firm had an unblemished record and would head the American end of the bond promotion together with Drexel, Morgan & Co. The European market could be safely left in the hands of Junius Morgan, the Barings, and Drexel, Harjes of Paris.

Boutwell was courteous but noncommittal. The whispers about two rival syndicates had inflamed critics in the press who accused the bankers of money grabbing. The government was advised to save on commission by selling direct to the public. Both sides, of course, opposed this and continued to argue acrimoniously before a Ways and Means Committee. Levi Morton reveled in the limelight, while Pierpont stayed in the wings, aloof from the hustling loud-mouthed lobbyists. His scorn for politicians had begun in his first days on Wall Street and grew stronger during the unsavory battle with Gould's gang. Now unavoidably finding himself in Washington, he treated even friendly senators with a crusty hauteur that contrasted with Morton's bonhomie. However, they still made a strong team and impressed the committee by pleading for only a reasonable share of the issue, while the Cooke-Belmont syndicate stubbornly demanded sole rights.

Secretary Boutwell at last intervened to divide the prize between them. The commission was whittled down to only .5 percent, but it launched Drexel, Morgan in the marketing of government securities. The allocation meant more than a loss of face for Cooke. He had been denied the funds on which he had so confidently counted and his resources would be dangerously stretched during the coming months as America entered another spell of recession.

During that summer of '73 money became tight all around. Several leading banks, already overextended, began to restrain credit. Wall Street, top-heavy with railroad stock, marked down prices and helped to scare off British investors. The crisis was further accelerated by a bumper wheat harvest and price slump that made high freight charges uneconomic. Grain rotted beside railroad tracks and ships stood idly by in New York harbor with empty holds.

Stocks and bonds continued to slide, starting a panic run on brokerage houses. Numerous small firms collapsed when banks, hit by an avalanche of withdrawals, called in loans. The New York Stock Exchange closed for the first time in its history. Undercapitalized western railroads like Union Pacific, long dependent on credit, cracked under the weight of distress selling, while Northern Pacific went into bankruptcy when the banks rejected Cooke's frantic s.o.s. On September 17, he had to shutter his Wall Street offices to keep out angry investors. Three days later he closed down his imposing headquarters on Third Street in Philadelphia.*

Gould, the supreme opportunist, benefited from the lean years by scooping up Union Pacific stock at almost paper-cheap prices. He now had two new partners, both of them subtler than Fisk and Daniel Drew and just as ruthless. Russell Sage, a former grocery clerk, had drifted into the flourishing world of real estate and railroad promotion in Troy, New York. He quickly surfaced as an expert in stock watering and political graft, equal qualifications for Jay Gould's approval. James R. Keene, a handsome iron-nerved gambler whose methods and hair earned him the nickname of "The Silver Fox," had emigrated from England in his youth and graduated as a California corporation lawyer before moving on to Wall Street. He always bought on margin, specializing in mining and railroad stock, and few had a keener nose for the market.

This trio spent many profitable hours together in the library of Gould's mansion at Forty-seventh and Fifth Avenue where they picked at railroad targets with sharp calipers, extracting those most vulnerable to stock manipulation and any others, like Missouri Pacific, running through wheat or coal country. They were helped by Gould's New York *World,* a handy medium for share-pushing, but he would gladly have traded it and much more for Commodore Vanderbilt's control of Western Union. He would not have to wait too long for that particular plum.

The five-year slump spared only those with ample capital and strong nerves. Edward H. Harriman was one of the few small brokers to survive, and indeed profit from, the crisis. He had bought Illinois Central shares at the bottom of the market and increased his holdings to secure himself a place on the board. By then he had married a daughter of William J. Averill, who ran a small line but within range of the great Pennsylvania Railroad.

---

*From his bankruptcy Cooke scraped together $3,000, which he cannily invested in a silver mine. By 1879 his take amounted to a cool million, more than enough to sweeten his last years. Drew was less resilient. He was wiped out after Jay Gould and other one-time associates ignored all appeals for help. Broken in health, he died in penury with only his watch and chain and a well-thumbed Bible to show for a long career of plunder.

Harriman worked on obtaining a stock majority so he could oust his father-in-law. At the same time he continued buying and selling on a modest commission for a clientele that occasionally included the Belmonts, but never the lordly firm of Drexel, Morgan of 23 Wall. By now, he was known as a railroad specialist with such a practical grasp of wage costs, freight, and track laying that quite a few agency tidbits fell to him from the chairman's desk in Grand Central Station.

The nominal value of the Vanderbilts' rolling stock had diminished during the recession, although New York Central still managed to pay 10 percent dividends. The Commodore had cobbled together a makeshift agreement with competitors to fix freight rates, but cynically offered secret rebates to the powerful Standard Oil combine and Andrew Carnegie. The latter's Pittsburgh mills and subsidiaries were valued at millions but, like almost everyone else in the first shock days of the slump, he still needed liquidity and did not despise an offer of $60,000 from Old Broad Street for some railroad stock that had gone sour. Junius appointed his son to settle the transaction that brought him together with Carnegie.

Pierpont sat at his rolltop desk in an office that blended tradition with the latest in contemporary taste. A blazing coal fire and thick carpet, opulent but dignified in color and design, recalled the old established City house whose paneled splendor Carnegie missed. Though prepared for the much-publicized elevators and chattering tickertapes, he must have been a trifle startled at being ushered into a glass-walled cage. The "open plan," destined to become a commonplace of office layout, was still a novelty that Pierpont, overcoming his natural instinct for camouflage, had approved so as to keep a close eye on his clerks, although he discouraged familiarities, interruptions, or queries by them. He expected them to observe an inflexible chain of command. Even Joseph Drexel and other senior executives learned to respect his quirky insistence on privacy in working hours except in rare cases of emergency. They seldom spoke to him after the morning conference in the board room at which he would also receive special clients or visitors from Washington arriving with confidential business.

Everything about Morgan, including the high wing collar,

flowing ascot cravat, starched cuffs, and heavy watch chain with its large bloodstone, implied wealth and breeding. His hair was already sparser and grizzling, but the well-tended moustache remained thick and trimmed in the walrus style favored by New England patricians. Andrew Carnegie was now too self-confident to quake under the cold hard stare that intimidated most callers, but he never forgot his first glimpse of the veined strawberry-like obscenity that was the proud young banker's nose.

Pierpont smoked nonstop and had barely clipped his second cigar before the meeting ended. He handed over the $60,000 check and another for $10,000 which, he explained offhandedly, also stood to the credit of Carnegie, who went off much impressed by an integrity rare in the contemporary financial climate. To Pierpont it was a routine affair executed in the Peabody-Morgan tradition of "doing only first-class business in a first-class way." The meeting failed to warm him toward the scrubby-bearded little ironmaster who was reputed to be "mad about money" and obsessed with Herbert Spencer's agnosticism. Pierpont's snobbish prejudice against those who did not come from the same upper-middle-class, well-bred, Episcopalian background as himself would later flaw his judgment of entrepreneurs like Harriman, Will Durant, and Bernard Baruch. At this stage, it blinded him completely to the brilliant enterprise of his visitor, who was one of the first to adopt the Bessemer process and was already starting to turn out America's first sixty-foot steel rails in his new plant at Braddock, Pennsylvania.

The Corner continued to flourish, with the junior partner steadily assuming more executive control. Anthony Drexel remained in charge of the head office in Philadelphia and the very active Paris branch. He also maintained cordial relations with Washington, an arrangement that suited Pierpont, who dismissed all politicians as either self-important fools or knaves who sold their principles to the highest bidder. Nevertheless he had accepted the Republican faith as the lesser of two political evils and endorsed that party's support of Rockefeller, Carnegie, and the railroad barons, all greedily expanding their empires into near-monopolies by keeping up prices, lowering wages, and crushing "revolutionary" strikes. He echoed the righteous indignation of the Rev. Henry Ward Beecher, who enjoyed a $20,000 a year stipend and from his Plymouth pulpit reminded his congregation: "The trade union, organized under the European system, destroys liberty . . . I do not say that a dollar a day is enough to support a man! Not enough to support a man and five children if he insists on smoking and drinking beer. . . . But the man who cannot live on bread and water is not fit to live. . . ."

Chainsmoking his large Havanas and living very comfortably within an income that would rarely drop below a quarter of a million dollars a year even in the depressed seventies, Pierpont Morgan considered himself a model Christian. Without personally venturing into the squalid alleys, he was ever ready to spread light and remove temptation from those who dwelt in their darkness. With William E. Dodge, a fellow committee member of the Y.M.C.A., he helped to form the New York Society for the Suppression of Vice, which aimed to keep the city's brothels under closer supervision and remove obscene literature from libraries and bookstands. He also helped to sponsor the Moody and Sankey revivalist meetings and joined in the fervent hymn singing. His response, strongly emotional, was matched by a taste for solemn protocol. He could never resist a big funeral and relished acting as pallbearer, a role to which he brought natural assets of physique as well as somber dignity.

On Sundays, when the family was in summer residence at Cragston, they occupied a prominent pew at Holy Innocents, where he had been elected to the vestry and soon took charge of its finances. He led the singing with enthusiasm, particularly if favorites like "Rock of Ages" and "Nearer, my God, to Thee" were chosen, but showed his displeasure by angrily jingling coins in his pocket if the pastor dared to select others less to his liking. His unfortunate wife and children endured his tuneless bullfrog voice after every Sunday supper.

His wishes were paramount in the family household, whether in New York or on the Hudson estate, where he sought relaxation from business pressures and a change of landscape, but he had no true feeling for scenery or the delights of Nature. Unlike the poet, he always needed a friend in his retreat to whom he might whisper, "Solitude is sweet." He preferred to indulge his taste for isolation within easy reach of guests whose society he could take or leave at whim. His succession of luxury yachts would prove ideal for this autocratic hedonism, but ashore Cragston suited him perfectly.

During summer weekends he often entertained up to a dozen guests in the six very comfortable chalets he had built on the grounds. He replaced his city derby with a wide-brimmed panama but remained dark-suited, adding a white waistcoat on exceptionally sunny days. He liked to organize elaborate picnics for houseguests and neighbors, sometimes including West Point cadets. He once persuaded the superintendent to give some of them a day's leave to sail his new steam launch, *Louise,* which could easily accommodate up to eighteen for river trips. *Louise* was also useful for meeting his train from New York and ferrying him across the Hudson to Highland Falls.

Cragston was always full for the Fourth of July, when he gave an elaborate dinner, topped off by an extravagant fireworks display. Following his father's example at Dover House, he laid out grass courts for tennis but was now too bulky and short-winded from overeating and heavy smoking to play more than a perfunctory set. He preferred a solitary walk with his pet mastiff, Hero, or a fairly sedate canter in the hills with one of the more attractive houseguests. As a special treat he harnessed a pair of trotters to a wagon and took the children on outings, although they were more at ease with their fun-loving mama. Fanny, an accomplished horsewoman, trained them to ride ponies and play exciting games of improvised polo. On hot days she would take them out on boating trips and rowed vigorously until her fourth pregnancy in '73. Baby Anne's arrival that summer completed their family of one son and three daughters, exactly duplicating that of Junius and his wife.

Fanny had tired noticeably after the last birth but remained a most dedicated mother and an excellent hostess, conscientiously arranging menus for the dinners, house parties, and lavish picnics that her husband insisted on at Cragston. Like his singing canaries, which were removed to East Fortieth Street each fall and languished until their return to Highland Falls in the spring, she always revived in the country and was not only a gracious hostess but obviously enjoyed the local church fêtes and garden shows. She was far more easygoing than her husband, who did not mix with his neighbors and who cursed Jay Gould for daring to pollute his eden by buying a magnificent mansion, Lyndhurst, set in five hundred of the most beautifully landscaped acres of Irvington-on-Hudson. There, while he nursed his weak lungs and plotted the expansion of his empire, Gould built conservatories filled with thousands of the world's rarest orchids.

The firm of Drexel, Morgan continued to function so smoothly that little disruption followed Joseph Drexel's retirement at the end of 1875. Pierpont had for some time acted on his own initiative and only consulted him on major policy. With Anthony's approval he now engaged three partners to cope with a heavier volume of business and to explore new outlets. Egisto P. Fabbri was a South Street broker specializing in shipping and foreign exchange; Charles Coster, an expert whose grasp of the most intricate statistics would underpin the firm's future railroad strategy; and J. Hood Wright, a seasoned member of the New York Stock Exchange. Each had an impeccable reputation and, quite as important to Pierpont Morgan, a willingness to work all hours and shoulder extra burdens when he was incapacitated by illness or became itchy for travel, which he often justified by remarking, "I can do a year's work in nine months, but not in twelve."

His father's approach resembled that of a consultant physician meticulously studying symptoms before prescribing. Pierpont was more the surgeon who acted fast and with supreme authority once satisfied with his own diagnosis. Dissecting columns of figures with Coster, he exhibited a microscopic eye for significant details or latent flaws. He displayed a similar scientific detachment in dealing with callers who needed advice or loans or who offered exchange. Humorless and distant, he would stare unblinkingly at visitors and deliver his verdicts with an imperial brevity that earned him the nickname of "Yes and No Morgan" on Wall Street. His ability to size up a problem quickly and take positive action had fast become legendary, but few appreciated that it was invariably based on sound preparatory work by a painstaking staff of departmental specialists. Once he had taken a decision, he never regretted it or allowed events to impair his confidence in his own judgment.

He concentrated interviews into minutes instead of hours by cutting smalltalk and prolix argument. This mandarin posture by a man still in his mid-thirties once irritated the dry goods magnate, Alexander T. Stewart, even more of a sourpuss. Like Carnegie in the early days of the crisis, he suddenly needed cash and presented himself at the Drexel Building. Without preamble he requested a short-term loan of a million dollars. Pierpont had studied the figures overnight and nodded approval. To his surprise, instead of thanking him or asking the rate of interest, Stewart prowled around the office and then demanded sharply, "Where does this carpet come from?" Pierpont named the supplier. Stewart at once picked up his hat and snapped, "If you won't buy carpets from *me*, I won't borrow money from *you*." Pierpont shrugged off the episode—they never did business together again—but rejoiced when Caroline Astor snobbishly excluded Stewart from her Four Hundred, explaining to her coterie, "Just because I buy my carpets from him, that is no reason why I should ask him to my house to *walk* on them."

Once his partners had settled in, Pierpont felt justified in taking his doctor's advice to break off for a long holiday. For some months past his dizzy spells had forced him to lie down on the long sofa in the boardroom at 23 Wall Street or ride home in a horse-drawn cab permanently on hire. His eczema remained troublesome but it reacted to treatment, unlike the angry pustules of *acne rosacea*, which spread across his nose to transform it into a strawberry. The condition (even now incurable) was already associated with vaso-motor instability and nervous tension, with a probable origin in chronic dyspepsia or gastritis. He chose to ignore medical hints that it might be aggravated by his taste for spicy condiments and perhaps an overindulgence in the heavier vintages.

His blood pressure was high, but he continued to eat too much and too fast, smoked his cigars all day, and rarely walked more than a few yards while in town. But he always recovered his spirits on his travels, particularly at sea. Dr. George Elliott inferred that, apart from the distressing rhinal affliction, his troubles were mainly psychological and self-induced by overwork and gluttony. He had no reason so far to suppose that his patient might be chafing under the restraints of what was an apparently harmonious marriage.

Pierpont sailed to Europe in mid-June 1876 with his wife and four children. They were soon installed at Dover House, where

Junius broke the sad news that he had planned a surprise gift but it had almost literally vanished into thin air. On May 6 a Gainsborough portrait of the naughty Georgiana, fifth Duchess of Devonshire, had been put up for auction. Originally bought from a Pall Mall dealer in 1839 for only 100 guineas, it was secured by Agnew's for 10,100 guineas and exhibited in their new gallery in Old Bond Street. For three solid weeks it drew the town. Among a host of admiring viewers was Junius Morgan, who had done considerable business with Agnew's and announced that he would buy the picture, arranging to settle terms and other formalities in a day or so. He was delighted with his Gainsborough and hoped it would help to cure Pierpont of his taste for deplorable landscapes.

Unfortunately, a thief had entered the gallery during the foggy night of May 25 and cut the portrait from its frame. Agnew's offered a reward of £1,000 and Scotland Yard combined forces with Pinkertons to trap a criminal they both suspected, but the picture disappeared for almost a quarter of a century. By then J. Pierpont Morgan would have acquired both a connoisseur's taste and a famed art collection including several far better Gainsboroughs, but he had not given up hope of one day seeing the missing Duchess on his walls.

At Dover House he played a little tennis with his brother-in-law, Walter, now Junius's right-hand man in London, while Fanny organized treasure hunts in the grounds for her older children and their cousins, May and Walter Burns. Every morning he traveled to the City in his father's coach and put in a full day's work at the office, although plagued by facial eczema during an abnormally hot July. The following month, when the Stock Exchange stagnated, he took his family up to the Lake District and on to the Scottish Highlands, where he admired some beautiful collies and resolved to start breeding them at Cragston. Discouraged by days of heavy rain, he shut himself away in his room and played solitaire hour after hour. Then he would emerge red-eyed and sullen.

He only revived when the family was comfortably installed in their suite at the Hotel Bristol in Paris, where they were joined for a few days by Walter and Mary Burns. Suddenly restless, he moved on to Switzerland and stayed overnight at Vevey, sentimentally revisiting the Institute. In Paris, between a grueling round of shopping and sightseeing that left Fanny exhausted, he still had the energy to spend several hours a day in the Drexel, Harjes office, maintain contact with 23 Wall Street, and he frequently crossed the Channel to consult with his father and Burns.

By the late fall he was again exhausted and starved for the sunshine that always tempted him to ignore his doctor's warnings about eczema. He quickly arranged a return visit to Egypt after a few days in Italy. By now many wealthy Americans took their families to the Land of the Pharaohs, staying in luxurious suites at Shepheard's and visiting the Sphinx and Pyramids as part of a ritual winter itinerary. The Morgans were among the more adventurous and leisurely who chartered Cook's steamers for cruises to Luxor and other sites. The men wore white ducks and their ladies braved sun and sand in long dresses, silken scarves, and gauntlets.

Pierpont and his family celebrated that Christmas at the Grand New Hotel in Cairo. The children missed the traditional tree but reveled in the bazaars where their father spent freely on antiquities, jewelry, rugs, and anything else that took his or Fanny's fancy. For this river trip he had engaged a Cairo doctor, a chef, and a retinue of native servants. Decked out in knickerbockers and topee, but still formal in a high-buttoned waistcoat with the familiar cravat and stiff winged collar, he led them off on expeditions whenever they stopped en route to Luxor. On Sundays he read morning and evening prayers on board. At one place their dragoman pointed out the local chief's harem. Pierpont mischievously persuaded Fanny to enter for a few minutes and protested with mock anger when he was sternly barred. Throughout the three-week cruise he remained exuberant, taking the children on bumpy donkey or camel rides, and often staging fireworks shows at night. He relaxed by playing piquet or whist with the doctor, who gave up trying to persuade him to eat sparingly of the chef's spicy fare and cut down on his dozens of cigars a day.

He had just returned from visiting the Temple of Karnak, which fascinated him, when the mail, including a batch of American newspapers, arrived in his cabin. The front pages were splashed with the news of Commodore Vanderbilt's death from peritonitis on January 4, 1877. There were pictures of flags at half-mast outside the Drexel Building and most other Wall Street offices. At 10 Washington Place hundreds filed past the coffin encased in pearl satin in which the deceased, packed in ice, had been laid out. Pierpont had often scorned the old rogue's senile vulgarity, but he was sorry to miss the ticket-only service at the Episcopal Church on Mercer Street and the cortège of sixty carriages that crunched through snowy streets, lined with scores of policemen, on its journey to the Staten Island Ferry and thence to Vanderbilt Landing for burial at New Dorp. He wrote a note of sympathy to William Henry and his sons, who were consoled by inheriting between them the bulk of the $105 million estate, including 87 percent of New York Central stock.

Poor Fanny had suffered on the choppy crossing back to Italy and was soon laid low by a fever. She had barely recovered before her husband bustled them back to the Bristol in Paris, where they were joined by his parents and Walter and Mary Burns, who had come over specially to celebrate his fortieth birthday on April 17. Mortlock, the Morgan butler emeritus, personally supervised a family banquet rounded off by a huge ornamental cake.

After an absence of almost a year, Morgan was restless to return home. They arrived back in America late in May, and he settled Fanny and the children into Cragston and resumed traveling daily to and from New York. Drexel, Morgan's affairs were flourishing, thanks to the drive of his new partners. Charles Coster brilliantly handled vast blocks of railroad securities and other investment capital, while Fabbri and Hood Wright probed every significant report from western mining locations and the now bubbling market in public utilities. Anthony Drexel had established sound diplomatic relations with Rutherford B. Hayes, who had taken over from Grant at the White House, but it was a bold initiative on Morgan's part, soon after returning from Europe, that won the government's approval and gratitude.

An active group of southern senators, resenting the appropriation of large funds for federal soldiers, had started campaigning vigorously to block the enabling legislation. While the politicians squabbled many soldiers on active duty in the South or the remote

West found their pay held up. They faced serious hardship until November when Congress would reassemble to pass a bill for the coming fiscal year. Pierpont wrote to the secretary of war suggesting that his firm would gladly fill the vacuum by cashing the men's pay vouchers, amounting to $550,000 a month, until the treasury could reimburse them for the loan, administrative costs, and a purely nominal rate of interest. The very generous offer was welcomed, and Pierpont personally took charge of distributing the huge payroll through a corps of trained cashiers who traveled back and forth all over the country for the next four months.

During that active summer, while preoccupied with the payroll crisis and the firm's move into the federal bond market—an inviting target since Cooke's departure—he spent only short weekends at Cragston. He booked into the old Fifth Avenue Hotel, built by Amos F. Eno on Twenty-third Street. It had a passenger elevator and a discreet staff, and it catered to those who valued their privacy. After a stressful day at the office he sometimes ate at the Union before a long session of whist, but more often he would bathe, shave, and change into evening clothes to dine out at Delmonico's with business friends, several of whom were at times partnered by vivacious members of the demimonde.

His own long career of dalliance almost certainly started during that summer of separation from his family, although he gave no outward hint of remaining anything but a devoted husband and father. He never failed to send his wife flowers at Easter, on her birthday, and the anniversary of their engagement, though oddly not of their wedding. He would always address her with civility and a respect perhaps too courtly for real warmth, but in obvious contrast to his usual brusqueness. Yet there were signs of cracks in this comfortable marriage. His hunger for foreign travel was natural enough for a man of imagination who had enjoyed a cosmopolitan schooling and could now gratify his taste for luxury and changes of scene. But at peaceful Cragston he seemed quite as feverishly eager for company and entertainment, while in town he had begun to spend several evenings a week dining or playing cards at the Union Club or the Union League.

Rich men like himself, who needed distraction from unexciting wives and office cares, could enjoy stimulating company in the

New York of that era with little risk of scandal. In Delmonico's private supper rooms the parties often included a quota of genteel but coquettish "widows" accompanied by shapely "nieces" or "cousins." These fashionably dressed ladies admitted to only modest private means but seemed to own small stylish houses or apartments in the city's best districts. The rewards for maintaining the anonymity of their protectors were handsome. Clients paid for favors with jewelry, charge accounts, or "loans," accepted with a fetching reluctance.

The masquerade suited Pierpont Morgan, who could not only afford the most attractive and ladylike courtesans on offer but, as his own master, found it easy to pursue a double life. He continued to support the Society for the Suppression of Vice and diligently performed his vestryman's duties at St. George's and Highland Falls. No word of gossip ever appeared in the newspapers to embarrass his wife, and no charmer could possibly seduce him from presiding at the family's Christmas and Thanksgiving dinners or the traditional Sunday suppers when he rapped a glass with his knife before offering a solemn blessing . . . unless, of course, some bishop happened to be available to perform that duty in his stead.

In the fall of '77, possibly due to these extramarital exertions, he began taking soothing Turkish baths and massage at the Windsor on Forty-sixth Street. He often found himself in the steam rooms beside the matching six-foot plus, 220-pound bulk of Billy Vanderbilt, who needed to relax not from adultery but from a blood pressure that had soared as a result of the bitter but unfruitful efforts of his brother and two sisters to upset the Commodore's will. On the eve of the hearing that November, Billy was much worried but dutifully attended the testimonial dinner that was given in New York for Junius Morgan to celebrate "his unselfish patriotism in the cause of upholding American credit in Europe." The aggregate wealth of the assembled bankers and merchant princes was estimated at $1 billion.

Not long after Junius's return to Europe he invited his son to come over and discuss future policy. Drexel, Morgan's trading year was closing with most satisfactory profits, but the elder Morgan's antennae had twitched at certain hints in Pierpont's twice-weekly letters and coded cable messages. They confirmed his own fears, half-formed during his brief visit to New York, that

America's railroad system could founder under its uneconomic fares and freight charges, quite apart from union agitation for higher wages. British investors were also disturbed by persistent reports that the Hayes administration might soon yield to a strong mining lobby and start minting silver dollars. This would seriously threaten the gold that the City of London and the Bourse had long hoarded as a sheet anchor in Wall Street's choppy waters.

Pierpont had at once responded to his father's summons, although he would miss spending Christmas at home and dressing up as Santa Claus for the children. After the ritual exchange of gifts, he always read out passages from *A Christmas Carol* and used to blow his nose at the Cratchits' sufferings. No Scrooge himself, he loaded a carriage every Christmas Eve with toys and food hampers for the needier parishioners of St. George's, with his son, Jack, lending a hand.

At the office or in Prince's Gate over late-night cognacs and cigars, Pierpont and Junius, usually in company with Walter Burns, talked business and agreed to mark time rather than diversify, as they would have preferred, until Hayes had clarified his monetary policy. The instability of railroad stock was still more troublesome than it had been, and they decided to watch closely for a likely threat from Gould and his mavericks now that the Commodore was out of the way. However, they believed that New York Central remained rock-steady under Billy Vanderbilt and Chauncey Depew.

The Corner at 23 Wall Street remained immune to the Stock Exchange's uneasy rumblings during the next few months and the firm's turnover climbed steadily. Before long the Treasury abandoned its silver policy and resumed payment in gold on legal tender notes. It automatically restored foreign confidence and facilitated the issue of $260 million in government bonds at 4 percent. This time there would be no haggling over the franchise. The Rothschilds and Seligman (a favorite of both Grant and President Hayes) agreed to join a syndicate with Levi Morton, Drexel, Morgan, and Junius's London house. The issue was smoothly handled on both sides of the Atlantic, each member of the syndicate showing a profit of close to five million dollars.

The railroad industry was far less satisfactory, with competing lines running too unprofitably to encourage European investors, who were still bruised from past encounters with Gould and other unscrupulous promoters. Pierpont's successful coup had gained him a most profitable holding in the Albany & Susquehanna; from time to time he bought cannily into other sound lines either for himself or the firm, but he was now far more involved with foreign exchange and government bond issues. Trains had little romantic or personal appeal to him—he much preferred river steamers and, of course, Atlantic liners—but he received a most welcome surprise in the winter of '79 while inspecting a few Midwest systems on behalf of interested clients. In Cairo, Illinois, he was touched when a company paid tribute to his father by naming one of its engines J. S. Morgan. He celebrated by unbuttoning his jacket to ride in the cab.

In October of 1879 he was unexpectedly thrust into a railroad deal that would transform the industry and add an entirely new dimension to merchant banking. Morgan had no inkling of what Billy Vanderbilt had in mind when he was asked to come over to the mansion on the corner of Fifth Avenue and Fortieth for a talk. As they served together on several committees, he had expected some discussion about a welfare scheme or possibly the Metropolitan's plans to underwrite its first archeological expedition to Egypt to which he, Billy, and his son Cornelius had each contributed generously.

But this meeting in Vanderbilt's library had a very different agenda. Pierpont was, as usual, pleased to see Chauncey Depew, whose wit had enlivened so many convivial dinners at the Union Club. He was genial enough but unexpectedly formal. He had become very corpulent over the years, which suited his boardroom *gravitas*. This evening he hovered by Vanderbilt's highbacked chair rather like a Tudor archbishop in the royal presence. Pierpont sensed, rightly as it turned out, that he had come in at the tail end of a long discussion.

William Henry sat bunched and silent for a moment or two while Depew made rather forced small talk. He then cleared his throat and bluntly announced that he had decided to dispose of almost half his holdings in New York Central. Pierpont and his father would be entrusted with the sale of 250,000 shares at the best price.

It would prove to be the most significant turning point in Morgan history since that day, a quarter of a century past, when George Peabody had offered Junius a partnership in his London firm.

CHAPTER SEVEN

William H. Vanderbilt's decision to sell part of the empire that his father had always vowed to keep in the family was prompted by the squalid litigation over the estate. Cartoons lampooned him as the undeserving heir to America's largest fortune. Lacking the Commodore's thick skin and his gift for ignoring any politician he could not seduce, Billy's natural shyness gave way to peppery arrogance. A devoted family man with solid Christian virtues, he never smoked, drank only an occasional glass of wine, and, apart from his taste for collecting bad pictures, had only one weakness: a passion for racing trotters. He never lost his boyhood thriftiness, which took on a touch of the ludicrous when he would insist on having lunch sent up to his office from a cheap restaurant near Grand Central Station. He once indignantly refused to pay for some coffee he had not ordered.

He grew paranoic and pompous, turning on a reporter to declare, "A public sentiment has been growing up opposed to the control of such a great property by a single man or a single family. It says we rule by might. We certainly have control of the property by right." He suspected anyone who threatened his wealth and overreacted when Congress made a vague attempt to tax railway revenues, hitherto exempt. This he chose to interpret as a sinister attack on New York Central.

More seriously, he had neither the training nor the temperament to handle grievances over pay or working conditions. Unlike his father, who drank and hobnobbed with the roughest laborers, he never felt at home with his employees and was outraged when they rejected his clumsy paternalism. Anger led him from one blunder to another. He responded to a drop in railroad revenue with a 10 percent wage cut which led to strikes followed by rioting in Baltimore, Pittsburgh, and Chicago, where other companies had unwisely followed his lead. At New York Central labor bosses demanded a 25 percent pay rise and sent a delegation to Saratoga where William H. was buying trotters for his maroon rig. He informed the spokesman that no concessions were negotiable without an immediate return to work. He then secretly requested Governor Robinson of New York State to send troops to Albany and pledged company funds to defray the full cost. The arrival of the militiamen forced the men back to work, but few were mollified by his $100,000 check for distribution among the strikers and their families. This largesse was naturally seen as a blatant bribe to accept the 10 percent pay cut.

Sniped at by Congress and press, unpopular with his fork force, he had almost decided to abdicate from New York Central in the summer of '79. He turned one day to Chauncey Depew and remarked bitterly, "We get kicked and cuffed by congressional committees, legislatures, and the public, and I feel inclined to have others take some of it, instead of taking it all myself." He now wished to spend more time on travel, philanthropy, and the enjoyment of his rightful place in society. He was tired of being snubbed by the Astors and Goelets. He commissioned Christian Herter and his brother to build him a fifty-eight room rococo palace at 640 Fifth Avenue, which would dwarf Mrs. Astor's chateau and also teach his own son a lesson. Willie K. had spent liberally on polo ponies, diamonds for his wife, Alva, and a dazzling extravaganza of a mansion complete with banquet hall, stained glass windows, and such little extras as a fully equipped gymnasium.

No longer willing to be upstaged, Billy Vanderbilt retaliated with a three-million-dollar mansion entered by bronze doors bought from an Italian prince. For several months a corps of Europe's leading sculptors and carvers strove valiantly to compete with the owner's lack of taste in tapestries, bronzes, and statuary. He favored the conventional paintings of Rosa Bonheur and feverishly handed over nearly $200,000 for seven Meissonier canvases. During that visit to Paris he had one of his attacks of economy and smuggled out of his hotel an old pair of brown boots that needed repairing. In his suite he received a procession of dealers, who soon learned that it was no use offering him Old Master, new Impressionists, or pictures of nudes. He preferred yards of landscapes glowing with pastoral innocence and replete with contented cattle.

With the Fifth Avenue mansion taking shape and occupying much of his time he grudged spending hours on tiresome office problems that only sent up his blood pressure. Chauncey Depew chose precisely the right moment to recommend that he sell some of his New York Central stock through the Morgans rather than dispose of it on the open market where Gould might be tempted to pounce on it.

William Henry was of course aware of 23 Wall Street's high reputation for marketing railroad and government securities. Depew now reminded him that J. S. Morgan and Company, a house of international prestige, enjoyed the confidence of the British investment public, a vital factor in disposing of the stock at a favorable figure. Practical considerations apart, the socially self-conscious Vanderbilt found it gratifying to employ the patrician Drexels and Morgans as his brokers.

After the preliminaries had been discussed in the closest secrecy, Pierpont confirmed the news in a coded cable to London. His father at once sailed for New York, arriving on November 2, 1879. He was met by Pierpont and young Jack, tall and strongly built for a twelve year old. He had a strong likeness to his father, although mercifully he was exempt from the dreaded eczema. Junius was quietly whisked off to the Brunswick Hotel where he received only a few business friends privy to the deal. Over the next three weeks he offered tactical advice while his son organized a syndicate to buy 150,000 of New York Central at $120, with an option on the remainder. The purchase was formally made on November 26, when J. S. Morgan & Co. became the railroad's London representatives and opened transfer books at 22 Old Broad Street.

The syndicate would include August Belmont (acting for the

Rothschilds), Morton, Bliss & Co., and, surprisingly, three of Gould's known associates, Solon Humphreys, Russell Sage, and Cyrus W. Field, the tall, white-bearded aristocrat who had laid the first transatlantic cable in 1866 and was one of Pierpont's cronies at the Union Club. His regard for Field's integrity may have influenced his decision to invite participation by the Gould interests, but it was a daring gamble calculated to avert a countermove that could have depressed the price of New York Central's stock and jeopardized the whole deal. By placating Gould he also hoped to ensure his good will, even if only temporarily, in the costly price cutting war. Fortunately, Billy Vanderbilt was anxious to settle the affair and had enough confidence in Pierpont's judgment not to question his cooperation with such a ruthless competitor.

When the sale was finally announced by the Corner after some days of rumor, New York Central climbed overnight to 130, soon adding a further five points. It returned the syndicate a handsome profit (Drexel, Morgan netting over $2 million) and added millions to the value of the stock still held by Vanderbilt. He showed his appreciation by presenting Pierpont with a handsome solid silver dinner service and won brief popular acclaim by investing his proceeds of $32 million in 4 percent government bonds. Over in London, investors continued to storm Junius's transfer office for every available scrap of stock. Altogether they bought shares worth $25 million. As Pierpont would hold the proxy votes and represent their interests, notably the guaranteed payment of an 8 percent dividend for the next five years, he had insisted on a place on New York Central's enlarged board. His argument was supported by Chauncey Depew, who reminded Vanderbilt that the London shareholders, so often victimized by shady American promotions, were entitled at last to a fair run for their money. Pierpont was duly appointed, much to the satisfaction of Depew, who would need a staunch ally if the two other new directors, Humphreys and Field, favored Jay Gould's interests.

This huge sale of securities by private negotiation established a precedent whose significance Pierpont at once appreciated. Until then Wall Street finance houses had been content to act as agents or intermediaries for a commission, with the banks pursuing their traditional role of moneylenders to promoters. He suddenly became aware that a finance house like his own, if backed by powerful muscle, might not only secure company directorships but, in the case of less powerful giants than New York Central, seize managerial control from boards desperate for more working capital in periods of crisis. Board power could be exercised for the judicious issue of stock with almost limitless scope to amalgamate weak units, like struggling, ill-managed railroads, into cohesive profit-making corporations that would attract investors disillusioned by men like Gould. In his mind's eye he had already begun to perceive the blueprint of the strategy that would transform the whole field of investment for almost the rest of his days.

He outlined his views to his father and Anthony Drexel, both of whom encouraged him to branch out into the railroad business. Not long after the successful sale of Vanderbilt's stock he smoothly organized a syndicate, but this time excluding Gould, to buy and distribute an issue of 6 percent first mortgage gold bonds, valued at $40 million at par, in Jay Cooke's ill-fated Northern Pacific, then almost literally at a standstill for lack of funds to extend its tracks from the Minnesota border to the west coast. The issue was well received and shareholders took heart when the company's revenues began to pick up with tighter management. A few months later, early in 1881, a further bond issue, backed by Junius and the Rothschilds in London, was heavily oversubscribed, with British investors much to the fore. Pierpont joined the board together with August Belmont, whom he liked personally although regretting his growing cooperation with Kuhn, Loeb & Co., the shrewd brokerage firm in Nassau Street that had now moved into railroad finance.

This was mainly due to the initiative of the junior partner, Jacob H. Schiff, who had arrived from Frankfurt in 1875, aged twenty-eight, and married Solomon Loeb's daughter, Therese, four months after joining the firm. A precise little man, five foot two, eyes of blue, like the girl in the future ditty, he was urbane, wily, and dignified. Pierpont despised his thick guttural accent and sneered at the inbreeding of the German Jews, but he had noted that the top London bankers liked to do business directly with conscientious Schiff, who was said to have inspected every mile of track on the Chicago & Northwestern Railway before promoting a bond issue in '77. That won Kuhn, Loeb a commission of $500,000. In a year or two Schiff's million-dollar fees became routine, but Pierpont, luxuriating in his unofficial title of "the Vanderbilt banker," saw no danger from a firm whose clients included seedy newcomers like E. H. Harriman, who had closed his own Wall Street office to develop Illinois Central with his partner, Stuyvesant Fish.

Drexel, Morgan could not afford to be overly complacent. Railroad finance had become chaotic with twice the length of track being laid as could be run at a profit. As the smaller companies collapsed, multimillionaire presidents like Vanderbilt and Gould expanded automatically, but even their vast capital reserves were threatened by the breakneck competition in passenger and freight rates. In the early eighties, witnessing the huge harvests of grain and cotton the country was producing, its rapid industrialization, and an increased output of manufactured goods that was heading for ten billion dollars a year, Morgan became convinced that the future of the national economy would depend upon the restoration of a balanced railroad system.

Depew sympathized with his views and attempted to enlist New York Central's support, but Billy Vanderbilt, purple with high blood pressure and made paranoid by even the slightest murmur of implied criticism, had apparently lost his business grip. He now devoted every spare moment to his trotters, his art "treasures," Vanderbilt University, and the completion of the family mausoleum on Staten Island. While making a cross-country tour by private train he stopped reluctantly at Michigan City, Indiana, to receive reporters who quizzed him on New York Central's policy and repeated the recent Congressional charge of monopoly. When one of them dared to suggest that the passenger fare of $15 for the New York-Chicago run was excessive, Billy lost his temper and accused the Pennsylvania Railroad of forcing him to charge a rate that was in fact "uneconomic and unfair" to his shareholders.

"But what about the public?" persisted the reporter.

"The public be damned!" he roared back. He later denied making the remark, which had embarrassed his board, especially Pierpont, who was discovering that being identified as the Vanderbilt banker could sometimes be a trial. After Jay Gould had set up a rival telegraph company, William Henry impulsively sold out his substantial holdings in Western Union and placed the proceeds in safe high-yielding government bonds. Gould moved in swiftly with the hope of winning an outright majority of voting shares and board control. He was blocked by, among others, Pierpont Morgan, who had become alarmed at the prospect of having his firm's confidential messages pass through such piratical hands. He soon bought himself on to the Western Union board.

Gould's threat to take over the railroad industry was far more serious. His primary target would be New York Central, and he had worked out a strategy recalling his earlier attacks on Erie and A. & S. With the Pullman Car bosses, who competed against the Wagner sleepers used by Vanderbilt's company, he formed the West Shore Company to build a rival 426-mile railway from New Jersey to Buffalo, with plans to extend it to Chicago. A syndicate was formed and shares issued to tempt the unwary. While Gould and Vanderbilt locked horns for a long and bitter tussle, the country's two most powerful industrialists, Carnegie and Rockefeller, seized the opportunity to extract preferential treatment for their freight. Through the elimination of weaker competitors and the imposition of harsh conditions on his helpless work force, Carnegie was by now heading for a steel monopoly. Standard Oil, a company originally capitalized at a million dollars, had swelled to a $70 million trust, which controlled 95 percent of America's entire refining capacity. By 1882 its nine trustees, headed by John D. Rockefeller and his brother, William, held two-thirds of all the stock and, in addition to their huge oil interests in Ohio, were investing heavily in steel mills, iron ore, copper, lumber, and real estate, chiefly in the Pacific Northwest.

Railroad business now absorbed most of Drexel, Morgan's attention, but the firm had remained alert for other outlets, among them Edison's laboratory in Menlo Park, New Jersey. Egisto Fabbri, a man of musical taste, had become interested in Edison's experiments with the phonograph, and even more fascinated by his plans to perfect the incandescent light bulb, which he claimed would replace gas once snags like high resistance had been overcome. Edison had won modest support from William H.

Vanderbilt and Norton Green, then president of Western Union, but Fabbri's enthusiasm finally persuaded him to form the Edison Electric Light Company in October 1878, with Drexel, Morgan as bankers.

It was floated with a capital of only $3 million in hundred-dollar shares, of which Edison would receive 2,500 plus $30,000 cash, in return for signing away his invention over the next five years. As company treasurer, Fabbri was soon being pressured for more money to continue the costly experiments with copper and platinum coils. He never lost faith and persuaded Hood Wright to buy a few shares, though Pierpont himself hedged until he had visited Menlo Park. Edison demonstrated his generators and platinum lamps but admitted that the system was still not practical and fused easily. Pierpont liked his frankness although he was physically repelled by his tobacco chewing and the sloppy coats he wore, each liberally sprinkled with a layer of dandruff.

Still unconvinced, Morgan attended a demonstration on New Year's Eve 1879 of a new dynamo weighing 1,100 pounds and nicknamed Long-Waisted Mary Ann because of its two upright columns. Edison had discoursed so long, so often, and so eloquently on his dream of a central generating station that could serve a whole city, that the company shares jumped from $20 to $600 before the rumors of more efficient systems perfected by Charles Brush and other competitors caused them to slump. Edison was not really taken seriously until he leased a mansion at 65 Fifth Avenue and kept the chandeliers blazing night and day in the luxurious offices and showrooms. Among his first supporters was James Gordon Bennett, who ordered his New York *Herald* to switch to electricity, and the shrewd shipping magnate Henry Villard, who sensing the potential of electrified railways privately advanced Edison a much-needed $40,000 to continue his experiments. Villard also ordered four Mary Anns for his new steamer, which sailed from New York to San Francisco via Cape Horn in May 1880. Even the sceptical Morgan was impressed to learn that the bulbs had burned brightly and without a single failure throughout the two-month voyage.

Although disinclined to invest a dollar of his own, Morgan soon approved the installation of 106 bulbs in the Drexel Building with power supplied from Edison's generators in Pearl Street. It worked smoothly, but the Vanderbilts had a less happy experience in their Fifth Avenue mansion. The steam engine and boiler had chugged away in harmony until one rainy afternoon when two wires became crossed in the picture gallery and set fire to some silk hangings. The power was at once shut off but Mrs. Vanderbilt became so hysterical that the whole installation had to be ripped out. Pierpont, however, was not deterred by this and he commissioned Edison to light his new three-story brownstone, 219 Madison Avenue, which he had just bought from the Phelps copper magnate family.

He and his wife had agreed that 6 East Fortieth had become too cramped for their family and quite unsuitable for entertaining a widening social and business circle. That summer, Pierpont was busy supervising the décor and structural alterations advised by Christian Herter, and he stayed most nights at the Fifth Avenue Hotel. Occasionally he even avoided weekends at Cragston in favor of livelier parties in Newport with yachting friends and one or two of the amiable widows from Delmonico's. However, he found time to install kennels at Cragston for the collies he had imported for breeding. When his pet mastiff died he adopted Shep, a beautiful reddish-brown collie who became passionately attached to him and always slept outside his door.

At Herter's suggestion, he moved the new front door of Circassian walnut around the corner to Thirty-sixth Street and had the façade refashioned to accommodate a huge bay window extending along the whole frontage on Madison Avenue. It was his own idea to build a basement gymnasium "in the Harvard style" largely for workouts by muscular young Jack, who would use it during his school vacations from St. Paul's in Concord, New Hampshire. Pierpont himself started off by dutifully waving a few dumbbells but soon gave it up. In town he seldom walked except on Sundays, when he strolled home from St. George's. He had now given up riding in Central Park and preferred driving in his open barouche with Fanny and the children. He kept his trotters in a brick stable at the back of the house.

The Romanesque dining room had a thick wainscoting of English oak which suited the solid fireplace, almost twelve feet wide. A large stained glass window was set in the heavy-beamed ceiling supported by columns of Siena marble. Even by contemporary

Victorian standards, the drawing room seemed a trifle ornate, Herter having introduced a Pompeiian touch in the ivory woodwork sprinkled with gold leaf and overspangled. Pierpont gave more attention to the library on the first floor, to which he could withdraw from the family to work on his papers, play solitaire and receive callers on private business. The high ceiling was adorned with allegorical paintings, strongly Biblical in theme, and he had the wainscoting richly paneled in black Santo Domingo mahogany. Accessible to the Black Library, as the servants always called it, was the long conservatory sited on the east side of the house to catch the morning sun. Orchids and a variety of climbing plants graced its tiled walls, but a visitor's eye was invariably caught by a black marble fountain, which poured water out of the mouth of a bronze lion. The children's schoolroom-nursery was tucked away on the third floor.

For a house of that size, it surprisingly provided only one guest room. Pierpont had engaged a black-coated English butler to run a smallish staff that included a cook, lady's maid, laundress, gardener, coachman, and a couple of chambermaids. The absence of liveried flunkeys, together with the solid comfortable furniture, stressed that the owner had no need of excessive gilt or marble to announce his breeding. But he owed more than he cared to admit to the discrimination of Henry Duveen, whom Herter had recommended so warmly that Pierpont somehow overcame his instinctive prejudice toward the plumpish young Jew with the walrus moustache and the thick Dutch accent that jarred his ear. Established in New York as a connoisseur of objets d'art, pictures, and pottery, his discernment and modesty impressed Morgan, who noted that Duveen could lay his hands on almost anything at short notice and good-humoredly accepted the brusquest criticism even when he disagreed with his client's taste.

While the house was being remodeled, Pierpont had confided to a friend, "I have no wish to add to the architectural monstrosities corrupting our skyline," but he was tolerant of the obelisk that Billy Vanderbilt put up in Central Park near the Metropolitan Museum. As Americans were currently going through a craze for Egyptian tombs and copies of the relics dug up by Englishmen like Flinders Petrie, the Khedive had decided to make a gift of a seventy-one-foot obelisk, popularly known as Cleopatra's Needle, although it was a monument to King Thatmose III who flourished several centuries before the siren queen. This seemed an academic quibble to William Henry, who spent $100,000 to have it transported and erected in New York. He was consoled by cheering spectators, some of whom shook his hand when it was reported that a bomb, happily soon defused, had just been delivered to his office.

Pierpont's housewarming at 219 Madison Avenue was a very modest affair beside the extravaganza and fancy-dress balls staged along Fifth Avenue by Mrs. Astor and her chosen Four Hundred, but he was gratified when the New York *Herald* reported: "Mr. Morgan's house is distinguished for being the first private dwelling in New York City in which the Edison electric light has been successfully introduced. He is able to light instantaneously the hall and every room on the first floor, basement, and cellar—a valuable precaution in case of burglars. The power that generates the electricity is a steam engine in the stable." So many friends and acquaintances had begged for a glimpse of the "illuminations" that he invited nearly four hundred for refreshments and a conducted tour. Among them were Whitelaw Reid, soon to be ambassador to Paris, and Darius Ogden Mills, the former San Francisco storekeeper who had made a fortune from gold mines in the Sierras and who built himself a palace opposite St. Patrick's Cathedral, spending nearly half a million dollars on decorations alone.

At ten the morning after, Mills arrived at 23 Wall Street, marched straight into Morgan's sacred glass booth, and placed an order for one thousand shares of Edison stock. Pierpont promptly bought a similar stake for himself, his first personal investment in the company; it soon trebled its capital issue, with Drexel, Morgan, and Western Union subscribing most of it between them. Sharp judges like August Belmont began snapping up the shares that eventually reached a fantastic $3,500. This was partly the result of the market's faith in Morgan backing, but it owed rather more to Thomas Alva Edison's personality and his emergence as an international celebrity.

Edison gave crowd-pulling demonstrations of his new twenty-seven-ton steam generator dynamo. It was named Jumbo after Barnum's elephant, and following his merger with Joseph Swan, the British lamp manufacturer and patentee, Edison quickly sold two to supply lighting for London's post office and certain other buildings. He also spotted the potential of a skinny Cockney clerk in the London office and took him back to America as his private secretary. Samuel Insull steadily developed into his majordomo and general manager. But in those early days he did not merit a second glance from Pierpont and was never invited to attend the board meetings in 23 Wall Street. He must have guessed what was going on, but seemed powerless to save his chief, whose inventive genius was paralleled by a childlike naiveté in company affairs. During the next few years, overexcited by the influx of capital to finance his plants, Edison would put up little opposition when the parent company, to whom he had rashly assigned his patents, also pressured him to part with his valuable rights in the manufacture of shafts, generators, and lamps in exchange for inflated stock.

Railroad business and the disruption of house moving had affected Pierpont's health during the fall of '81. His nose grew so swollen and suffused that he consulted a leading dermatologist, who predicted that the condition was unlikely to improve and might indeed deteriorate. This sensitive and proud man, exceptionally reserved from boyhood, now saw himself condemned to a lifetime of ridicule. The condition seemed nearly as intolerable as being afflicted with a humped back or a club foot. Already abrupt in manner, Morgan became testier and more splenetic, and there is little doubt that he compensated for his disfigurement with abnormal amorous gusto and a sadomasochistic urge to be seen with and to master beautiful women.

Low in spirits that winter, he had welcomed his father's invitation to come over for more talks and then join him for a Mediterranean cruise in the steam yacht he had chartered. It would mean missing Christmas at home, but he would celebrate with his parents and the Burns family. In mid-December he sailed from New York by Cunard liner with three of Fanny's cousins, one of whom was recovering from an illness. He saw little of them during a very rough crossing, which kept even him confined to his cabin. Already peevish by the time they finally docked at Liverpool on Christmas Eve, he became still more irritable when the stewards, eager to be off home once they had pocketed their tips, proved less than helpful with the baggage. Morgan stumped off angrily to catch the London train and vowed to sail White Star in future. His vendetta with Cunard would smolder for years and would be, in part, responsible for one of his costliest misjudgments.

Fussed over in Prince's Gate and at the Hotel Windsor in Paris, he was almost cheerful by the time he traveled south to Nice with his parents and their guests to join the *Pandora*. They spent several days touring Palestine and visited the Church of the Holy Sepulchre where, as he wrote to his wife, he had fallen to his knees before the shrine. It was the emotional response of a man whose faith, though sincere and deeply felt, was reflected in neither humility nor self-denial. He was so taken with the comfort and luxurious privacy of cruising that, while spending several weeks working at the office and enjoying London's social distractions, he wrote to his friend, George Bowdoin, requesting him to buy on his behalf a single-screw steam yacht, *Corsair,* which he had previously inspected as a possible replacement for his launch.

Returning home at the end of May, he was delighted with the 165-foot black-hulled vessel. She was slow—taking over three hours to steam the fifty miles to Cragston—but suitable enough for short cruises or for ferrying him and his weekend guests between New York and Highland Falls. Morgan kept his suite at the Fifth Avenue Hotel, as *Corsair*'s cabins were none too well ventilated for summer comfort, but it was his intention to live aboard as much as possible. He planned to use the boat for secret business meetings, away from prying reporters, and to entertain cronies like Depew, Bowdoin, and Charles Lanier or, whenever possible, intimate women friends. The crew had been carefully selected for both nautical skill and discretion.

That autumn of 1882, with the new house at last redecorated and furnished to his satisfaction, the proud owner of *Corsair* seemed unusually relaxed when the vestry of St. George's assembled in his library at 219 Madison Avenue to consider the most likely candidate for rector. He was Dr. William S. Rainsford, a bearded young revivalist whose controversial sermons had drawn large congregations to his Toronto church. St. George's, then suffering from poor attendance, too few pew holders, and an obstinately persistent overdraft, would obviously benefit from a vigorous pastor, but some of the conservative elders still hesitated to appoint such an acknowledged radical.

Pierpont smoked his black cigar in silence while the other wardens began their cross-examination. He liked Rainsford's easy Irish charm but was equally impressed by two less obvious assets. He had graduated from Cambridge University in England. This meant much to Pierpont, who would consistently endorse Henry James's snobbish indictment of their common homeland: "No sovereign, no court . . . no country gentlemen . . . no palaces, no castles, nor manors, nor old country houses, no great Universities, no Oxford, nor Eton, nor Harrow, no Epsom nor Ascot!" The candidate also stood six foot four, a commendation in itself. As the descendant of a clan notable for its imposing stature, Morgan cultivated an idiosyncratic contempt for "dwarfs" like Gould, Carnegie, Harriman, and Jacob Schiff.

He warmed at once to the silver-tongued giant, although startled by his proposal to abolish all paid-for pews and his flat demand for a fund of $10,000 for three years to administer as he thought fit. Pierpont grunted, then recommended the appointment. Once it was made, however, he soon discovered that it would no longer always be possible to have his way by simply waving a check. He and Rainsford breakfasted together most Mondays on Madison Avenue to discuss church affairs mostly without argument, but Pierpont had to swallow hard when the rector said he thought that women should be admitted to the choir. He was even less enthusiastic about the number of "unwashed poor" who now regularly crowded into St. George's to hear Rainsford's eloquent sermons.

One wealthy elder offered Rainsford $200,000 to build a Memorial House that would accommodate assistant clergy, with recreational facilities for parish workers and local youngsters. The gift was subject to the rector's quietly dropping such radical innovations as lady choristers. He was firmly shown the door. The project, dear to Rainsford's heart, was shelved until Pierpont, by then senior warden, drove up to the rectory and handed over a check for a quarter of a million dollars, with only one simple condition: the new Memorial House should be dedicated to the memory of Fanny's parents, Charles and Louise Tracy.

While it was being built, Rainsford had wrecked one of their amiable Monday breakfasts by bluntly opposing Pierpont's plan to reduce vestry membership. Quite the contrary, objected the rector, who argued that his new working-class parishioners were entitled to at least one representative. Pierpont said tersely, "I do *not* want the vestry democratized. I want it to remain a body of gentlemen whom I can ask to meet me in my study." Rainsford reminded him that he had been promised a free hand. That afternoon Pierpont sent in his resignation, which Rainsford refused to accept.

They breakfasted together on the following three Mondays, continuing to discuss parish affairs but with nods, grunts, and tight-lipped monosyllables on both sides. The deadlock was only broken when the banker sailed for Europe. Rainsford had decided not to part without one last attempt at reconciliation. He hovered in the background while family and friends thronged the dock. Pierpont spotted him, shook his hand, and invited him into his state room to talk in private. Rainsford often recalled his astonishment when the banker impulsively embraced him and exclaimed, "Pray for me, pray for me." It was his first glimpse of the hidden pressures behind the crusty mask and of the melancholia that often followed sudden spells of illness.

In his memoirs he would record: "Mr. Morgan had the peace and power of religious assurance. . . . His mental qualities drew him strongly to the ecclesiastical side of the Episcopal Church's life. Its very archaic element, its atmosphere of withdrawal from the common everyday affairs of man, answered to some need of his soul. . . . We would never have another falling-out over church matters."

Although the rector received far more consideration than others, he did not blind himself to Morgan's faults. He was grateful when the banker generously paid all his costly medical expenses after a breakdown due to overwork, but he was not so delighted that, while he was convalescing, the senior warden thought fit to station himself outside St. George's and greet the congregation rather too much like a feudal English lord of the manor with his tenantry.

In the years ahead when Pierpont Morgan attempted to dominate everyone who opposed him, from the president of the United States to the trade union leaders pressing for more humane

133

conditions, Rainsford would find it difficult to forgive the way in which the banker neglected the brotherly love that was enjoined by the Sermon on the Mount and showed a quite clear preference for the harsh Judaic doctrine of an eye for an eye, a tooth for a tooth.

CHAPTER EIGHT

Corsair had not been bought for vulgar display. She was far more modest than the 250-foot *Atalanta,* which cost Jay Gould $1,000 a week to run. Gould never sailed without his doctor and a chef who prepared the special diet imposed by chronic dyspepsia. Pierpont himself was astonishingly immune from stomach troubles despite continuous cigar smoking and a massive daily intake of food and drink. At breakfast, often in the company of one of his daughters (for Fanny preferred a tray of coffee and toast in her own room), he consumed eggs with steaks or chops, sliced tomatoes, and pancakes with fresh cream, washed down by several cups of coffee before he lit the second or third of his long black cigars. His luncheon at the office was light and usually eaten alone in the partners' room. He nibbled at a chicken or turkey sandwich and swallowed a dozen raw oysters plus a few sticks of rhubarb and always a mince pie. He drank plain water until sundown and expected his staff to follow this salutary example. At night he downed an eight-course dinner, with another dozen oysters, sluiced by his favorite vintage wines, Montrachet or Château Latour, and he often had cognac with his coffee.

He showed few aftereffects from alcohol, but so much food and almost no physical exercise, except between the sheets, induced spells of insomnia aggravated by a habit of taking catnaps on the boardroom sofa and a short snooze in his library before dressing for dinner. After the birth of their last child, Anne, he and his wife began to occupy separate bedrooms, allegedly because of his insomnia, his snoring, and the irregular hours prescribed by business and social engagements. Only the most unworldly of their friends had failed to note that he spent less time at Cragston than aboard his yacht during the summer months. He enjoyed convivial dinners, followed by whist or sing-songs, with cronies like Depew, Charles Lanier, and Bowdoin, whom he had recruited into the firm from Morton, Bliss & Co. These gatherings became so congenial to him that he decided to form the Corsair Club whose members periodically dined together, each playing host in turn while the yacht was laid up. He naturally selected the membership, which grew from the original five to a maximum of a dozen, and would later include attorneys Joseph Choate, Lewis Cass Ledyard, and Charles Steele; Jack Morgan (when he was old enough for election); and John D. Rockefeller's brother, William, a hard-drinking extrovert with a taste for bawdy stories.

For Pierpont the yacht was a welcome refuge when he needed to think or be alone. At such times no one dared intrude on his privacy. Long after his father's death, Jack would recall an occasion when he had asked a Harvard classmate for a weekend at Cragston and arranged for him to board the *Corsair* at the New York Yacht Club landing. Upon doing so, he politely introduced himself to the owner, who grunted and resumed his solitaire. The young Harvard man slipped into a deckchair to read his newspaper, hardly daring to rustle the pages. Not a word passed between them. At the pier in Highland Falls, Pierpont greeted his son affectionately and murmured, "Glad you asked that young fellow up. One of the nicest chaps I've ever met."

His intimates often disagreed with Morgan's snap judgments, for they could turn as much on his instinctive likes or dislikes as on the solid criteria of a man's social background and business record. He was proved right in resigning from the board of the Northern Pacific Railroad because he disapproved of the personality and devious methods of Henry Villard, but he shocked Chauncey Depew and other party loyalists by abandoning the Republican ticket in 1884 for the first and only time in his life. Although he shared their suspicion of Cleveland's low-tariff policies, he respected the man's blunt-spoken integrity and preferred him to his opponent, James G. Blaine, who had played an unsavory part in the Crédit Mobilier scandal and, during his term as Speaker in Congress, supported dubious franchises on Cooke's behalf.

Pierpont had brought his father-in-law, Charles Tracy, around to his own way of thinking but he was unable to convince Depew, Choate, and other friends who rallied to Blaine. They assembled at Delmonico's for the "Millionaires' Banquet," chiefly notable for its saggy wallets and soggy prostates. The guests, among them such worthies as Gould, Russell Sage, and the Chicago pork-packer, Philip D. Armour, failed to save Blaine. However, Gould had characteristically won himself enough time to unload blocks of shares before the market slumped in response to the news of Cleveland's victory.

Cleveland's administration took on a legacy of high unemployment, rising prices, and acute labor unrest. Wall Street, already overextended by wildcat railroad finance, was soon rocked by scandals over Manhattan Elevated, which Gould and Russell Sage had manipulated for quick profits. Although they had brazenly exploited the name and prestige of Cyrus Field to attract investors, he grew uneasy at the excessive passenger fares imposed by his partners. Finally, they agreed to sell him their holdings at an inflated price. They then beared the market to buy the stock back cheaply, a maneuver that cost Field his entire fortune. Broken in health and reputation, he spent his last years in penury. Pierpont did not hesitate when one of Field's daughters, who happened to be a most beautiful young woman, secretly implored him to continue the premiums on her father's last few insurance policies.

With all his faults, Pierpont was always a foul weather friend, as he also proved by later rescuing Charles Lanier, who had unwisely involved himself with Gould, Villard, and George Pullman in 1883 by promoting the shaky West Shore Railroad. This line went into receivership in June the following year thanks to mismanagement and a suicidal rate-cutting tussle with New York Central whose own heavy losses alarmed Pierpont, already much disturbed by Billy Vanderbilt's irresponsibility. Peevish, sick, and always paranoid, Vanderbilt had overreacted to a threat from George H. Roberts, the dour president of Pennsylvania

Railroad, who was buying up West Shore's low-priced mortgaged bonds. Encouraged by Carnegie and Rockefeller, Vanderbilt had, early in 1885, sanctioned a $5 million outlay to build a new line, the South Pennsylvania, in the hope of driving Roberts out of business and seizing his profitable coal freight.

Unless this extravagant move were checked, Pierpont saw another railroad war ahead, with the gravest consequences for New York Central. Its stock had already slumped due to the crippling struggle with West Shore. Investors, nettled by a newspaper report estimating Vanderbilt's income at $20 a minute, now learned with dismay that he was switching his personal holdings into government bonds. He had also halved the 8 percent dividend as soon as the five-year guarantee, negotiated in November '79, expired. As proxy holder for numerous foreign investors, Pierpont felt himself let down by Vanderbilt's arbitrary action but equally concerned for the good name of his father, who had placed so much New York Central stock in the London market. Unless confidence could be restored in that line and other vulnerable American railroad securities, the disillusioned British public would no doubt condemn 22 Old Broad Street for failing to protect them.

After a friendly talk with Chauncey Depew, now president of New York Central and himself nervous at Billy Vanderbilt's rampaging, Pierpont sailed for England in March 1885. Junius was then in his seventies and, although hale for his years, had not yet recovered from the loss of his wife a few months earlier. Depressed by the emptiness of Prince's Gate, he stayed more often at Dover House and occupied himself with his model dairy and the company of a few chosen friends on weekends. He planned to spend his winters in the villa he had bought himself in Monte Carlo and expected to leave much of the firm's running to his son-in-law, Walter Burns, assisted by young Jack Morgan when he graduated from Harvard.

This pleasant semiretirement was now seriously challenged, but he took heart when Pierpont outlined a bold strategy to negotiate peace between the rival Pennsylvania railroads. He thought that New York Central would be well-advised to buy bankrupt Lake Shore rather than let Roberts absorb it. As a quid pro quo, Roberts might take over the new South Pennsylvania line after reimbursing New York Central for its investment. But it would not be easy to reconcile the two embittered and suspicious chieftains. Roberts was a hard-bitten roughneck who had started as a rodman and clawed his way up to Pennsylvania's presidency. He hated the autocratic multimillionaire and would relish any chance of humbling him. And Vanderbilt was unlikely to welcome the idea of purchasing West Shore which he had already denounced as "a miserable common thief caught with its hands in my pocket."

Pierpont guessed that his chief obstacle would be the personal antipathy between them, but he remained convinced that self-interest and survival might still bridge the gap. His first and most urgent priority would be to persuade Billy Vanderbilt to buy back into New York Central. By a lucky chance he happened to be in Europe enriching art dealers and intended to stop off briefly in London before sailing home. Pierpont at once decided to join him on the voyage as it would provide an almost ideal opportunity for private business talks.

The crossing was smooth and Vanderbilt expansive while he bored his captive audience with a tedious catalogue of the paintings, bibelots, and bric-à-brac purchased during his French and Italian shopping spree. As Pierpont had feared, he scoffed at a peace parley with Roberts over the two competing Pennsylvania networks, and his eyes almost popped with fury at any hint of purchasing the West Shore line. Grumpily, however, he agreed to leave that issue open for further examination. One objective was achieved: by the time they docked he had consented to reinvest in New York Central. The stock shot up within a few days.

Although delighted by the substantial profit accruing to him and the favorable publicity his "generous" action produced, Vanderbilt still resisted Drexel, Morgan's advice to buy up Lake Shore. Pierpont persevered. With Depew in his corner and backed by the detailed statistics Charles Coster's tireless team at 23 Wall Street had compiled, he persuaded Vanderbilt that the near-bankrupt line, if overhauled and properly financed, could be restored to health. That would effectively stop Roberts from gaining a majority and running his trains from Jersey City to Buffalo. To clinch the deal he offered his firm's services for only out-of-pocket expenses and without charging any fee or commission. He also agreed to accept Vanderbilt's nominee, former Judge Ashbel Green, who would cooperate in handling the very intricate transfer of the line's rundown and disorganized properties.

Green soon discovered who would be in charge when Pierpont drew up a detailed memorandum to lease West Shore for 999 years to New York Central by taking up mortgage bonds to a value of $50 million.

"I don't think it can be done legally," objected Green.

Pierpont eyed him coldly. "I asked you to tell me how it *could* be done legally," he snapped. "Come back and tell me how it *can* be done." Next day the old judge returned with the necessary ammunition, but a minority group of West Shore stockholders, scenting a fat killing, promptly issued an injunction to prevent the takeover. They had to be bought off after much haggling during the sizzling summer of 1885. Pierpont, suffering from a bout of influenza, often dragged himself from a sleepless bed to confer with Green or travel with him to Albany for the court hearings.

The deal, though troublesome, proved far easier to implement than his plan to have Roberts take over Pennsylvania South from Billy Vanderbilt on payment of $5 million. Chauncey Depew employed all his diplomatic skills, but made little impression on that truculent railroad man. Jug-eared, with a muttonchop moustache permanently stained from tobacco juice, Roberts rocked back and forth in his chair while he smoked a foul cob. After a particularly fruitless interview, Depew reported glumly that the fellow seemed quite determined to humiliate Vanderbilt for plotting his downfall with Carnegie and Rockefeller.

Pierpont was less defeatist and guessed that Roberts, a self-made Philadelphian, might secretly be impressed by the Drexels' grandeur and the prestige enjoyed by the Morgans on both sides of the Atlantic. Some of his brokerage business was already being handled by 23 Wall, but relations became less amicable when the firm openly identified itself with the Vanderbilts' interests. Pierpont had made little headway with Roberts during several visits to Philadelphia, although the vice-president, Frank Thomson, seemed rather more conciliatory. At one of their meetings in Thomson's stifling office he hinted casually that Roberts might perhaps enjoy a pleasant day's cruise on *Corsair,* with Depew

J. P. Morgan as photographed in 1903 by Edward Steichen. *(Courtesy The Museum of Modern Art)*

Amelia ("Mimi") Sturges, Pierpo
Morgan's first wife. Her trag
death, after four months of ma
riage, was a blow from which h
never fully recovered. *(Courtes*
The Pierpont Morgan Library)

French Government 6% Loan.

This loan contract, written on a single sheet of notepaper
at Tours in November 1870, during the Franco-Prussian
War, marked Junius Morgan's debut in international
finance. The bonds, issued at £85, slumped fast but were
later redeemed at par, netting the Morgan syndicate a
profit of a million pounds sterling. *(Courtesy The Pierpont
Morgan Library)*

Junius Spencer Morgan, Pierpont's father, who joined George Peabody's merchant banking firm in London in 1854. With his son in charge of the New York office, the Morgan firm transacted a major share of the turnover in Anglo-American securities. Junius was a multi-millionaire when he was killed by accident in 1890. *(Courtesy The Pierpont Morgan Library)*

J. P. Morgan, aged 44, during a visit to London in 1881. Later that year he bought his first yacht. A few months before, he sold 250,000 shares in New York Central on behalf of William Henry Vanderbilt, the first of a series of deals that would make him the most powerful figure in American railroad finance. *(Courtesy The Pierpont Morgan Library)*

The Pierpont Morgan Library on East 36th Street, New York City, was designed by Charles McKim and completed at a cost of several million dollars in 1905. It houses the banker's collection of rare books, first editions, and art treasures. In 1928 an annex was built at the site of the Morgan mansion on the corner at 219 Madison Avenue. *(Courtesy The Pierpont Morgan Library, c 1956 Ezra Stoller/Esto)*

The library's West or "Red" Room, with its walls in crimson damask from the Chigi Palace in Rome, was not only Pierpont Morgan's venue for receiving special visitors and holding important business meetings, but his chosen retreat to work out strategy in privacy. It led off into a huge vault containing a priceless cache of manuscripts, including Leonardo's notebooks, four Shakespeare Folios, and a five-page letter from George Washington. *(Courtesy The Pierpont Morgan Library c 1956 Ezra Stoller/Esto)*

The lavish East Room, furnished in the Florentine style, was add by superb tapestries, like that over the monumental fireplace tiers of Circassian walnut shelves glow with volumes bound in enamel, and ivory. Here J. P. Morgan assembled the leading New bank presidents and dictated his plans for dealing with the Panic. *(Courtesy The Pierpont Morgan Library c 1956 Stoller/Esto)*

Watching the Yale-Harvard race, June 1910, from the deck of *Corsair III*, J. P. Morgan's twin-screwed luxury yacht, 302 foot, manned by a crew of 69. She was used in home waters for lavish parties and secret business meetings. *Corsair* was regularly sailed across the Atlantic to be joined by the banker for Mediterranean cruises. Kaiser Wilhelm II was among his guests at Kiel Regattas. *(Courtesy The Pierpont Morgan Library)*

J. P. Morgan, Jr. (1867-1943) succeeded his father as head of the firm but did not inherit his business dynamism. He was unpopular with the Woodrow Wilson administration and also became a target for bitter labor criticism. The firm enjoyed a boom in World War One but was hard hit in the 1929 Wall Street Crash. Staunchly Anglophile, he entertained King George VI at his grouse-shooting parties and presented *Corsair IV* to the Royal Navy for use as a patrol vessel in 1940. *(Courtesy The Pierpont Morgan Library)*

joining them for lunch. He stressed that they would be able to talk business away from telephones and unwelcome reporters whose papers had been carrying hostile rumors about a possible merger. Roberts took the social bait but assured Thomson that nothing would induce him to change his mind about any deal with Vanderbilt.

They joined *Corsair* in Jersey City and sailed up the Hudson in glorious late-July weather. After a gourmet luncheon, they settled down to coffee, cognac, and cigars—except for George Roberts, who pulled out his pipe and puffed away. Depew argued smoothly that Vanderbilt would be risking a fortune to absorb West Shore, a competitor just as troublesome to the Pennsylvania Railroad as to New York Central. Roberts looked scornful and Depew, forcing himself to remain polite, repeated that he stood to win freedom from ruinous competition, as well as potential revenue, by taking over the South Pennsylvania.

Throughout the next few hours of rancorous argument, as Roberts indulged in clumsy sneers at Vanderbilt's hidden motives, Pierpont only intervened to offer the relevant facts and figures. During one lull, while glasses were yet again being freshened, he fixed Roberts with a cold eye and suddenly assured him that, unless he yielded now, his company would be driven to accept far less generous terms. Vanderbilt, he pointed out, could continue to fight indefinitely. Roberts flushed angrily at this switch from Depew's diplomacy.

The *Corsair* reached Jersey City at seven that evening. Roberts and his vice-president headed for the special train to Philadelphia, presumably to start the next phase of the battle for the Pennsylvania. On the gangway Roberts shook Pierpont's hand, thanked him for his hospitality and declared with a broad grin, "I agree to your plan and will do my part." Vanderbilt's approval followed with reluctance, but he could neither afford to withdraw Depew's provisional terms nor to repudiate Pierpont Morgan's authority to negotiate on his behalf.

On December 9, only a couple of days after Pierpont and Ashbel Green had finalized the West Shore lease, Billy Vanderbilt died from a heart attack at 640 Fifth Avenue. That same evening Pierpont joined a small group of leading financiers at Depew's house on Fifty-fourth Street. Among them they agreed to guarantee up to $15 million to cushion the market against a possible slump. After conferring with Depew, Pierpont cabled his father an assurance that Vanderbilt's stocks would not be dumped on the London market. Jay Gould also called a meeting of his associates, together with a director from Drexel, Morgan. It was provisionally decided to buy 250,000 shares of New York Central to maintain the price. None of these emergency measures proved necessary.

A few bears moved in to depress Lake Shore stock, but Wall Street took heart when the details of Billy Vanderbilt's estate became known. It was valued at over $200 million, double the amount left by the Commodore. The bulk would be split between the two oldest sons: serious unsmiling Cornelius II, who had dedicated himself to church affairs and philanthropy, and William Kissam, playboy yachtsman and polo player. Both would continue to act as nominal chairmen of various companies in the railroad empire, but they were content to leave New York Central under the presidency of Chauncey Depew. Morgan was presented with a solid gold dinner service for his successful coup and now took his place as the senior member of the board.

Christmas that year passed much as it usually did at the Morgan household. Pierpont dispatched his traditional ornamental caskets of tea to relatives and friends all over the country and, accompanied by Jack, distributed food parcels and toys to the needy. After Christmas dinner, the family joined in carols led by the choir from St. George's. Fanny and the children were given the usual costly gifts, and Pierpont received several brocaded waistcoats that he sported on cruises on the *Corsair* or for celebration dinners at the New York Yacht Club. He specially cherished a silver tankard from Ashbel Green. It commemorated a most considerate and seasonable gesture toward the West Shore employees whose back pay had been held up for several weeks while the new corporation emerged from the legal thicket. Without fuss or publicity Pierpont arranged for Drexel, Morgan to advance enough to cover all arrears, plus paychecks extending over the holiday period.

In accordance with the policy he had initiated with the Drexels' approval, his staff was given their usual bonus ranging from an extra year's pay for partners to lesser sums, graded by years of service, for the lower orders.

There were a few changes at the top. Fabbri's health had already cracked. Before long Hood Wright would drop dead while waiting for his train after an exhausting day at 23 Wall Street. But Charles Coster, Samuel Spencer, and Bowdoin continued to travel thousands of miles cross-country to check running costs, overheads, and likely sources of new revenue so that they might salvage the Baltimore and Ohio, the Lake Erie and Western, and the Chesapeake and Ohio. The firm was no longer acting for expenses only as New York Central's go-between, but pioneering an entirely new field in investment banking.

Pierpont's strategy was based on issuing stock and increasing working capital to integrate several weak competing lines into a profitable unit. Within a few years he would be in position to merge thirty-five small lines into the vast Southern Railway complex, capitalized at $375 million. By then he had successfully developed the voting trust formula, which became known on Wall Street as "Morganization." Instead of accepting a commission, often amounting to a million dollars or more for structuring a merger, The Corner would demand a relatively small proportion of the fee in cash and take the rest in voting stock with a place on the board for Pierpont or one of his associates. Operating through intricate and interlocking directorates, the firm enriched itself with each amalgamation while adding another link to the chain of railroad monopoly.

Gould still controlled 10,000 miles of track (together with Manhattan El and Western Union), but he and the other railroad magnates had at first minimized the potential threat from Morgan's system of capital syndicates, which Justice Brandeis would later blast: "Adding the duties of undertaker to those of midwife, the investment bankers became, in times of corporate disaster, members of security holders' 'Protective Committees'; then they participated as 'Reorganization Managers' in the reincarnation of the unsuccessful corporations, and ultimately became directors. When a banker entered the Board his group proved tenacious and his influence usually supreme; for he controlled the supply of new money." In other words, the tugs seemed to end up by owning the vessels they had salvaged.

Morgan could justify his drive toward monopoly by claiming that it eliminated waste and inefficiency and was beneficial to the shareholders (and, naturally enough, to his own firm, as managers!). Others were less happy, including the passengers, who would pay higher fares; workers less able to bargain for shorter hours and better pay; and, above all, the smaller companies, which now faced rising freight costs while monoliths like Carnegie and Rockefeller enjoyed privileged rebates.

Pleased at the significant gains made in railroad securities as a result of the wave of takeovers, Wall Street naturally welcomed these advances in investment banking and viewed Morgan's every intervention as a talisman of success. His reputation for wizardlike skill in reorganization was nourished by his congenital horror of publicity. He gave no interviews and wrote only once in his career to a newspaper editor—to protest angrily that his Christian name had been wrongly spelled, a phobia dating back to his schooldays. On another occasion he flung back a document to a terrified clerk and shouted, "I am Pierpont, *not* Pierrepoint." He did not deign to thank Henry Clews who wrote flatteringly of him, "He has the driving force of a locomotive. He cares nothing for show; he is a plain man of action. He strikes hard blows, he is naturally aggressive. In speech he is candid to the verge of bluntness; in action he is short, sharp and decisive."

He liked attending bankers' dinners but could never be persuaded to make a speech. He usually preferred to let Coster or Bowdoin represent the firm at company meetings, but nobody dared ignore him when he put in an appearance. A minor railroad president once ruefully observed to a colleague, "Wherever Morgan sits on a board is the head of the table, even if he has but a single share." He sometimes sat in on the New York, New Haven, and Hartford board meetings because of his sentimental link with that line since his childhood. At one of their meetings in the Grand Central Depot, he stood up and growled, "I have been told that you are very slow about paying your bills. I hear that some of your creditors have been held up, or staved off, sometimes for as long as six months. I think this railroad ought to pay its just bills as soon as they are due. If you haven't the ready money on hand to pay them, I will advance it." He then picked up his hat, stomping out without a second glance at the others.

By the time he celebrated his fiftieth birthday in April 1887 his personal holdings and stocks were being freely estimated at around $25 million, a fortune smaller than those of Gould, Carne-

144

gie, Rockefeller, and the Vanderbilt brothers, but in terms of financial power he already controlled more capital investment from rail mileage, telegraphy, and Edison franchises than any of them. At Wall and Broad the office lights burned so late, night after night, that they soon sparked off the legend of an all-powerful general, with a huge red nose and a jutting black cigar, tirelessly deploying armies of greenbacks from his marble fortress.

The facts were rather different. Before driving to the office at ten sharp each morning, he would already have studied the cables received from London or Paris and noted the latest stock quotations on his ticker tape. With Fanny still tucked away in her bedroom, he would be joined at breakfast by Louisa or Juliet, both dutifully sympathetic if he had slept badly. The youngest girl, Annie, sometimes offended his sense of decorum with her casual clothes and dislike of "ladylike" deportment, but she alone could coax him out of his grizzly bearskin.

At the office he joined his chief executives in the partners' room for a brief conference. As this was strictly confidential, no secretary was ever present to take notes. He then made his ritual visit to the stock desk and the securities department to update himself on the firm's cash position. He had a predatory eye for the tiniest discrepancy in a long row of figures and would sharply reprimand clerks for any negligence or ambiguity. To enable him to deal expeditiously with callers, he expected his partners and departmental specialists to provide detailed analyses at short notice. He astonished clients with his mastery of figures and the speed with which he came to a decision after asking no more than a few leading questions, but this was often based on expert staff research and weeks of patient legwork. Nevertheless, he could not have coped with a demanding work schedule without a remarkable capacity to concentrate intensively on the most intricate problems and produce not only *ad hoc* solutions but often the blueprint for a long-term strategy. He was helped by a complete faith in his own judgments or prejudices. If his verdict on some client clashed with a partner's, he would end all further argument by sniffing, "He's not to be trusted," or "I don't like him." There was no right of appeal.

After his luncheon and nap, followed by an hour or so to clear

145

outstanding correspondence, he would leave promptly at three o'clock for his club or a tête-à-tête with a lady friend. His colleagues had to accommodate themselves to his brief office hours and his insatiable appetite for outside committee work. He continued to support the Metropolitan Art Museum and the New York Yacht Club, in whose affairs he took an increasing part. After attending his first Episcopal Convention in Chicago as a lay representative of St. George's, he had characteristically volunteered to supervise the entertainment and all travel arrangements for the delegates and their wives. Once plans had matured to erect the immense Cathedral of St. John the Divine in New York, he subscribed lavishly to the building fund, agreeing to act as treasurer responsible for administering several million dollars on a project that would involve him in long years of frustration.

However, he did not neglect his senior warden duties at St. George's and always made time for Dr. Rainsford's welfare projects. When the rector hinted that many mothers and their babies suffered cruelly from the summer heat on New York's East Side, he accompanied him to Rockaway Park, Long Island, approved a suitable plot, and endowed a Seaside Rest with excellent residential and bathing amenities for fifty families. Rainsford soon mentioned various other schemes to help deserving parishioners, but he went on at such length at one of their Monday breakfasts that Pierpont brusquely interrupted, "Go ahead, meet your expenses as far as you can, then bring in a statement every quarter or six months and I'll make good any deficit."

Morgan's philanthropy was impulsive, sentimental, and limited almost exclusively to those with some personal claim to his regard. It did not stretch to strikers clamoring for an eight-hour day or business clients who failed to meet his exalted standards of social breeding and education. One small industrialist, too importunate in requesting a much-needed loan, was escorted out to the street where Pierpont's hansom stood waiting to take him over to the Union Club. Morgan shrugged off the man, who had dared to grasp his arm, and snapped with whiplash sarcasm, "I'll walk with you as far as the Stock Exchange. After all, being *seen* with me might be worth more to you in the long run than the loan which, on the facts presented, does not hold sufficient appeal to my firm." Another victim, whose credit rating was none too high, grew so desperate after several fruitless appeals for an interview

146

that he buttonholed the banker when he was leaving 219 Madison Avenue one morning. "Will you lend me your ear?" he stammered. "Certainly," said Pierpont. "But nothing else."

Such anecdotes became part of Wall Street's folklore, but his network of trusts was so intricate and covert that, outside the banking hierarchy, he remained a shadowy figure. This preserved him from dissatisfied shareholders and, quite as welcome to a man of his reserve, insulated him from the bitterness employees felt toward the railroads, Standard Oil, and Carnegie's iron and steel empire. In the fall of 1866, while cocooned with his bishops in Chicago at the Triennial Episcopal Convention, he had piously approved locking out strikers from the McCormick Harvester works. Riots started and a bomb exploded in Haymarket Square, killing a policeman and wounding many others. Four of the ringleaders were brought to trial and hanged.

Against the sequel of industrial turmoil, Congress reacted by attacking the insidious growth of trusts, particularly in the railroads, whose "consolidated" systems now apparently controlled 45 percent of the country's entire mileage. Early in 1887 Cleveland's shaky administration had made a frantic bid for popularity by rushing through the Interstate Commerce Act to abolish secret rebates and agreements that favored the powerful combines but maintained punitive rates for passenger and freight traffic. A commission set up to enforce it fizzled into impotence as railroad presidents fought and won every case on appeal to the Supreme Court.

Pierpont Morgan was never mentioned by name, but in the privacy of the Union Club no one more violently attacked government "interference." He had long repented his support of Cleveland, whose low-tariff policies had depressed the economy and outraged the country's industrialists, farmers, and manufacturers seeking bigger markets at home and overseas. Cleveland became so unpopular that Chauncey Depew thought of putting himself forward for the presidential nomination but the Republican party managers considered that as chief of New York Central, he would be a certain vote loser. He withdrew in favor of plodding Benjamin Harrison, a former Civil War general from Indiana, with Wall Street's favorite son, Levi P. Morton, as his running mate.

Morgan strongly supported both candidates on this winning

ticket although he was less enchanted by the appointment of shady James G. Blaine as Secretary of State. For the moment he welcomed the administration, believing it would check the growth of the new Populist movement pledged to destroy Big Business, trusts, and monopolies. This he dismissed as "typical of the new anarchy," and thought it unlikely to interrupt his triumphant run of "Morganization."

While tightening his hold on the Chesapeake & Ohio, the Richmond & Allegheny, and other lines, he had practically ignored insignificant-looking Illinois Central, one of the few independents paying its way, thanks to the efficient management of E. H. Harriman. It owned the lease of the small but strategic Dubuque & Sioux Railroad, which it hoped to renew at the old and very economical figure or possibly buy outright on a current low valuation. Alerted to this move in 1887, Drexel, Morgan at last became interested and Dubuque's shareholders elected Pierpont to the board with proxy votes for two-thirds of the stock. At the general meeting some weeks later, Harriman and his associate on Illinois Central, Stuyvesant Fish, objected that Drexel, Morgan had no power to use this majority holding since the necessary forms had been signed as proxies and not trustees, as required by the laws of Iowa. On this technical flaw, due to rare negligence by the firm's local agents, Harriman won the first round. Litigation followed, but it was so costly that the Dubuque shareholders lost heart and before the end of that year accepted the "take it or leave it" offer for their stock from Illinois Central. After what he condemned as "a snide trick," Pierpont declined to invite Harriman to attend his historic conference of railroad chiefs at 219 Madison Avenue early in January 1889. By then it was clear, even to the most optimistic Republicans, that President Harrison's high-tariff policies would have little effect on the shaky national economy and were even less likely to placate trade union leaders now openly accusing the administration of "holding the people down while the Trusts went through their pockets." With the railroads obviously next in line for attack, and probable disruptive strike action to follow, Pierpont judged the moment ripe to restore order and stability to the industry. Although it now controlled more track mileage than the whole of Europe's systems, rampant overspeculation and mismanagement had bankrupted many of the smaller lines and depressed investor confidence in Wall Street and the City of London.

Pierpont served his guests an excellent dinner and then adjourned to the library where his partner, Samuel Spencer, took the minutes. Some presidents had refused to attend, objecting that they were responsible to their own shareholders and not Wall Street, but those who accepted Drexel, Morgan's invitation still represented two-thirds of the nation's railroads. Jay Gould, now a shrunken figure ravaged by terminal tuberculosis, sat beside his son, George, to defend their interests in Missouri & Pacific; Pennsylvania's George Roberts looked even more truculent and suspicious than usual; others present included Collis P. Huntington of Central and Southern Pacific and representatives of the two powerful Midwestern networks who, it was thought, were unlikely to abandon their maverick policy. New York Central's Chauncey Depew and patrician Charles Francis Adams of Union Pacific both looked ill at ease amongst these men who had gouged their way to power and influence. Adams would later recall his embarrassment at sitting down with "this coarse, realistic, bargaining crowd," and he was plainly in a minority when he spoke out sharply against "the covetousness, want of good faith, and low moral tone of railway managers."

Pierpont began calmly enough by urging the need for an association to maintain "public, reasonable, uniform, and stable rates." Irritated by the scepticism of most of his listeners, he soon began talking down to them with a disapproval verging on contempt. He concluded by frostily rebuking "those who take the law into their own hands, which is not elsewhere customary in civilized communities." Jay Gould glowered and Huntington smiled cynically. Roberts, puffing hard on his corn cob, could not resist hitting back at "bankers responsible for the building of damfool competing lines." He conceded, however, "despite Mr. Morgan's pretty harsh language," that he would not oppose the setting up of an advisory board to centralize rate controls and decide all matters of common interest. Several others grudgingly nodded but A. B. Stickney, the roughneck chieftain of the Chicago, St. Paul, and Kansas City, would not endorse what he saw as snobbish window dressing for a further extension of banking rule. Hands on hips, he looked around belligerently and sneered, "I have the utmost respect for you gentlemen, but as railroad presidents I wouldn't trust you with my watch out of sight!"

The so-called Gentlemen's Agreement, welcomed in a New York *Sun* editorial as "a revolutionary substitution of straightforward business principles for chicanery and corruption," was more remarkable as an example of its creator's towering presence than as a significant move toward harmonizing the nation's rail system. The new association, united only by its opposition to the Interstate Commerce Act, had no real authority to impose sanctions. Since members could withdraw after ninety days' notice there seemed little hope that freebooters like Gould, Huntington, Roberts, and particularly the hardbitten Midwesterners would observe more stringent controls or deny the oil and steel kings their old privileges on freight. But if that meeting in the library of 219 Madison Avenue achieved little else, it reminded Congress, labor leaders, and industrialists like Carnegie and the Rockefellers that Pierpont had for the first time clearly identified himself as the champion of investment power, a power that could be imposed on stockholders and independent operators more docile than Ned Harriman.

Edison, for one, soon learned that Morganization would not be restricted to the railroad business. Pierpont had recently helped to float the North American Phonograph Company and was one of the first to install the new apparatus for home entertainment. He used the machine to record the voices of his children and guests on the crude early cylinders that were, alas, soon broken. He showed little interest in Edison's experiments with the Kinetoscope, the forerunner of motion pictures, and became impatient with his repeated demands for cash and his very unbusinesslike methods.

The inventor raised loans far too impetuously for his own good. Once he had to be rescued by Henry Villard to meet the weekly payroll for his workforce, now swollen to 3,000. Pierpont's friend and ally, James A. Stillman of the National City Bank, was less helpful when approached for an advance to develop a new process for concentrating magnetic ore. "You don't need a banker," Stillman remarked coldly. "What you want is a partner." Edison had no doubt whom Stillman had in mind after Drexel, Morgan harshly exacted interest at 20 percent on a loan of $20,000.

By the end of the decade he was being harassed both by patent pirates and competitors like Westinghouse and the British firm of Thomson-Houston, who dominated the supply of arc lighting for street lamps. Although carrying millions of dollars' worth of securities in municipal utility companies and boasting a full order book, he remained chronically short of ready cash for research and new factories. At one point he came so near bankruptcy that he turned to Insull and observed wryly, "Well, Sammy, I can always earn my living as a telegraph operator, and you will never starve as a stenographer!"

His liquidity problems were temporarily resolved in the spring of 1888 when Villard integrated most of the manufacturing offshoots into the parent firm under the title of the Edison General Electrical Company, launched with new stock to the value of $3.5 million at par. Another $4 million of stock was soon issued, with Drexel, Morgan and Berlin's Deutsche Bank (acting for Siemens) handling most of it. Edison held 10 percent of all the stock. The sale of his shops and other assets to the new company yielded him a further $1.7 million, which left him freer to work on his Kinetoscope and other inventions. He and Insull were given places on the board, but Pierpont, with Coster as treasurer, exerted far more control.

The Morgan relationship with Henry Villard, already strained by bitter disagreements over the Northern Pacific and Lake Shore railroads, had burst into open enmity when Pierpont began buying more and more stock in General Electrical for his own firm and favored clients like Ogden Mills and Hamilton Twombly, the late Billy Vanderbilt's son-in-law. Villard retained faith in his German bankers, Siemens, to repel this or any other challenge, although uneasy at rumors that the Morgans might be planning a secret deal with the Thomson-Houston firm.

This possible merger was indeed very much in Pierpont's mind when he sailed for England in late March 1890 with his eldest daughter, Louisa. The Edison Company's complex future and the still unresolved railroad situation would head the agenda for discussion with his father, but otherwise he hoped for a work-free holiday, including a week or two at the Monte Carlo villa. After some shopping in London he intended to visit booksellers and bibliophiles to buy more first editions for his library.

The collection had started modestly with the manuscript of Scott's *Guy Mannering,* a gift from Junius. On his last visit to London, his nephew, Sarah's son, had introduced a young book-dealer named Wheeler, who had secured an original Thackeray manuscript from the novelist's daughter.

Pierpont asked brusquely, "How much?"

"One hundred pounds."

"How much for cash?"

"Ninety pounds," stammered Wheeler, who would later bring him many other treasures including first editions of *Robinson Crusoe* and Spenser's *Faerie Queene.*

At meals he was exceptionally cheerful as the liner neared the Irish coast but complained to Louisa that Jack, who had graduated from Harvard and was just starting at 23 Wall Street, seemed too hasty in planning to marry by the end of the year. As was his habit, he insisted on a barometer in his cabin and had daily weather reports sent down to him by the captain.

At Queenstown he was handed a sheaf of telegrams announcing his father's accidental death. His office had sought to soften the blow by sending at intervals one that announced his injury, another that spoke of his serious condition, and a third that revealed his death, but Pierpont received them simultaneously and opened the last one first. Junius Morgan's death had a melodramatic air for one who had lived his life in the cool, sober terms of double entry bookkeeping. On April 4, he had been out for a sedate drive on the Beaulieu-Eze road when a train hurtled by on the adjacent track, causing the horses to bolt. Junius was thrown out of the carriage and struck his head on a rock. Taken to the hospital unconscious, he died on the ninth.

Grief-stricken, Pierpont hurried to Monte Carlo where his sister, Mary Burns, had already arranged for the body to be embalmed. They returned together to America with the coffin and Pierpont finalized details for the funeral and the burial in the Cedar Hill cemetery at Hartford. The estate was conservatively valued at $9,211,740, of which $3 million was left to each of the two elder daughters, Sarah and Mary, but a million less to the youngest, who had wilfully married a clergyman Junius disliked. In his will drawn only a few months before the fatal accident Junius had specified that her share in the plate, and so forth, should only be for life and "such use and enjoyment to be personal and independent of any present or any future husband." The cruel parting sting could hardly be reconciled with an obituary that lamented the passing of "a bright, kindly, lovable and generous man."

His son and heir was the residuary legatee, inheriting 13 Prince's Gate and Dover House, Roehampton, plus a million dollars in cash and his quarter share in Junius Morgan's handsome collection of plate and paintings. Before sailing from New York in June 1890 to settle his father's estate in England and formally take over as senior partner of J. S. Morgan & Co., he requested Frederick Tams, a fellow member of the Union and Yacht Clubs to supervise the building of a new yacht, which would be faster and larger than *Corsair* but still maneuverable on the New York-Highland Falls ferry run. He wanted a vessel with less vibration and better ventilation for longer cruises. Although she would have a similar black hull and single funnel, *Corsair II* was to be much more opulent, a liberal budget ensuring the most luxurious cabin accommodations and tasteful furnishings, though it would still fall short of the standard set by William Kissam Vanderbilt's ocean-going *Alva,* which had a private bathroom for each mahogany paneled stateroom.

CHAPTER NINE

Pierpont swiftly made plans to refurbish Prince's Gate and perhaps add to the collection of paintings that his father had built up over the years, often with the guidance of Alfred de Rothschild, the debonair bachelor and *bon vivant* whose own treasures in Seamore Place, just off Park Lane, were the envy of the world's connoisseurs. Disraeli, who moved into the mansion when he left 10 Downing Street, had described it as "the most charming house in London, the magnificence of its decorations and furniture equaled by their good taste." Alfred played host to guests led by the Prince of Wales, the Prime Minister, Lord Rosebery (who had married Hannah Rothschild), and the cream of the diplomatic corps. Pierpont turned to him for advice on pictures, and the acquaintance warmed into close friendship, despite growing anti-Jewish prejudice among New England's blue bloods, who took an unhealthy interest in Houston Stewart Chamberlain's theories of "Aryan" racial superiority, which were being widely trumpeted on the Continent.

Morgan found it impossible, however, to patronize the powerful Rothschilds and, like almost everyone else in European society, from crowned heads downward, had come to regard them not as a Jewish clan of former moneychangers but as some exotic breed with the social status of Maharajahs.

Alfred himself chanced to be so blond and fair-skinned that he might have slipped into even Houston Chamberlain's Valhalla without attracting any attention. He had also recently become a director of the Bank of England, the first of his race to be so honored. Coming from a country where Jacob Schiff might have found it easier to walk on water than pass the hall porter of the New York Yacht Club, Pierpont was impressed by Alfred's houseparties at Cowes and his membership in London's most exclusive clubs. He was soon captivated by his charm, wit, and the eccentric spirit that induced him to conduct his symphony orchestra with an ivory, diamond-encrusted baton at Halton House in Buckinghamshire. There he maintained a private circus and drove around in a zebra-drawn carriage. Even Pierpont, who prided himself on his own $1.50 Regalia de Morgan cigars specially imported from Havana, goggled when the host casually presented him on leaving with a casket of one hundred guinea panatellas. Nor would he forget how "dear Alfred," the kindliest of men, kept the Prince of Wales slavering for his dinner until past nine o'clock so that the staff could finish their own evening meal in comfort.

Alfred's hospitality was an oasis compared to the bleak landscape he confronted from the firm's London headquarters in Old Broad Street. Every day brought some sharp reminder of a growing lack of confidence in the American economy. The Gentlemen's Agreement had not prevented many of the minor railroads from buckling, and British investors took fright. The City of London became even more uneasy over a recent act of Congress enabling the Treasury to coin silver and place it on a parity with gold. The ensuing glut of silver in certificates and bullion soon led to a run on America's quickly declining gold reserves just when Lombard Street was itself attempting to stem an abnormal gold outflow. In early November 1890, when Argentina was hit by a disastrous crop failure and began to impose panic taxes on foreign banks, the Bank of England rate shot up to 6 percent and its effects were soon passed on to Wall Street.

The old established London house of Baring Brothers, which carried huge blocks of unsalable Argentine bonds and had incurred liabilities of over £20 million, suddenly faced insolvency. Although Pierpont's firm was not involved (he had always prudently advised Junius to avoid "gaucho finance"), he grew nervous about likely damage to the whole stock market. He was only

156

partially reassured by his influential friend Sir Everard Hambro, whose almost godlike Viking looks and stature he admired almost as much as the prestige of his banking dynasty.

Late one night Hambro called on Lord Revelstoke, Baring's arrogant chairman, and came away much disturbed. By eight next morning he had hurried off to confer with the Rothschild directors, who agreed that the City risked a severe crisis of confidence if Baring Brothers suspended payments. He then visited the Bank of England, whose Governor, William Lidderdale, admitted that his gold reserves of under £11 million would be inadequate to save the Barings. An Argentine Committee, chaired by Lord Rothschild, hastily negotiateed a loan of three million sterling in gold from the Banque de France and bought another million pounds' worth from Russia.

On Friday, November 14, 1890, a guarantee fund was launched for £3.2 million, the Bank of England authorizing the first million. The fund was soon doubled and indeed reached £14 million after the five major stock banks, together with the Rothschilds and Hambros, had made substantial contributions. Pierpont also pledged the credit of J. S. Morgan & Co. and Drexel, Morgan for guarantees of £100,000 each. Within a few hours the crisis had passed. Baring Brothers was reconstituted as a limited company with a million-pound capital base and paid off all its obligations within three years.

Like the other guarantors, the Morgan firms lost not a penny piece in the salvage operation but it helped to propel Pierpont's name into the highest echelons of international banking. His prompt response had won warm City approval, although the American *Tribune* overdid the gush in applauding him for "working out the salvation of the financial world after the Argentine collapse." Lord Rothschild soon recommended to his committee that J. S. Morgan & Co., with its connections in London, Paris, and New York, seemed ideally placed to refund Argentina's national debt by underwriting a $75 million loan at 6 percent.

It went so smoothly that Pierpont was tempted to venture further into Latin American finance. In 1890 he joined a consortium with the Seligmans of Paris and New York and Charles Lanier's Wall Street firm to float stock in the French Panama Canal Company to acquire and expand the country's small, rundown railroad. Unhappily, fraud and mismanagement, reminiscent of the Crédit Mobilier scandal, soon sent the shares into a sharp decline.

American investors protested that the stock had been grossly overpriced, and several radicals on Capitol Hill caught the whiff of monopoly. The consortium was rebuked in Congress for flouting the Monroe Doctrine by supporting a crooked "French project." A congressional committee, set up after the operation had collapsed, expressed its blunt disapproval.

Pierpont would always maintain that he had taken only a minor role in the promotion, but in fact his firm was paid $400,000 for its services, precisely the same fee as the Seligmans. Predictably, the Jewish firm was soon singled out for condemnation as cynical operators who had ignored the national interest.

With American sentiment continuing to be violently critical of the Panama affair and its unpleasant aftermath, a small clique in the Union League Club, of which Jesse Seligman was a vice-president, went into action when his lawyer son, Theodore, a Harvard graduate, applied for membership. Although sponsored by General Horace Porter, Joseph Choate, and Elihu Root, he was blackballed. The committee, with overwhelming support of the members, blandly assured his father that the objection "was not personal in any way but purely racial!" Jesse never again set foot in the premises although the committee refused to accept his resignation. New York's Mayor Gilroy signed a public protest deploring the club's racism. He died a few months later, brokenhearted it is said, leaving a fortune of $30 million, but the great firm of J. & W. Seligman lost its early prominence and declined steadily, while J. P. Morgan not only survived the Panama Canal scandal but soared in influence.

One direct but significant bonus accrued to the firm from the Baring crisis and its damaging effect on a Wall Street still depressed by the federal government's silver policy. The Edison General Electrical Company continued to stack up sales revenues, but it had to grapple simultaneously with vast capital expenditure, a crippling floating debt, and incessant price cutting by foreign patentees. It became harder to raise investment cash both in New York and London, and Pierpont saw no future in rescuing the company while Villard remained as president. Instead he instructed Coster to buy up stock secretly through nominees, while he himself dropped hints of a possible merger to Charles Coffin, whose organizing drive had multiplied the profits of Thomson-Houston, Edison's most formidable competitor.

With the shaky Northern Pacific Railroad still on his hands, Villard faced stark ruin when his German backers, Siemens, decided to sell out their Edison holdings, leaving the door wide open for Drexel, Morgan to draft terms for the long-planned amalgamation. It was launched with a capitalization of $35 million, more than half the stock going to Thomson-Houston. Villard had to resign, and the inventor suffered the indignity of seeing his name removed from the new company, which emerged as General Electric. He was also squeezed out of all the final negotiations, which J. P. Morgan handled in association with Ogden Mills and Hamilton McKown Twombly. Edison rarely attended even the first G.E.C. meetings at 23 Wall Street and soon gave up a directorship that was almost offensively nominal.*

While in London, though busily engaged with the Baring crisis and the Argentine loan, Pierpont found time to make certain staff changes. He also issued a directive that startled his brother-in-law, Walter Burns, and other office veterans who had always considered him far more of a martinet than Junius. Although still insisting on rigid discipline from his employees, he expressed disapproval of the obsequious bowing and bobbing to seniors traditional in the City's conservative banking houses.

It was a quirky gesture of protest against a code which he found personally offensive and un-American, rather than a conversion to democracy. If anything, he had grown more peevishly autocratic with greater affluence, power, and prestige. The Union Club's committee made this painful discovery after rashly black-

---

*Samuel Insull was practical enough to see the logic of the merger but could not bring himself to play second or third fiddle to Coffin, the newly elected president. He preferred to go west and start a small company that he called Chicago Edison, although his disillusioned old chief took no part in it. Insull appointed himself president and parleyed a $250,000 loan from Marshall Field into a huge public utilities empire through crooked franchises and inflated bond issues. His billion-dollar pyramid of sand and paper would collapse in the Wall Street crash.

balling one of his nominees for membership. He decided not to resign but retaliated by forming a syndicate with Depew and others to build a rival club at the corner of Sixtieth and Fifth Avenue, one of Manhattan's choicest sites. The Metropolitan was soon being nicknamed the Millionaire's Club from the wealth and social position of its members, whose fine carriages drew up in the cobbled courtyard. For many months after the opening he and his friends ostentatiously avoided the Union's yellow dining room and only returned in triumph when they considered the committee adequately humiliated. The Metropolitan was designed by Stanford White, whose firm was also responsible for Madison Square Garden, built in 1890 for nearly four million dollars through a syndicate organized by Morgan.

The success of that operation was rather soured by Jack's marriage later that year. Pierpont approved of the charming bride, Jane ("Jessie") Grew, who came of flawless New England stock, but showed his displeasure when her parents insisted on having the wedding reception in Boston and the ceremony at their own church in Arlington Street, politely rejecting his offer to stage-manage the entire affair in New York. That problem did not, of course, arise in April 1894 when his second daughter, Juliet, married eligible William Pierson Hamilton. This time he personally took over, from the elaborate floral arrangements in St. George's to the wedding breakfast menu at 219 Madison Avenue, where Louis Sherry was kept on the hop to meet his every whim. The bride, bridesmaids, and Fanny were fetchingly gowned by M. Worth with Pierpont's vote naturally settling any little argument over style and design.

By 1894 Jack had become a partner in Drexel, Morgan and its associate houses in Philadelphia and Paris. Sent over to work in the Old Broad Street offices, he and his wife both found London most agreeable. They had settled comfortably into 13 Prince's Gate, with Dover House a pleasant summer retreat and ideal for weekend parties. Jack was conscientious but took every chance to sail home with Jessie and proudly display their first-born, Junius Spencer Morgan III, to his grandparents in New York and Boston. As tall as his father, though far more muscular and athletic, Jack plainly lacked his outstanding business drive and acumen, but an urbane manner won him many friends once they had accepted his irritating air of superiority and clipped English accent.

The Philadelphia & Reading Railroad was one of the systems whose finances Morgan had restored to credit some years earlier. The mileage was insignificant but it crossed territory containing some half of Pennsylvania's anthracite deposits. Drexel, Morgan acted as the fiscal agents, and the Vanderbilts owned some of the stock, as did Pierpont's prickly old foe, George Roberts. The majority holding remained in the hands of the president, Archibald McLeod, and his fellow directors, George M. Pullman and John Wanamaker, who, seeing their chance to extend into the manufacturing areas of Pennsylvania and New England, bought into the Boston & Maine and other smallish lines. They hoped to present a threat to Roberts and also to New York Central.

Depew and the Vanderbilt brothers agreed with Pierpont Morgan that the upstart line would have to be put out of business after McLeod arrogantly rejected a polite overture for a merger. "I would rather run a peanut stand than be dictated to by J. P. Morgan," he snorted. But his grandiose attempts to absorb other networks were soon blocked by Morgan counteroffers backed by Vanderbilt cash and malicious whispers impugning his financial stability. To raise capital he had to pay high rates of interest to Speyers and further impoverished himself by hastily unloading securities on a falling market. Once Pullman and Wanamaker decided to sell their stock, he turned to Kuhn, Loeb & Co., but Jacob Schiff, never the man to go into battle when outgunned, backed off from confronting the powerful Morgan-Vanderbilt coalition.

While McLeod headed for disaster, George Roberts played the market from the sidelines. With various business friends, among them C. Stuart Patterson, Sr., father of Chippy, the famed hard-drinking criminal attorney), he moved in for the kill on February 17, 1893, when almost half a million P.R.R. shares were dumped on the market. He saw a clear prospect of absorbing the line into his Pennsylvania combine but found himself checkmated four days later when a Morgan partner became receiver of the stricken line. This time, comforted by his fat profits, he took defeat gracefully. With Patterson and other members of his abortive consortium he accepted an invitation for a brief Caribbean cruise on the *Corsair* to celebrate Morgan's intervention.

Jaunty Willie K. Vanderbilt came on board as New York Central's representative and soon returned Pierpont's hospitality on his new yacht. It had replaced the *Alva,* which had sunk after a collision near Martha's Vineyard. Like other magnates, Willie Vanderbilt had deserted Saratoga Springs for the more fashionable delights of Newport, where he had built himself a $9 million white marble palace. He was still out-dazzled, however, by his brother, Cornelius, whose socially ravenous wife had goaded him into putting up a seventy-room palazzo, The Breakers. The staff, including sixteen footmen in wigs and silk breeches, waited at dinner on up to two hundred guests. Tapestries and fireplaces had been imported from Italy and France, and even the billiard room was an ornate creation of marble and mahogany.

This Italianate rococo fantasy typified the spendthrift flamboyance that flourished during the nineties in a working-class climate of sweated labor, hunger riots, and strikes. Ogden Mills did not hesitate to allocate $450,000 to decorating his Fifth Avenue mansion opposite St. Patrick's, bragging that his chefs and trained lackeys could serve a banquet for a hundred at an hour's notice. Adolphus Busch casually arranged with Pullman to have chilled beer piped into each stateroom on his private car. At some Delmonico parties the ladies would find gold bracelets tucked into their napkins for dessert, and *demimondaines* became accustomed to receiving appearance money in the form of packs of cigarettes wrapped in one-hundred dollar bills.

But just as he had disdained building himself a Renaissance château on Fifth Avenue, Pierpont despised the parvenu craving for buying Europe's blue blood with American greenbacks. He remained content to marry his own children into New England's solid *haute bourgeoisie* and took a sardonic pleasure in the matrimonial disasters that overtook the Vanderbilts and others who launched themselves into Burke's *Peerage* or the *Almanach de Gotha.*

He had been among the many dry-eyed mourners in December 1892 at the funeral of Jay Gould, whose unenviable title of "the most-hated man in America" was immediately shared out between John D. Rockefeller and Andrew Carnegie. Gould had left well over $100 million in trust for his sons and daughters, one of whom, plain sallow Anna, seemed quite irresistible to a French dandy, philanderer, and gambler, Count Boni de Castellane, then hard-pressed to pay off his creditors.

Pierpont had a spasm of anxiety when Boni, checking the field through his lorgnette, showed a distinct interest in his youngest daughter, Anne, who spoke fluent French and was culturally well above the run of rich American fillies, although rather too addicted to strenuous tennis and sailing for his exquisite taste. She was enchanted by the witty dilettante but far too shrewd to be seduced by his flattery. He soon found easier and more opulent prey than the Morgan girl, whose sire had such a daunting business reputation.

He married Anna Gould at brother George's mansion, to the romantic strains of Victor Herbert's orchestra. The bride's veil alone cost $6,000. She seemed a trifle dazed by the splendor but cautiously refused to become a Catholic, thus leaving herself an emergency exit. The couple departed for Paris where Count Boni rapidly squandered the huge dowry on Versailles-like fêtes and a stable of hungry cocottes. On the birth of his first son he had objected to naming him "after a thief."

"But you don't mind living on the money of a thief," the Countess reminded him sharply.

She divorced him after a few years and, still thirsting for nobility, married his distant cousin, the Duc de Talleyrand. Boni fell on hard times and became a tout for antique dealers. Morgan would later savor the delight of snapping up some beautiful blue and pink Gobelin tapestries that Boni had acquired back in the days when Jay Gould's mountain of dollars first cascaded through his manicured claws.

Anna's ill-starred marriage was matched by an even grander fiasco engineered by Alva, Willie K. Vanderbilt's ambitious wife. She married off their beautiful 18-year-old daughter, Consuelo, to the ninth Duke of Marlborough, who graciously accepted $2.5 million in railroad stock, an allowance of $100,000 a year, and a generous contribution to restore Blenheim Palace. It was no love match—Consuelo would have preferred Winthrop Rutherford, a charming young attorney, to the pop-eyed Duke—and the unhappy union drifted into divorce, although not for several years as Marlborough had embraced the Roman Catholic faith.

The Morgans had attended the ceremony in St. Thomas's Episcopal Church and the glittering reception that followed. Pierpont could not resist a good party, and he generally attended Caroline Astor's overpowering annual ball each January. There she would queen it in a velvet robe, usually in regal purple, with a stomacher of diamonds, a pearl dog-collar, and the mandatory tiara. He was greatly amused to hear that she had long hesitated to include him in her list of the so-called Four Hundred and had told Ward McAllister, her social adviser, that "Mr. Morgan seems to have become rather *bohemian.*" He made frequent appearances at Delmonico's and Sherry's as escort to Edna May or Lillian Russell, but his favorite haunt was the mahogany-paneled Men's Bar at the Waldorf-Astoria, the hotel put up at the corner of Fifth Avenue and Thirty-Fourth after Mrs. Astor had swept uptown. Here he could chat and drink with Depew, Willie Vanderbilt, and William Rockefeller. This would usually be followed by a stag dinner or some charity hundred-dollar a plate banquet cooked by a $10,000 a year chef under the lordly eye of "Oscar" Tshirky, who had left Delmonico's.

By contemporary millionaire standards Morgan's scale of entertainment was almost modest. In the summer months he offered pleasant though unextravagant hospitality at Cragston or on *Corsair.* When the family was back in residence at 219 Madison Avenue, he gave formal dinners for a small circle of friends like his doctor, James W. Markoe, the yachting expert, Beavor Webb, and the firm's attorney, Francis Lynde Stetson, Grover Cleveland's one-time law partner. A bishop, or James Stillman of the National City Bank, or some influential Washington friend of Chauncey Depew's might round off the list. The "intellectual" and artistic world would be represented only by a fellow trustee of the Metropolitan Museum or possibly a visiting connoisseur from Europe. Fanny, still a handsome and tastefully elegant woman in her fifties, always acted the polished hostess, without the overpowering airs of the snobbish Astor or Vanderbilt matrons. She gave no hint of anything but a serene marriage but could not have been unaware of her husband's visits to clubs and his attendance at the raffish supper-parties at Delmonico's. His infidelities, however discreetly managed, were by now common knowledge.

After dinner the men invariably took their cigars and brandy in the Black Library where Pierpont liked to exhibit his latest finds. The harvest of first editions, original letters, and royal autographs now included manuscripts of his favorite author, Charles Dickens, with several of the original Phiz illustrations for *Pickwick Papers,* as well as Dumas, Keats, Byron, Charlotte Brontë, and James Fenimore Cooper. He had already started collecting rare early Bibles but took special pride in a handsomely bound copy of the Revised Prayer Book he had had privately printed in a limited 250-copy edition after attending the Triennial Convention of the Episcopal Church.

Unlike Carnegie, John D. Rockefeller, and the Vanderbilts, whose gifts to churches, libraries, and universities attracted welcome press coverage, he insisted on the strictest privacy for his own philanthropies. He responded generously to most appeals, if satisfied of their authenticity, but his manner could be churlish. He once offended Mayor William R. Grau of New York, whose banking house did a profitable business with Drexel, Morgan in refunding Latin American securities. He had called one morning at 23 Wall Street to request a contribution for some municipal charity and went on rather too long. Pierpont became impatient but remained apathetic. Grau picked up his hat in exasperation and turned for the door.

"Where are you going?" Morgan growled.

"I'm leaving. Pardon me for worrying you with this little matter."

"Wait a minute." He then wrote a check for $5,000 and said almost affably, "Come in again when you're going by and tell me how you are getting on."

His dislike of publicity was acutely jarred by sniggering gossip when he sponsored Dr. Markoe's plans for a new Lying-in Hospital. The handsome athlete and yachtsman was a regular guest on the *Corsair* and at Cragston weekend house parties, but neither his millionaire friends nor a Park Avenue practice had blunted a sensitive social conscience. He was genuinely shocked by the plight of New York's tenement population who had to suffer malnutrition, poor gynecology, and inadequate postnatal care. He soon persuaded wealthier patients that his ramshackle Lower East Side dispensary was scandalously ill-equipped.

Pierpont had readily agreed to serve on his new Hospital Committee, and his liberal checks, sometimes for as much as a million dollars, could not be kept out of the newspapers. This generosity, coupled with his reputation for womanizing, inspired the calumny that one of his mistresses had persuaded him to endow the hospital after Markoe had delivered their baby. He was indignant but far too preoccupied with large-scale railroad finance to dignify such gossip with rebuttal.

In the summer of 1892, when the Harrison administration was clearly heading for defeat by the Democrats, railroad shares were among the chief casualties in a depressed stock market. Morgan was called in by the board and creditors of Union Pacific, now almost bankrupt through years of mismanagement and corrupt practices. Its stock had slumped to the point that operators like E. H. Harriman picked up blocks of shares, once valued at $150, for as little as four cents. Morgan headed a committee of five in a rescue bid to keep the line running by issuing over $5 million in gold collateral trust notes against the company's securities, valued at $100 million at par.

Soon after Cleveland took office the following March, Drexel, Morgan started to plan the reorganization of Northern Pacific, then in receivership, but found this less easy than a similar operation on behalf of the bankrupt Erie Line. This time Morgan was vigorously opposed by a group hastily formed by August Belmont, the U.S. Trust Co., and E. H. Harriman, who had the backing of Kuhn, Loeb's wily Jacob Schiff. It collapsed after Pierpont won a vote of confidence at the Erie stockholders' meeting, although Harriman used his second mortgage bonds to fight on alone for months until the Supreme Court ruled against him.

Railroads were among the many casualties of the recession that gripped the country from May 1893. President Cleveland had inherited an economy crippled by the free coinage of silver and a parallel drain on gold by nervous foreign investors. By the end of the year almost 600 banks had failed, and most Wall Street stocks had halved in value. Food prices continued to rise while wages slumped, and unemployment was soaring to the million mark.

Cleveland's troubles were not helped by a growing pressure group within his own party. The Populists were led by William Jennings Bryan, a handsome, politically ambitious attorney and outstanding orator, who had identified himself from the late eighties with the depressed Midwest rural areas. In the Senate he preached tirelessly for the Populist manifesto, which demanded shorter hours and better pay for all workers, with the right to form unions and, above all, the virtues of cheap money (anathema to all good Republicans). He scoffed at Cleveland's hasty imposition of a 2 percent tax on incomes over $4,000 a year and won still more supporters when the face-saving measure was ruled unconstitutional by a Supreme Court majority.

Every attempt at union strike action was denounced as "treasonable" by J. P. Morgan and other Wall Street bankers, who still suspected and mistrusted industrialists like Carnegie but identified with the policy of free enterprise so ruthlessly executed by Henry Clay Frick, his chief associate. Frick was a fearsome boss, black-bearded, short of build, words, and temper. Through hard work and early help from his heiress wife and the Pittsburgh Mellons, he had invested in coal-bearing land and went on to build coke ovens on a huge scale. By 1879 he was already worth a million dollars and supplied coke to Carnegie, who appointed him general manager of his steel company with a substantial stockholding. Those who dared to oppose his twelve-hour, six-day week were replaced by more docile immigrants.

His aggression was partly balanced by Charles M. Schwab, who rose from a dollar-a-day ostler to become Carnegie's personal aide. Subtler than he appeared and dedicated to protecting his employer's interests when they coincided with his own, he lacked Frick's brutality and technical know-how, but his bland jovial personality charmed all except the most radical among the company's 30,000 workers. The dimpled smile never cracked even under extreme heat. He liked to recall, "At 17 I had never worn a suit of clothes that was not made by my mother. Yet in seven years I was president of the Edgar Thomson Steel Works and a few years later had built the Homestead plant. . . . And for 22 years I never spoke a harsh word to anybody in the entire organization of the Carnegie works."

In the summer of 1892 when the plants seethed with discontent, Carnegie took refuge in Skibo Castle, set in a 40,000-acre estate in the Scottish Highlands. Early in July, Frick ringed the Homestead plant with barbed wire and locked out 4,200 stubborn workers. He then imported a corps of armed Pinkerton toughs to repel strikers who had attempted to storm "Fort Frick." As the situation turned uglier, thousands of Pennsylvania's National Guard arrived. The threatened strike was only broken after several casualties, some fatal, on both sides. From Skibo, Carnegie sanctimoniously disclaimed personal responsibility for the military intervention. However, Homestead would continue to operate with cheap nonunion labor.

Later that month a Russo-Polish agitator, Alexander Berkman, burst into Frick's office in downtown Pittsburgh, shot him twice, and inflicted several knife wounds. Frick refused an anesthetic while a bullet was removed from his neck and assured reporters that the company would not change its policy," whether I die or not." Public opinion switched overnight from the strikers and "anarchists" to heroic Frick. Among the shoal of sympathetic messages was a cable from Standard Oil's John D. Rockefeller, who was just then avidly seizing control of huge iron deposits in the Messabi Range of Minnesota.

While Frick made a slow recovery, Carnegie moved young Schwab from the Braddock plant across the river to take charge of Homestead. He duly soft-soaped the workers into a sort of truce, but Carnegie was not forgiven for his hypocrisy. The St. Louis *Post-Dispatch* summed up the verdict of countless trade unionists and even a few capitalists, including J. P. Morgan, in editorializing, "Say what you will of Frick; he is a brave man. Say what you will of Carnegie; he is a coward. And gods and men hate cowards." Schwab stayed at the works from July 6 until Christmas, often sleeping on a blanket on the floor of his office.

The five-month dispute cost Carnegie Steel $2 million, one third of that year's net profits. Its costly triumph, however, temporarily relieved the pressure on other trusts and monopolies. Morgan, for one, could now proceed to his major mergers without troubling himself too much over what the railroad labor leaders might be thinking.

Lack of opposition reinforced his arrogance. When the New York and Northern, an independent 52-mile line, became insolvent and was put up for sale at the Yonkers Station, he arrived on December 28, 1893, with New York Central's counsel, Ashbel Green. Declining to wait in the crowded main room, he took over a small outer office and smoked a last cigar before entering with Green on the stroke of noon for the start of the auction. It was over barely a minute after he had curtly offered one million dollars on Central's behalf. Nobody dared to challenge the bid. He wrote a check for the $100,000 deposit and stalked off without so much as a nod.

His grouchiness was not confined to business affairs. Visiting the Chicago World's Fair in the summer of '93, he strode through the Palace of Fine Arts and brushed aside a noisy cohort of guides and overeager dealers. Asked his opinion of the pictures, he told a reporter, "The French exhibits must have been selected by chambermaids." He behaved with even more hauteur during one of his visits to Monte Carlo. While there he stayed at the Hotel de Paris which was in convenient proximity to the Casino and to parties given by Russian Grand Dukes and by the owner of the *New York Herald*, James Gordon Bennett, whose luxury yacht boasted a Turkish bath and an Alderney cow to provide fresh milk and cream.

Morgan also enjoyed the ambiance of Camille Blanc's private gaming salon, where Europe's most beautiful cocottes were always available to top off a successful session at the tables. But one night he angrily and permanently withdrew his patronage. Unlike some of the princelings who recklessly squandered fortunes on the turn of a roulette wheel, he was perfectly aware that the odds of thirty-five to one gave the house a mathematical advantage with thirty-six numbers and a zero. He usually emerged with a tidy profit by playing the martingale system of doubling up, but on this occasion he ran into a losing streak and could only recoup his losses by insisting on a no-limit maximum. When the *chef de parti* reminded him politely that the limit on a single number was 12,000 francs (then $2,400), he scooped up his remaining chips, tossed them contemptuously to the croupier as a gratuity, and went off in a fury to play double-pack solitaire in his hotel suite.

Most of his local friends took his side, especially Leopold II, King of the Belgians, who had settled into a villa at Cap Ferrat, to the great relief of the Monegasque authorities. For years he had been notorious for his orgies and for what was widely regarded as the kidnapping of young girls. He had scandalized his own subjects by taking up with a sluttish sixteen-year-old virago, ennobled as the Baroness Vaughan, by whom he had a series of illegitimate children. Although far more discreet in his own amours, Pierpont could never resist parties aboard the royal yacht *Alberta* in the company of courtesans even more inviting than the food and drink. The host himself, obscenely fat and sporting a nose of Morganesque proportions, made a less than appetizing spectacle when he stripped and flopped overboard with his long white beard tucked into a rubber envelope.

Social delights apart, Morgan was flattered to act as the King's adviser on investments that extended to railway concessions in China and the development of the million square-mile Congo Free State's rubber and ivory. Too proud and independent ever to act the courtier, he nevertheless reveled in socializing with the unsavory despot, whose policies he felt no compulsion to look into so long as they served his own financial interests. Morgan shared Edward VII's easygoing view that the Belgian was "an admirable king, very clever and extremely agreeable," and for several years he disregarded the atrocity stories that leaked out of the Congo.

Back home, Pierpont busied himself with the firm's reorganization made necessary by the sudden death of Anthony Drexel in Karlsbad. He automatically assumed absolute control. Allied to his accession as senior partner of the London house, this confirmed his status as both a prominent international banker and the architect of America's increasingly cohesive railroad system.

The economic situation had meantime become highly volatile since Grover Cleveland's return to the White House. His administration's uncertain handling of the troublesome silver-gold issue quickly forfeited the confidence of Wall Street and the foreign money markets. Congress at last stopped buying gold, but this angered Cleveland's supporters almost as much as Republicans with powerful vested interests in western mining. By then the Treasury's dwindling gold reserves caused foreign investors to start "bearing" most American securities, especially railroads. During the mounting crisis of 1894, the Treasury's issue of over $100 million in 5 percent gold bonds failed conspicuously to relieve the pressure. Speculators still hoarded their gold while Lazard Frères and other banking houses continued to ship bullion overseas.

On New Year's Day 1895, Drexel, Morgan had formally re-opened for business under the new title of J. P. Morgan & Co. One of Pierpont's first acts as chairman was to direct the London office to do all possible to restore confidence in American stocks, but few City houses would touch them without a solid gold back-up. By the morning of the 28th, the U.S. Treasury held a reserve of less than half the statutory minimum of $100 million required to maintain payments in gold. With daily withdrawals approaching $3 million, it would run out within three weeks. In near-panic, Cleveland asked Congress authority to issue more gold bonds to avert imminent bankruptcy and ensure "the perservation of our national honor and credit," but Wall Street looked unlikely to rush for certificates redeemable over fifty years at only 3 percent.

On the 30th, William E. Curtis, Assistant Secretary of the Treasury, arrived in New York to confer urgently with August Belmont, who warned him that the London Rothschilds were less than enthusiastic about the proposed government issue. They had suggested that J. P. Morgan & Co. should be co-opted in a *private* bankers' syndicate to sell half the bonds abroad. Pierpont at once agreed to join forces with Belmont, Speyer's, the National City Bank of New York, in which Standard Oil had a big footing, and the First National with whom Drexel, Morgan had long done a substantial business in underwriting and distributing corporate bonds.

On the afternoon of Sunday, February 3, 1895, he sat in his library playing solitaire and smoking nonstop while waiting for a telephone call from Washington. This would decide whether or not the president would agree to the terms he had outlined to Curtis. The syndicate proposed handling $62 million of bonds at 4 percent. Curtis had objected that 3½ percent was a generous yield, but Pierpont stressed that few British investors would be attracted to the issue for less than 3¾ percent guaranteed interest.

Curtis at last came on the line, obviously worried. Instead of at once confirming government approval, as the syndicate had anticipated, he informed Pierpont that a message was on the way by special courier. Next morning a letter arrived, signed by Treasury Secretary Carlisle, announcing that the administration had rejected the syndicate's terms and would rely instead on a direct public issue. Cleveland had plainly been swayed by his party's traditional suspicion of Wall Street plus the Populist antigold lobby, led by William Jennings Bryan, the fiery demagogue from Nebraska who scourged all bankers as worshippers of the Golden Calf and still believed that only the free coinage of silver could save the nation. A vigorous press campaign, promoted by Joseph Pulitzer, also predicted that the public would respond to a 3 percent issue.

Pierpont was astounded and dismayed by Cleveland's decision, which, in his view, could only end in a national disaster if the low-interest bonds failed to subscribe. He hurriedly telephoned Belmont, who agreed that a final attempt should be made to dissuade the Treasury from scrapping the syndicate's plan. He then called Carlisle, who reluctantly consented to delay announcing a public loan for a day or so.

Next morning Belmont left for Washington by the ten o'clock train. Pierpont followed that afternoon on the Congressional Limited, accompanied by his counsel, Francis Lynde Stetson (an old friend of Cleveland's), and young Robert Bacon, who had recently joined the firm as a junior partner. He symbolized Morgan's cult of the athletic Adonis that would become almost obsessive in later years.

It has always challenged students of his personality. His obvious preference for executives with handsome profiles and sporting distinction was never linked to any hint of homosexuality, even by the most scabrous gossips. Wall Street simply echoed the verdict of one waggish broker who quipped, "When the angels of God took unto themselves wives among the daughters of men,

172

the result was the Morgan partners." In the light of modern psychology one may infer that his own ugliness attracted him to exceptionally goodlooking subordinates whose dependence helped to soothe a bruised ego. His staff policy also had a strong element of snobbery. Bacon and others all discovered that, in joining Wall Street's most prominent investment bankers, they had become members of an exclusive ultraconservative club that few could penetrate without family pedigree, a college education (preferably Harvard), and a quality of dress and bearing up to the standards of the British Diplomatic Service. Racial background was also significant. Morgan did not object to, and was almost certainly influenced by, attitudes of his time that affirmed "Aryan" racial superiority. The American banking tradition of that era automatically barred Jews, however talented, from any hope of a partnership or indeed an appointment at senior executive level, at 23 Wall, at the London office, or at Morgan, Harjes of Paris.

But for the lack of a millimeter or so of foreskin, Bernard Baruch might have sat at one of the mahogany rolltop desks. The son of a respected physician from South Carolina, he stood six-foot three and was a noted boxer and all-round sportsman. After graduating from City College, he had joined a New York broker and used to deliver securities and market reports personally to Morgan at The Corner. At various boys' clubs, of which the banker was a patron, Baruch took gym classes, thinking wistfully that he might catch the great man's eye and perhaps end up with a junior partnership. By the midnineties, years before Morgan's supreme triumph in U. S. Steel, this was already equated in Wall Street circles with receiving a cardinal's hat from the Pontiff.

Baruch developed into an outstanding bond salesman, specializing in mines and raw materials. By the time he was barely thirty-two, his bold speculative coups had netted him a fortune of $3 million. His further operations in association with Kuhn, Loeb, the Guggenheims, and other coreligionists brought still more wealth and an independence he could never have achieved with "Jupiter" Morgan, as the banker was beginning to be called. It is fair to note, however, that irrespective of his German-Jewish ancestry, Baruch's plunging on bearish markets, his drinking, and his weakness for the race track would have invited instant dismissal had he ever worked for Morgan.

In every respect—background, character, ability—Bacon qualified as the golden epitome of Pierpont's ideal. He was the descendant of English settlers who had arrived in Massachusetts only three years after Miles Morgan. A Harvard alumnus, he had graduated with Theodore Roosevelt who reported to a friend, "Bob Bacon is the handsomest man in the Class and is as pleasant as he is handsome." They had often sparred together in the gymnasium. Bacon, endowed with an exceptional physique, excelled at boxing, football, baseball, athletics, and rowing. He was tall, crinkly haired and blond, with a sunny disposition charming men and women alike. After graduation he had made a round-the-world trip, including the Far East and England, becoming as Anglophile as any Morgan. He then entered a Boston banking firm with whom Morgan, Drexel had pleasant relations. Pierpont was impressed enough by his negotiating skill to offer him a desk in the fall of '94.

"Your job is to *think*," Morgan told him tersely as they shook hands on his arrival. During his first few months Bacon proved that he could both think and, given the chance, show initiative without ruffling older feathers. He also discovered that the rewards could be exceptionally generous in cash and prestige for those who worked conscientiously and were prepared to stake their health and possibly their marriages.

"Jupiter" was not given to praise. He preferred to acknowledge outstanding service with the gift of a prize collie from the Cragston Kennels or occasionally a casket of his favorite cigars, a munificence mainly restricted to fellow connoisseurs of the Corsair Club.* As sole owner of the firm after Tony Drexel's death, he took 51 percent of all profits, assessed each New Year's Eve, with the balance split equally between the other partners, who also shared in those of the London and Paris houses. But none held stock or voting power, and all were liable to summary

---

*It was a rare gesture. He once came ashore from *Corsair*, asked a pierman for a match and impulsively handed him one of his choicest Santa Claras. To his horror the man crumbled the precious leaves into his pipe.

dismissal, without right of appeal, if they failed in their duties or personally offended him. With his approval they might invest in affiliated companies and draw directors' fees that would become substantial with the firm's phenomenal expansion during the next decade. (Coster was on the boards of fifty-nine corporations when he died at the turn of the century!)

Partners were expected to pool their experience and take joint responsibility for decisions. Seldom indeed would a specialized branch of the business be assigned exclusively to any one individual, however senior. The closest confidentiality was mandatory for all employees of a firm that stubbornly rejected any inspection of its books by government officials. No statements were ever issued to depositors or clients, who would be vetted almost as thoroughly as the staff for their background and suitability.

It was a wholly autocratic structure. As Bacon later told his biographer, James Brown Scott, "There was one head to the company. [Morgan's] Partners were lieutenants, not commanders. They were associated with him in such matters as he chose to have them handle with him personally, or to carry out under his direction."

When they set out together for Washington on February 4, 1895, to try and talk some horse sense into President Cleveland, Bacon already knew that his junior partnership was no sinecure, but he had no inkling that this delicate mission would establish him as Morgan's personal assistant, still less that he was to become almost a second son. In retrospect it seems inevitable that the grouchy, reserved, and often isolated banker should have warmed to an aide whose loyalty was matched by unstinting self-sacrifice. It may be claimed without exaggeration that Robert Bacon at last filled something of the aching loneliness that had built up in Morgan in the long years since Mimi's death. It would not diminish his deep affection for his heir, but he tended to regard him more like a younger brother. This was not altogether surprising; Jack had been away at school for much of his youth, and his graduation from Harvard had been followed almost at once by his early marriage and long duty spell in the London office.

Bacon not only became Morgan's chief confidant and traveling companion but took over as personal deputy during his frequent overseas trips. It says much for his charm, modesty, and tact that neither Jack Morgan nor any of the senior partners appeared to resent this very privileged status.

CHAPTER TEN

They arrived in chilly windswept Washington to hear from Daniel Lamont, the secretary of war, that Cleveland would not receive them. "I have come down to see the president," snapped Morgan, "and I am going to stay here until I see him." Stetson was not successful in changing Cleveland's decision, and Belmont telephoned to say that he had tried in vain to budge Carlisle. Pierpont glowered and decided with an effort to send Bob Bacon over to attempt to charm Richard Olney, the attorney general. The result was a vague half-promise to set up a conference next day in the White House.

After Bacon had left the Arlington Hotel at midnight, Morgan stayed up for several hours playing solitaire while he pondered the next step. Cleveland could persuade Congress to authorize a gold issue, with the sale of bonds limited to public subscription, but this would take time and might be too late to replenish the government's dangerously low stock of bullion. Morgan was absolutely certain that only speedy action by his syndicate to replenish the Treasury's fast-diminishing stocks of bullion, at a fair and agreed price, could avoid irreparable damage to American credit. He appreciated, however, that even if he could convince Cleveland to change his decision, a hostile and suspicious Congress was likely to stall or block it.

What was needed was some short cut that could save the

presidential face and justify antagonizing his own party supporters. Pierpont suddenly recalled that, thirty years earlier, Lincoln
had secured Congressional approval to buy bullion from New
York bankers in exchange for government bonds.

Next morning he alerted Bacon, who checked and confirmed
that Treasury Secretary Chase had duly bought coin "at such
rates and upon such terms ... as were deemed most advantageous
to the public interest." If the act had not been repealed, it was a
precedent that Cleveland might use, subject to his having the
nerve to risk unpopularity by aligning himself with the syndicate.

Pierpont and Bob Bacon ate a gloomy breakfast, discouraged by
calls from 23 Wall Street that the Subtreasury was running out of
gold and the London market expected prompt action by Washington. Before they had finished their coffee, Olney called to say that
the president would receive Morgan and Belmont in his office.

They drove over to the White House through a snowy blizzard.
Cleveland, flanked by Carlisle and the attorney general, sat
upright behind his desk and wasted no time on polite preliminaries. He curtly repeated that a public issue of gold bonds had
now been decided. The atmosphere was far different from the old
days of his first administration when he and Morgan had chatted
amiably over a jigger of rye and had exchanged cigars. This time
Cleveland was not smoking and did not invite his visitors to light
up. He listened carefully to their case for the syndicate, but was
often interrupted by the ringing of the telephone and was obliged
to make several exits to see members of his staff on other Cabinet
business.

The meeting dragged on with Morgan, still not daring to smoke
without permission, chomping on his unlit Havana. He managed
to control his irritation and stressed that his own firm, with
Belmont and the others, had acted in the country's best interests
by provisionally arranging to secure $50 million in gold from
Europe. He vehemently refuted newspaper reports that any
member of the proposed syndicate had shipped gold abroad to
drain the Treasury's reserve. He also reminded Cleveland that,
according to private information received that very morning from
his New York office, the Subtreasury was facing heavy withdrawals including an imminent $10 million draft for repayment
in gold. Cleveland looked almost offensively sceptical until

178

Carlisle read from a yellow slip just handed in by a clerk. It disclosed that only $9 million in gold coin now remained in the vaults.

Pierpont bent forward and commented, "Well, if that $10 million draft is presented and you can't meet it, it will all be over before three o'clock." Cleveland exchanged a startled glance with Carlisle who nodded glumly. "Have you anything to suggest, Mr. Morgan?" the president then asked in a low voice. This was the banker's cue to quote the precedent of the 1862 act, which Olney at once confirmed had not been repealed. Himself a lawyer of long experience, Cleveland needed only to glance at Section 3700 of the Revised Statutes to establish that it offered a lever for setting the syndicate's rescue bid into almost immediate operation. But he remained suspicious.

"If we adopt the plan, what guarantee have we that the gold will not be reshipped abroad for a profit after it comes in?" he demanded. "Can you guarantee that this will not happen?"

Pierpont answered crisply, "Mr. President, I will so guarantee during the life of the syndicate." Cleveland looked impressed by this blunt assurance, which implied considerable risk for the Morgan firm if any of the others broke the undertaking. He hesitated for a second or two and then agreed to dictate a special message to Congress. As Morgan stood up, the remains of his crumbling unsmoked cigar dropped from his lapels and trousers to make a dusty pile on the carpet. The president smiled as if in half-apology, fished out a large box of Havanas from his desk drawer, and invited him to stay behind for a few minutes before joining the others for luncheon.

Morgan returned to New York to organize the syndicate. It would grow to sixty-one in number, with each member pledged not to send any gold out of the country until the agreement was formally signed and the Treasury's reserve replenished to safety level. But Congress reacted violently, and many accused Cleveland of being a tool of a Wall Street gang who were exploiting national misfortune to drive a harsh bargain. Bryan, still fanatically defending silver, denounced "a scandalous surrender of credit" on which the bankers could gorge, and some newspapers even hinted darkly that presidential goodwill had been rewarded by a fat slice of the spoils.

The outflow of gold ceased dramatically even before signature of the agreement by which the Treasury would receive $65 million in gold over the next six months (half of it from Europe). The syndicate was authorized to issue 4 percent bonds for over $62 million on a thirty-year basis. Allowing for the government's cut, this still offered investors an attractive 3¾ percent, precisely what Pierpont had originally proposed. He and Belmont jointly signed the documents on behalf of the syndicate, Belmont commemorating the occasion by the gift of a handsome bronze collar for one of the prize collies in the Cragston Kennels. It was inscribed, "EMERGENCY. Presented by August Belmont to J. P. Morgan as a souvenir of February 1895." Pierpont appreciated the gesture but, when Bob Bacon pointed out how the collar glinted in the sun, he couldn't help commenting ungraciously, "You will notice it isn't gold!"

On February 20, the new bonds went on sale in Wall Street and the City of London at 112. Heavily oversubscribed, they soon touched 120 and even higher, thanks to the coincidental rise in South African gold mining stocks. By the time Pierpont arrived in England, accompanied by Louisa, the London Stock Exchange was luxuriating in "the Kaffir Boom" promoted by Barney Barnato, who had sensationally hit pay dirt in the Rand after losing out to Rhodes in the De Beers amalgamation. The city now fêted the flashy Jewish financier, but Pierpont pointedly avoided all the dinners in Barnato's honor, including one given by the Lord Mayor. He hurried off instead to the Continent to buy pictures and bric-à-brac.

In May he came back to London to work out a merger between the Great Northern Railroad, which James J. Hill had aggressively transformed into a profit-making system, and the very shaky Northern Pacific. For the past two years Pierpont and Charles Coster had been quietly planning to eliminate competition between these two main lines in the Northwest. Like Hill, they saw the danger from Harriman, who was threatening to move into the rich territories west of the Mississippi. With heavy cash backing from the Rockefellers, and Kuhn, Loeb's expertise, he would be a formidable opponent unless quickly stopped. After some hesitation, Pierpont had suggested that Hill might care to come to England and discuss a possible coalition.

Hill was flattered and was much impressed by the plan for a huge stock issue to be promoted by J. P. Morgan & Co., the Deutsche Bank of Berlin, and August Belmont representing the Rothschild interests. Pierpont, quite out of character, displayed a cordiality only explicable by his anxiety to cement the merger. Unkempt, ill dressed and rough in manner, Hill was a chunky, piratical character with one eye and black hair worn shoulder length like Buffalo Bill Cody. From Canada he had originally drifted to Minnesota and into steamboats, finally advancing, like old Commodore Vanderbilt, into railroads (and by very similar methods). From 1890 onward he was unquestionably the most powerful magnate in the Northwest, but it was still difficult to imagine a more unlikely dinner guest in Prince's Gate, seated at the right hand of the patrician banker who had saved America's international credit.

Between them, together with the Deutsche Bank's representative, they soon hammered out the structure of a new company to be floated with issues of $200 million in bonds and $100 million of stock. Hill and his associates would benefit by half of Northern Pacific's new capital stock, but although Hill's Great Northern would retain considerable influence in the conglomerate and operate the combined railroads, financial power would be vested in the voting trust set up by Morgan, Belmont, and the German bank.

The move was opposed by a group of Northern Pacific stockholders who won a Supreme Court decision declaring the merger unconstitutional. Pierpont promptly restructured the new company to overcome any further legal objections. Once Hill's vigorous management had again made Northern Pacific profitable, its stock soared and no more was heard from the dissidents. J. P. Morgan was delighted to secure a strong footing in another 11,000 miles of railroad track.

When he arrived back in June, to be welcomed by Fanny and his family on the *Corsair,* the Treasury's gold reserve had topped a comfortable $107 million but Bryan and others continued to attack him for making "millions" from his rescue operation. The fact was, however, that the Morgan firms in New York, London, and Paris together collected less than half a million in profits and management commissions by the time the syndicate's books closed that autumn. Grover Cleveland, at least, nursed no regrets for his last-minute change of heart. Long afterward, looking back on that dramatic meeting in his office, he paid generous tribute to the financier: "I found I was in negotiation with a man of large business comprehension and of remarkable knowledge and presence. . . . He was not looking for a personal bargain, but sat there, a great patriot, concerting with me and my advisers to avert peril, determined to do his best in a severe and trying crisis."

That summer Pierpont, exhausted by the gold operation and his work on the alliance with James J. Hill, found it difficult to relax at the usual Cragston houseparties. He preferred to cruise back and forth to Newport with Depew, William Rockefeller, Bob Bacon, Dr. Markoe, and a decorative lady friend or two. On one of these cruises, he could not resist the chance of another talk with President Cleveland, who was then resting at Buzzards Bay aboard a friend's yacht, the *Oneida*. With persistent hints from Wall Street that other speculators might follow the recent example of a coffee importer who had shipped gold to Brazil, he thought it timely to confirm the administration's continued support of gold.

The *Oneida* lay at anchor in a cove off Gardiner's Island when Pierpont went over by launch from his yacht. After a pleasant dinner he explained that, as the syndicate's resources were coming to an end, another bond issue would be desirable to avoid the scale of withdrawals responsible for the earlier crisis. The president listened politely but doubted whether Congress would give statutory approval to maintain the gold standard in perpetuity, as Wall Street and the foreign bankers seemed to be expecting.

Pierpont returned to *Corsair II,* still hopeful that the Democrats might yet resist the pressure from Bryan's noisy "Free Silver" bloc, but distinctly uneasy over Cleveland's ability to hold Congress together much longer. Through all the bonhomie and clouds of cigar smoke, he had clearly caught signals of demoralization. Cleveland would not easily win back trade union sympathy after sending in federal troops to crush the Pullman strike in Chicago and jailing the strikers' leader, Eugene V. Debs, without a jury trial. And he was still smarting over his failure to break Havemeyer's American Sugar Refining Company, a monopoly as blatant as Standard Oil or Carnegie Steel. The Supreme Court had overruled the Department of Justice's action as unconstitutional.

They next met in Washington on December 23 at the special invitation of the president, who wished to discuss the currency situation, which had become grave as a result of deteriorating diplomatic relations with Great Britain over the government's policy toward Venezuela. Bullion was being heavily withdrawn under pressure from the City of London, and the two countries seemed to be drifting perilously close to war. That was unthinkable, but meanwhile, another large bond issue would be necessary to protect the Gold Standard and restore market stability. Cleveland thought it prudent to consult Pierpont Morgan on his views before Congress reassembled in the New Year.

This crisis had first erupted when, following a long-simmering boundary dispute between Venezuela and British Guiana, the Venezuelans invaded British territory and fired on a gunboat. This stimulated Cleveland to invoke the Monroe Doctrine and warn that the United States would consider it "a willful aggression" if Great Britain retaliated by seizing any lands "which we have determined as of right to belong to Venezuela." This rather bumptious expression of national sentiment was applauded in America and bitterly resented by British jingoists, who called on the Salisbury government to teach Washington a sharp lesson, by force of arms if necessary. The City of London reacted at once against Wall Street. As head of a banking house traditionally dedicated to Anglo-American accord, Pierpont now bluntly reminded Cleveland that his saber rattling could inflict lasting damage on the national economy even if war were averted.

The president bristled at this rough criticism but declined to comment. He turned back to the Gold Standard question on which Congress remained deadlocked. He had to admit that Bryan's bimetallist lobby was gaining too much ground and agreed that it might soon be necessary to rebuild the Treasury's gold reserve, which was below $60 million. But when it came to the proposal to form another syndicate, broadly based on the previous one, Cleveland hedged. Pierpont left the White House profoundly gloomy over the Venezuelan affair and the imminent prospect of another currency crisis.

In the boardroom at 23 Wall, he conferred with National City's

James A. Stillman, a handsome Texan with whom he had established a rapport. They shared similar social backgrounds and a taste for good pictures, as well as an affection for William Rockefeller, two of whose sons would marry Stillman daughters. With John D. Rockefeller's recent retirement to live on milk and graham crackers, William was virtually running the empire and turning more and more to Stillman, whose bank would soon become identified as almost a Standard Oil property.

Assured of Stillman's support and that of other interested parties, Pierpont wrote to Cleveland formally proposing a new syndicate to raise $200 million in gold from Europe, mainly from Paris (through the Morgan, Harjes office) and the Deutsche Bank in Berlin. This time, however, in view of continuing Anglo-American tension, he diplomatically excluded August Belmont, the Rothschilds' go-between. He was so confident of success that, when a Wall Street acquaintance buttonholed him for inside information about the rumored new issue, he said gruffly, "If you want to make some money and have got the gold, subscribe. If not, au revoir."

Morgan had gravely overestimated Cleveland's capacity to withstand the sound and fury that exploded as soon as the news leaked that the wicked bankers once again had the Treasury by the throat. Pulitzer's *World* pushed to the attack, supported by William Jennings Bryan, who told Congress that Morgan and his confederates had already gulped "millions of dollars" and were now avid for a second helping. Although the war threat had subsided with an agreement to submit the Venezuelan boundary dispute to arbitration, the violent anti-British sentiment persisted. It found a welcome echo in Congress's implacable suspicion of J. P. Morgan's links with the City of London. In this hostile context the Treasury hurriedly decided to offer the public its own new $100 million gold issue.

Pierpont had always prided himself on being a good American. During the gloomiest days of his tussle with Cleveland he had predicted, "The man who is a bear on the future of the United States will always go broke." (Years later he invited Jules S. Bache, then a rising young banker, to dine with him at the Windsor in Paris and said, "Boy, here's a piece of advice. Never sell a first-class American stock. Buy them and keep them.")

He was convinced that the president was making a grave error but saw no alternative to dissolving the private syndicate after it had bid for a share in the new issue. Morgan and his friends were allotted $38 million worth of bonds at 110.6, which showed them a satisfactory profit but failed to soothe Pierpont's bruised pride.

He turned to his next project, the reorganization of Union Pacific's still unwieldy, loss-producing structure. It proved far less simple than his major surgery on the Erie Railroad or the smooth grafting of Northern Pacific onto James Hill's complex. His plans for refunding Union Pacific's huge debts were blocked by a strong antitrust congressional lobby.

Impatient of what he called "political wire-pulling," he surprised Wall Street—and his own partners—by accepting an offer from Jacob Schiff to take the Union Pacific reorganization off his hands. No doubt Morgan saw the prospect of certain disaster for the thrusting German-Jewish firm, then second only to The Corner in its turnover of bonds and securities, and could not imagine they might succeed where he had failed. Whatever his motives for so uncharacteristically abdicating, it was a tactical blunder that strengthened Kuhn, Loeb and catapulted Edward Harriman into the very forefront of railroad imperialism.

Kuhn, Loeb was soon being denounced by Congress and press alike for adopting the hated technique of Morganization. Its move into Union Pacific was further thwarted by heavy buying from mysterious nominees, with shareholders suddenly demanding exorbitant prices for their holdings. Schiff at once suspected the long hand of 23 Wall Street, but Pierpont had justly denied all complicity and intimated that Harriman, already holding much cheaply bought stock, might be the culprit. "That fellow's an undesirable citizen," he warned Schiff, who acted on the hint.

Harriman cheerfully admitted to him that he had indeed been buying secretly into Union Pacific with the aim of soon linking it to Illinois Central. He boasted, a touch optimistically, of having all the necessary seed capital, but astonished Schiff even more with his grasp of railroad construction and costing, an asset denied to financiers like Morgan and Schiff himself. It became plain that he had traveled far and wide to determine Union Pacific's viability, and Schiff began to understand the reaction of the stunned branch superintendent who told a colleague, "The little feller saw every poor tie, blistered rail, and loose bolt on my division."

Schiff now appreciated that Harriman's plan to carry through a $25 million program to modernize and reequip the line, once he had a majority holding, was no empty boast. He passed his findings on to Otto Kahn and the other partners in Nassau Street. Harriman also won tentative promises of support from such hard-nosed bankers as George Jay Gould and even James Stillman, whose personal friendship with Pierpont did not blind him to a rich investment outlet for some of National City's enormous Rockefeller deposits.

Harriman's ace in the hole was influential Jacob Schiff, whose decision to support him may not have been entirely motivated by business rivalry with the Morgan firm. The wealth and prestige he had won himself in Wall Street had not healed childhood memories of anti-Semitism in Germany nor made him any less sensitive to snobbish American prejudice. Back in 1893 he had already entered his son for Groton and suggested that Mortimer, brought up as an orthodox Jew, should be excused chapel. The headmaster, backed by the Board of Trustees that included a number of Pierpont's friendly Episcopalian bishops, rejected his plea. Schiff swallowed his wrath and sent the boy to Amherst. He was a good hater, all the more dangerous for sometimes concealing his enmity behind the smooth facade of deference that Jupiter naturally accepted as his due.

Morgan sailed for Liverpool in March 1896 with his daughter Louisa, satisfied with his business affairs and indifferent to the effects of having so short-sightedly relinquished Union Pacific. Within the next four years Harriman would improve its rolling stock, modernize from top to bottom, and start making profits from it, before absorbing Southern Pacific as well. He would then control another 15,000 miles of invaluable track.

Pierpont stayed at Prince's Gate with Jack, Jessie, and their children and soon plunged into the delights of the London season with Alfred de Rothschild and other congenial friends. He found time to acquire a two-volume Mazarin Bible and a Gutenberg, several Church of England Rituals, a Folio Shakespeare in four volumes, and some handwritten Mozart scores, which meant nothing to his unmusical soul but were too rare to resist. He had also visited Worth's in Paris to make his usual personal selection for Fanny and his daughters.

Arriving back in mid-June, he was far less concerned with reports of the Harriman-Schiff coalition, which he still thought insignificant, than the imperative need to replace Grover Cleveland with a Republican administration dedicated to the gold standard. The first priority was to crush the Democratic presidential nominee, William Jennings Bryan, who would soon barnstorm the country with his passionate plea, "You shall not press down upon the brow of labor this crown of thorns. You shall not crucify mankind upon a cross of gold."

Like several other diehard Republicans, Pierpont thought Levi P. Morton (who, in spite of his name, possessed no Jewish blood) an ideal candidate for the White House, but "Dollar Mark" Hanna, the Ohio Senator and party chairman, considered his Wall Street background disqualified him. Since Hanna was himself a millionaire with considerable interests in iron and steamship companies, Pierpont treated his views with more respect than he normally accorded to professional politicians. He invited him aboard the *Corsair* for talks and subsequently to Sunday dinner at 219 Madison Avenue, where Hanna argued persuasively in favor of William McKinley, a former governor of Ohio, who had little personal magnetism but could claim long congressional service. He would make a safe candidate, pledged to support gold, and certain to attract hundreds of thousands of campaign dollars from the beef and sugar trusts, Standard Oil, and Carnegie Steel. Though only half-convinced, Morgan had to agree that the party must now stop behaving "like a lot of scared hens" and go all out for victory at the polls.

That June, after McKinley had been duly nominated in St. Louis, Pierpont was sharply reminded of Congress's hostility when a senatorial finance committee summoned him to defend his part in the alleged "conspiracy" with Cleveland over the first gold bond syndicate. Speaking without a single note or the benefit of counsel, he ignored questions about his firm's profits but confirmed with a shrug that no member of the administration

187

had personally benefited. He also repeated huffily that his sole reason for seeking foreign gold was to save the country from certain disaster.

Senator West made a last despairing attempt to shake him. "If you were actuated by the desire to prevent a panic," he asked with heavy sarcasm, "why were you not willing that other people should do it, if they wanted to?"

"They could not do it," he chillingly retorted.

On the eve of the presidential election, 80,000 McKinley supporters marched through New York City, joined by scores of employees from Wall Street offices. They raised a special cheer when J. P. Morgan, an unmistakable figure in his long black topcoat with the lamb's wool collar, arrived by cab at The Corner. He acknowledged their greeting by slightly lifting his high-brimmed hat, a unique cross between a derby and a topper, already almost as distinctive as the bulbous, crimson nose.

Bryan steadily lost ground, in spite of eloquent stump oratory and his well-publicized daily prayers on the campaign train. McKinley triumphed, and Hanna sent him an ecstatic wire, "God's in his Heaven—all's right with the world." It seemed that the Almighty had indeed blessed the trusts and all who sailed in them, notably Standard Oil, whose revenues would multiply phenomenally when automobiles started burning the Rockefellers' gasoline. A host of other promoters and financiers also felt handsomely compensated for their generosity to Hanna's war chest. George Jay Gould could now sleep more easily in the bed that had cost him $25,000. Schiff's partner, Otto Kahn, would lavish $2 million on transforming the Metropolitan into a truly international home of grand opera, and have enough to spare for his new estate on Long Island, where he gained a sea view by having tons of stone and sand hauled up to create an artificial hill.

In January '97 Pierpont had given thanks for both McKinley's election and his own firm's bumper harvest by donating a further million dollars toward Dr. Markoe's Lying-in Hospital on Second Avenue. This time his munificent gift escaped muckraking innuendoes from newspapers preoccupied with the political scene. His departure later that month for a short camping vacation in the Adirondacks did not rate even a paragraph in the social columns. Enchanted by the beauty and privacy of the forests, he took a mortgage on the 1,000-acre estate, including the whole of Lake Mohican, from his host, W. West Durant, whose finances chanced to be a little shaky. After a visit by Fanny, who shared his enthusiasm, he bought the property at a knockdown price as a second holiday retreat and renamed it Cape Uncas. He then purchased a few sites to protect his house on Madison Avenue from unwelcome development. It would also bring his family closer. Before long he arranged to build a house on Thirty-sixth Street for his married daughter, Juliet Pearson Hamilton, and earmarked another plot at the corner of Madison Avenue and Thirty-seventh. This would suit Jack when he returned from London to take up his duties at 23 Wall Street as successor-designate.

More immediately he had to find room for his expanding collection of manuscripts and first editions. They had overflowed from his library into the basement and now filled the small warehouse he had rented on East Forty-second Street. Having recently taken extra space for a stable, he planned a new fireproof library, next door to his mansion, but with a separate entrance on Thirty-sixth Street.

Only a supreme egoist with an exceptional capacity for self-deception could have assured Chauncey Depew, after showing him over Cape Uncas, "All I really need is a place to live in and a lot in the cemetery!" It did not surprise his friends when, in addition to the brownstone on Madison Avenue, his huge black yacht, the estate of Cragston, the London mansion, and elegant Dover House in Roehampton, he quietly bought himself a fishing box at Newport and an apartment at the fashionable Jekyll Island Club in Georgia, which had emerged as a millionaire's refuge from New York winters.

At the end of March 1897 he sailed once again to England with Louisa. He was tempted to stay over for the Queen's Diamond Jubilee, with London *en fête* for the triumphal procession to St. Paul's, but, as its newly elected commodore, felt impelled to return early in June to supervise the races of the New York Yacht Club. He had given several gold and silver cups for race winners and also provisionally agreed to present the site for a new clubhouse.

Soon after Christmas he once more sailed across the Atlantic on the White Star liner *Majestic* to spend the New Year with Jack and his family. This visit, planned to last into late spring, had to be cut short because an explosion sank the U.S. cruiser *Maine* in Havana Harbor on February 15, 1898. Few Americans disagreed with Assistant Secretary of the Navy Theodore Roosevelt, who denounced "an act of treachery on the part of the Spaniards." The government's reluctance to declare war also prompted his famous comment, "McKinley has no more backbone than a chocolate éclair."

Pierpont was one of many Republicans startled by Roosevelt's term as New York's police commissioner. It was one thing to clean up the force and blast Tammany Hall's corruption, but his campaign for slum clearance came uncomfortably close to the Democratic platform. Even his enemies in both parties had to admit, however, that the navy was in splendid shape when he dramatically resigned, had himself fitted with a Brooks Brothers uniform, and organized a volunteer cavalry unit, the Rough Riders, which would storm San Juan Hill under withering fire and make him a national hero. To Hanna he would always be "a damned cowboy," and Anglophile J. P. Morgan would never forgive or forget his hotheaded reaction to the Venezuelan crisis: "If I were asked what the greatest boon I could confer upon this nation was, I should answer, an immediate war with Great Britain for the conquest of Canada. . . . I will do my very best to bring about the day . . ."

Pierpont's part in the short Spanish-American War was minor but painful. He had at once accepted the navy's very modest valuation of $225,000 for the *Corsair II*, which was recommissioned as a gunboat and had part of her mast blown off in Cuban waters. He speedily engaged Beavor Webb to build him another boat of similar design but a hundred feet longer, faster, and with twin screws. She would carry a crew of sixty-nine. He demanded the same fittings and furnishings as before. When Webb pointed out that the factory had ceased making the carpets, he insisted that the patterns should be woven to the former specifications, at whatever the cost. To a Wall Street acquaintance who confided that he was thinking of buying himself a yacht and wondered what the running costs would be, Morgan replied disdainfully, "Anybody who even has to *think* about the cost had better not get one. Remember also that no man who is short of friends congenial to himself and ready to spend long days afloat, should ever consider owning a yacht, which can be the loneliest place in the world." He continued to restrict his own guests to a selected coterie and said, "You can do business with anyone, but you can only sail a boat with a gentleman."

By the time *Corsair III* was ready for her maiden trip, the war with Spain had ended. Cuba's "independence" was followed by American dominion over Puerto Rico and the Philippines. More significantly from Wall Street's angle, the new era of imperialism coincided with America's debut in global finance, but now as a lender instead of in her traditional borrowing role. The Morgan firm automatically organized the syndicate that took up nearly $250 million in bonds to finance Britain's war with the Boers. It also handled the American end of enormous issues for the governments of Sweden, Germany, and Russia. A million-dollar commission for financing Mexico's national debt, in association with the Deutsche Bank, was almost routine.

Thanks to the McKinley administration, which had cynically castrated the Sherman Antitrust Act and encouraged the Morgan strategy of forming conglomerates through stock ownership, The Corner continued to tighten its hold on the country's major railroads, directly or as fiscal agents, apart from dominating the policies of General Electric, International Harvester, and Western Union. It was also starting to expand its capital resources by investing in life insurance companies that, by the end of the century, had built up huge assets.

The Republican climate was wholly favorable. The New Jersey Holding Company Act offered a wide umbrella for promoters like John W. ("Bet-a-Million") Gates, a vulgar and flamboyant gambler, who had started as a hardware clerk in San Antonio after the Civil War at $25 a month and had first made real money peddling fence wire to the cattlemen. By the late nineties he was said to be a multimillionaire, had formed the American Steel and Wire Company of New Jersey, and had ambitious plans to organize a cartel for fixing prices.

The idea was sound enough and contained the seed of the future U.S. Steel Corporation, but he lacked the banking muscle or the prestige to withstand inevitable competition from Carnegie. Wall Street's hierarchy mocked a shirtsleeved maverick who sported three large diamonds in each of his suspender buckles and had earned his nickname by offering to lay up to a million dollars on a horse when the race track imposed an official $10,000 bet limit. However, he somehow won the confidence of Elbert H. Gary, who had astonishingly survived eight years as a Du Page County judge without a whisper of corruption and gone on to a flourishing corporation practice in Chicago. A devout Methodist, his high-minded horror of liquor and card playing did not preclude a discerning eye for women and the main chance. As counsel to Marshall Field's Illinois Steel, which supplied rods for Gates's wire plants, he had found it expedient to accept the flashy gambler as a client.

Toward the end of 1897, Gary advised Gates that his best chance of amalgamating the steel wire business might be to invite J. P. Morgan & Co. to promote and finance a holding company. Until then the firm's only interest in this area had been a couple of directorships, representing stockholders of Illinois Steel and the Minnesota Iron Company, although Pierpont had noted the growing overseas demand for American iron and steel. The industry was obviously heading for a boom but, like the earlier railroads, seemed bedeviled by quarrelsome small operators. Their only community of interest was a justified fear of being gobbled up by Carnegie, now by far the largest supplier of crude steel, who openly squeezed rebates from the Pennsylvania Railroad and other transport lines.

On paper, the independents, headed by Illinois Steel, Gates's barbwire plants and the tinplate steel hoop business of former attorney William H. Moore, had significant resources, but, even unified, they would still form only a modest bloc against the Carnegie monolith. Nevertheless, Pierpont had shown some interest in Gary's suggestion that he might intervene. He was impressed by the lawyer's solemn dignity and his grasp of the intricate steel industry, but he could not stomach Gates, who reminded him of the late Jim Fisk. The outbreak of war with Spain gave him an excuse to defer a decision. Gates soon lost patience and formed the American Steel and Wire Company of New Jersey, grossly overcapitalized at $90 million, with much of the stock siphoned into the hands of the promoter and his associates.

Illinois Steel, weary of being overcharged for Carnegie's ore, now planned to merge with the Minnesota Iron Company. Morgan made the necessary arrangements, which were completed, with the expert back-up of Judge Gary and Coster, in three months. The Federal Steel Company was floated with an optimistic capital value of $200 million, divided equally between common and preferred stock. Gary had been reluctant to give up his Chicago law practice but, strongly pressured by Pierpont, agreed to become president. He thought Gates's large holding in Illinois Steel qualified his client for a directorship in the new company, but on this point Pierpont stuck. "I don't think property is safe in his hands," he rasped. Gary had to yield. The board would include Bob Bacon, representing his firm, which had been paid a $200,000 commission for organizing Federal Steel, plus a substantial block of stock. H. H. Rogers of Standard Oil was also appointed on the recommendation of Pierpont Morgan, who wanted Rockefeller support if and when Carnegie retaliated.

Soon afterward Morgan sailed into New York harbor in his sparkling new yacht, pennants gaily fluttering, to take Fanny off the White Star liner on which she had returned from England. Impatient to show her *Corsair III,* he had set off impatiently by launch in a choppy sea as soon as the port's health officer left the liner at Quarantine Point.

Many of those aboard the *Oceanic* crowded to the rails and watched in amazement as the portly banker, with a white panama jammed on his head and a long black cigar between his teeth, climbed the sixty feet by swaying rope ladder. Bets were laid that he would fall or have to turn back as he mounted with sweat pouring down his cheeks. Some raised a cheer while he made his painful ascent. Finally he heaved a leaden leg over the rail and brushing off a steward's helping hand, snapped "Where is Mrs. Morgan?" He was obviously exhausted but still erect and puffing at his cigar as a ship's officer escorted him to her stateroom.

The exploit had demonstrated the remarkable stamina of a

62-year-old weighing over 220 pounds who was anything but athletic except in bedrooms. Morgan regularly patronized two ladies in Bar Harbour and, while taking the waters at Aix-les-Bains, had met an attractive Frenchwoman for whom he rented a nearby château. Like most of his favorites, she was yet another full-bosomed brunette of mature years who did not threaten the idealized image of his frail girl bride. He still continued his pilgrimages to the grave and was among the first to help endow the sanatorium that his friend Dr. Alfred Loomis had opened in New York State to treat needy victims of tuberculosis.

His numerous extramarital affairs, though conducted discreetly, have spawned a startling quantity of fanciful imaginings. In contrast to Satterlee, who tactfully ignored his father-in-law's amours altogether, John Winkler's biography suggests that "women were attracted to him irresistibly," while a woman author has recently written breathlessly of "his beautiful manners . . . and brilliant compelling eyes."

The facts must have been rather less romantic. His aura of power could have acted as an aphrodisiac, but one cannot exclude the appeal of comfortable love nests, lavish charge accounts, stock market tips, and the little black bag of diamonds he always brought back from London or Paris. His mistresses, so often seasoned theatrical veterans, must have needed dramatic talent in order to swoon convincingly in the arms of an elderly and obese lover with a monstrous nose and smoke-laden lungs that wheezed under pressure like a bagpipe. Even allowing for the plushy fringe benefits, one suspects that these bedroom mergers throbbed with all the careless rapture of an Amish honeymoon.

His amorous gusto inevitably fostered legends. Hearsay credited him with a penis so huge and durable as to rank with the weaponry of notorious womanizers in the Maupassant and Frank Harris bracket. Scandalmongers spread the malicious tale, wholly uncorroborated, that one of his favorites had waited in a private railroad car drawn up on a siding while he attended a convention of the Episcopal Church. It was whispered just as implausibly that several interns at Dr. Markoe's Lying-in Hospital had graduated to Park Avenue practices after marrying former Morgan mistresses, each of them provided with "the usual" dowry of $100,000. This canard has been trotted out over the years but without a scrap of evidence. The idea of a "fixed tariff" for services rendered does not fit the banker's character, although the figure quoted reflects his generosity to his favorites and to contemporary beauties like Lillian Russell, whom he was pleased to escort in public or entertain on his yacht. It was reported by one nervous gossip columnist that Morgan called regularly on Miss Russell "to advise her on her valuable collection of Chinese porcelain." It was widely assumed, however, that she supplemented "Diamond Jim" Brady's lavish gifts to her with tokens from the banker's little black bag. Another close friend was the attractive Mrs. John B. Markoe, a relative of the doctor by marriage. She often figured on the passenger list when Morgan crossed the Atlantic and joined several of his yachting cruises. Satterlee mentions discreetly that his father-in-law enjoyed "playing dominoes with her."

During his three years as commodore of the New York Yacht Club nothing gave Morgan more pleasure than the defeat in September 1901 of Sir Thomas Lipton's *Shamrock,* which had challenged the *Columbia,* built by a Morgan-financed syndicate, for the America's Cup. He considered it almost a personal triumph, although one newspaper reporter sneered at "the fawning flotilla" that had greeted *Corsair*'s every appearance with fireworks and popping champagne corks. His guests included the six-foot-six yachtsman, corporation lawyer, and investment consultant Tom Chadbourne, who but for his divorce would have been a natural choice for a Morgan partnership. He and his second wife, Grace, were close friends of actress Maxine Elliott, and introduced her to the commodore.

Morgan was at once dazzled by the slender and elegant goddess, whose jet-black curls set off her ivory skin and quite perfect Grecian features. Like everyone else he was repelled by her husband, Nat Goodwin, a squat, ginger-haired comedian who sported loud checked suits and too much jewelry. Several years older than Maxine, all his previous marriages had been wrecked by two-fisted drinking, and gambling sprees. He doted on her, but the marriage was already heading for the rocks when she met Pierpont Morgan.

She was then still in her early thirties but her velvety eyes had already seen a lot. A native of Rockland, Maine, daughter of an immigrant Irish sea captain, she was briefly married to a flashy lawyer-politician, one of Mayor Grace's unsavory henchmen in Tammany Hall. After several small parts in repertory, during which she acquired a series of lovers including John Drew, she won more praise for her beauty than her acting from critics in London and New York. Seeing her at a première, Ethel Barrymore had stammered, "My God, it's the Venus de Milo with arms!"

She had first met Nat Goodwin in San Francisco and toured Australia with his stock company. They married in February 1898. Nat spent recklessly both on himself and Maxine, who persuaded him to buy a suburban mansion, Jackwood Hall, while they were playing London. Her looks and style soon enslaved connoisseurs like Alfred de Rothschild and George Keppel.

Goodwin's company commuted between England and America with many ups and downs, largely surviving through her glamorous appeal. Wearing thousand-dollar creations by Worth or Poïrot and glittering with diamonds supplied by her love-struck husband while he was in funds, and by various protectors when his luck ran out, her light comedy roles always drew huge audiences. But Maxine had lost patience with her husband's vulgarity and alcoholic fits of jealousy and secretly planned to run her own company, with herself as star. She yearned to emulate Lily Langtry, who had so successfully combined a theatrical career with the life of a royal courtesan. In America she began openly cuckolding Goodwin.

Her liaison with Pierpont Morgan was conducted with great discretion, however, and this must have demanded iron self-restraint from such an extrovert. One of her few lapses is recorded at a party aboard *Corsair III* when the Commodore sat relaxing on deck in his wicker chair, smoking an after-dinner cigar and chatting with Depew, William Rockefeller, and Morton Paton, a retired corporation lawyer whose witty but inaudible quips irritated Maxine. Bored with woman talk and missing the limelight, she called out, "Why, you men in Wall Street are like a lot of cannibals. You just devour anything that comes along—if it's edible!" Morgan joined in the laughter, although he disapproved of such familiarity in the presence of his daughters. They were quite accustomed to seeing their father's favorites on yachting parties or transatlantic crossings but had come to expect a measure of decorum.

After Maxine's divorce, Pierpont met her more often, although still in the strictest privacy and preferably when she was playing out of town. He would always deny that he had financed the Maxine Elliott Theatre and, to protect himself from gossip, he avoided smothering her with traceable furs or jewels. It was both simpler and less conspicuous to "advise" her on investments, which, with the help of her own financial flair, proved so rewarding that Tom Chadbourne, tongue locked in cheek, once enthused, "If Maxine had been a man, Schiff would have been her secretary and Carnegie her office boy!"

She reveled in her social triumphs, notably in London, and seldom failed to hint archly that in her time she had turned down marriage proposals from two of England's wealthiest and most distinguished widowers, Lord Curzon, former viceroy of India, and a one-time prime minister, the Earl of Rosebery. However, she had all their letters destroyed, possibly to preserve the romantic legend after the spotlight was switched off.

If she and Morgan ever exchanged letters or *billets-doux,* which is most unlikely, nothing has ever come to light, but she always spoke with affection and admiration of the man whose name, as her biographer, Diane Forbes-Robertson, has rightly observed, "spelled more concentrated power than the entire British aristocracy put together." Long after his death, when Maxine had grown grotesquely obese, she would intrigue Winston Churchill and other guests at her luxurious Château de l'Horizon, near Cannes, with sprightly accounts of dining with King Edward VII at Marienbad and greeting the Kaiser aboard *Corsair III.*

For all her snobbishness and frivolity she had preserved a very practical and lasting respect for Big Business. One suspects that none of her conquests, however eminent, outranked the banker who put together the world's first billion-dollar merger.

CHAPTER ELEVEN

In the last year of the century, with the demand for American steel nearing peak levels, Morgan appreciated that, while Federal Steel was thriving under Judge Gary's leadership, it could not hope to survive an embrace by the Pittsburgh octopus. The industry's best hope of dominating the world market appeared to rest on the creation of a centralized combine, preferably organized and financed from 23 Wall Street. The policy had worked smoothly enough on the railroads, despite a few jagged ends like Harriman's Union Pacific, and Morgan was further encouraged by rumors of Carnegie's intention to retire from business and spend his millions on free public libraries and other educational endowments.

Coster had unfortunately died after a short illness aggravated by overwork, and the relentless pressure was already taxing Bob Bacon, who was conscientious to a fault and tended to crack during his chief's lengthy spells abroad. Coster's mathematical genius would be missed, but he was soon replaced by George W. Perkins, a vice-president of the New York Life Insurance Company, which had a large stake in various Morgan-controlled railroad and traction companies. His flair for directing vast reservoirs of capital to strategic points would be invaluable at a time when, as the *United States Investor* noted, "Big deals are no longer possible if banking assistance is withheld."

Perkins was an exception to the general upper-class mold of Morgan executives. A one-time grocery clerk, he cheerfully admitted, "I began life sorting lemons and I have been doing it ever since." He insisted on keeping his vice-presidency with New York Life and had even extorted an agent's commission for taking out a policy with them when he became a partner at 23 Wall Street!

Carnegie scoffed, "Mr. Morgan buys his partners. I prefer to grow my own." The sneer was ill-timed considering the recent upheaval in Pittsburgh that had lost him his right-hand man and troubleshooter. Frick had for years supplemented his large income from Carnegie Steel by speculating in realty, which he unloaded on the company at inflated prices. He also overcharged for his coke. With the little Scot's approaching retirement, Frick saw himself as the undisputed successor and began to intrigue for a takeover that would yield him a still larger share of the spoils.

In May 1899 he secretly approached J. W. Moore, a sharp Midwest attorney and company promoter, who with his brother had set up factories turning out tin plate and steel hoops. They approved Frick's plan to acquire a ninety-day option on Carnegie Steel for a purchase price of $158 million. From his own pocket Frick contributed part of the million-dollar deposit but lost it when the Moores failed to raise the necessary capital. The plan crashed because First National and other banks friendly to Morgan and the Rockefellers declined to finance a deal that would have destroyed Federal Steel.

By the end of the year, after violent board quarrels, Charles Schwab became chairman in place of Frick, who still retained a considerable minority holding. Carnegie now planned a strategy to weaken the small rebel groups and squeeze a higher price for his huge conglomerate. A meeting was arranged between Gary and Schwab, who hinted that a merger with Federal Steel might be mutually advantageous. Pierpont accurately dismissed the overture as kite flying to spread alarm and despondency among the independents. He was just as sceptical about Schwab's approaches to Standard Oil. Carnegie, who detested the Rockefellers almost as much as he did Morgan, had by now raised the price tag on his corporation to $250 million, justifying the increase by recently published bumper profits. The Rockefellers expressed no more than polite interest, but Gates and the Moores took alarm. They decided to challenge Carnegie by manufacturing their own steel. National Tube and other small companies soon followed suit.

Carnegie retaliated swiftly. From Skibo Castle he cabled Schwab, "Only one policy open. Start at once hoop, rod, wire, nail mills. Extend coal and coke roads, also tubes." Schwab hurried to Scotland to assure him that he could produce tubes at least $10 a ton cheaper than any competitor and also undercut them right across the board. He had already earmarked a factory site at Conneaut on Lake Erie. "Go right ahead," ordered Carnegie, who further approved setting up a vast rod mill in Pittsburgh to drive Gates clean out of business.

The rebels at once began to panic, imploring Gary of Federal Steel to use his influence with 23 Wall Street to avert a ruinous trade war. Pierpont still suspected a bluff to boost the price, but he was far more disturbed by Carnegie's threat to link Pittsburgh with the Atlantic ports and his proposed alliance with George Jay Gould, who had revived his father's vision of a transcontinental line to San Francisco. He remained outwardly calm, even when reports reached him that a corps of surveyors was already mapping out routes under the direction of Schwab and Gould, but glumly commented to Judge Gary, "Carnegie is going to demoralize the railroads as he has demoralized steel."

Gary was less pessimistic. His talks with Charles Schwab had convinced him that the grasping little ironmaster seriously intended to sell out and had at last made up his mind that only J. P. Morgan & Co., with its control of financial resources through trusts, banks, and the three leading insurance companies, could raise the huge purchase price and weld all the disparate parts of the steel industry into one mammoth unit.

Pierpont was intrigued by the challenge, though uncertain that he could organize the cash Carnegie expected, even if the Rockefellers, Gates, and the Moores sank their differences. Throughout the summer months of 1900 he played a waiting game and preferred to buy more books and pictures while making plans for his daughter's wedding. Louisa would marry Herbert Livingston Satterlee, a Harvard graduate and thirty-seven-year-old corporation lawyer specializing in railroad finance.

Pierpont made his usual spring trip to Europe, during which he paid £100,000 for Raphael's Colonna Altarpiece, but he did not forget the Metropolitan, which benefited from a rare collection of ancient Greek ornaments. In Paris, between relays of dealers at the Hotel Bristol, he escorted poor Louisa to Worth's where he selected every single item in her elaborate trousseau as well as the outfits to be worn by Fanny and the bridesmaids. In London he attended services at St. Paul's. Noting that the beautiful dome was badly lit and lost much of its grandeur after dark, he volunteered to foot the entire cost of installing a modern, subdued lighting system. The Chapter accepted his generous offer and he wrote out a check for the estimated cost of $25,000. It rose to $85,000 by the time the work was completed.

On returning home he engaged Charles F. McKim, the distinguished architect, to design his new marble library on East Thirty-sixth Street. It was needed to store his ever-growing collection of rare books and manuscripts, but he also had visions of a beautiful retreat in which he could take his ease, receiving visitors more privately than was possible at 23 Wall or in his home. After several breakfast meetings in the house at Madison Avenue, poring over blueprints, designs, and details of materials, it was obvious that the library would take years to build and would require a budget running to several million dollars. Even McKim was amazed when, after wistfully remarking that the walls of the Erechtheum in Athens had been built from blocks without a trace of mortar, Morgan at once demanded similar tightly sealed joints. McKim explained that the cost for such an almost invisible refinement would be high. Pressed, he estimated an outlay of at least $50,000, perhaps even double that figure. "Go ahead," the banker told him.

Morgan moved with equal speed when representatives from Harvard called at his office to canvass support for the Medical School on Huntington Avenue. He took only a few minutes to examine the plans before provisionally agreeing to contribute one million dollars to put up three of the five new buildings. He soon confirmed the arrangement, subject only to the extension being

202

known as a memorial to his father, "a native of Massachusetts and for many years a merchant in Boston."

His free-spending mood was no doubt stimulated by the reelection of McKinley, who was firmly pledged to adopt the gold standard and would certainly support the potential steel merger or indeed any other trust that had Wall Street's blessing. Pierpont had been less enthusiastic over the choice of Colonel Theodore Roosevelt as running mate. As police commissioner of New York City and governor of New York State he had won more approval from the Democrats than from his own party for his slum-clearance program and his all-out attacks on sweatshop employers. However, he seemed to enjoy the uncritical admiration of his old Harvard classmate Bob Bacon. Rainsford and Judge Gary also welcomed the nomination. Mark Hanna continued to mistrust the Rough Rider, but predicted his emasculation in the office of vice-president.

Soon after the election Roosevelt invited Pierpont to dine with him. It was a calculated gesture to reassure Wall Street, as he intimated self-mockingly to Secretary of War Elihu Root: "You see, it represents an effort on my part to become a conservative man in touch with the influential classes. . . . Hitherto, I have given dinners only to professional politicians or more or less wild-eyed radicals." Pierpont appeared wholly disarmed by his host's graceful congratulations on Louisa Morgan's marriage to Herbert Satterlee, who had served as a naval officer in the Spanish War.

Louisa's wedding on November 15, 1900, typified Pierpont's autocratic control of family matters. He had overruled the couple's pleas for a quiet ceremony with a small reception afterward at Cragston. He insisted instead on an elaborate invitation-only service in St. George's, followed by a party at 219 Madison Avenue that spilled over into his adjacent lots, where a huge marquee with a specially laid dance floor was put up for the 2,400 guests. Pierpont had supervised every detail of the catering, personally helped to hang the floral decorations, and even rearranged the lighting.

Three weeks later he attended a tribute dinner to Charles Schwab at the University Club. The unpopular Laird of Skibo (who discreetly kept away) vetted the guest list, which included

Gates, the Moores, and others who had no love for Carnegie Steel but were anxious to secure its new president's goodwill. J. P. Morgan, seated at his right hand, leaned back, cigar in mouth, to enjoy another of Schwab's witty after-dinner speeches, but "Smiling Charlie" was unusually serious as he outlined the prospects for the steel industry if it could be induced to end wasteful competition. "In the United States no one plant makes steel cars exclusively," he observed. "Instead of having one mill make ten, twenty, or fifty products, why not have one making one product, and that continuously?" He recommended a single trust powerful enough to boost output, keep down prices, and compete profitably overseas. He ended with a buoyant forecast of his own company's plans for expansion.

His speech was an olive branch wrapped in barbed wire. It plainly warned Gates and others what to expect if they continued their tactics, but Pierpont surprised them all by standing up to lead the applause. With a rare gesture of cordiality he even took Schwab by the arm and steered him to a corner of the room, where he questioned him on several points and seemed impressed by his answers.

Next morning he conferred with his associates. They agreed that a further talk with Schwab might be useful, but Gary thought that Gates, as a key figure among the independents, should be brought in. Pierpont yielded reluctantly. A meeting was duly arranged at 219 Madison Avenue, with food and drinks served in the library, for a session lasting until well past midnight. Prompted by Bob Bacon, Pierpont for once did most of the talking. Schwab listened intently without committing himself, while Gates, overawed though suspicious, restrained his normal aggression. It was decided that the Morgan firm should attempt to buy an option on Carnegie's corporation, to be followed by a merger with Federal Steel and its two affiliated companies, National Tube and American Bridge. Pierpont would then arrange to acquire the interests of Gates, the Moores, and the Rockefellers.

Schwab went off to report to Carnegie, who happened to be playing a round of golf at the St. Andrews Club in Westchester County. He at once rejected any idea of an option, but Schwab convinced him that nothing would be lost by at least quoting a purchase price. Scratching his beard and still grunting doubts that Morgan was seriously in the market, he at last jotted down his price. It was nearly $450 million, payable in cash and bonds. His own share would total $217,720,000.

Schwab called at 23 Wall Street the following day, handed over the slip of paper and calmly announced, "Here is the figure, Mr. Morgan." After briefly consulting Judge Gary, who had meantime secured the approval of Marshall Field and other Federal Steel directors, Pierpont informed Schwab that the terms were acceptable. He then decided to invite Carnegie over to The Corner for a friendly talk, but the ironmaster, so often affronted in the past by Morgan's condescension, objected that, as his senior, (he was two years older), it would be more fitting if he did the honors. Pierpont went to the Steel Corporation's offices on Fifty-first Street, stayed only an uncomfortable quarter of an hour, and then shook hands, remarking with an effort at affability, "Mr. Carnegie, I want to congratulate you on being the richest man in the world!"

"Thank you, *Pierpont*" the dour little Scot responded. Morgan, wincing at the familiarity, took his leave with a stiff bow.

Gates could not forgive Morgan for excluding him from the Federal Steel board. He now hit back by demanding an excessive price for his American Steel and Wire Company. One night, after losing a big hand at stud poker, he had chuckled, "Never mind, I'll put it on old Livernose's bill."

Gary summoned him and his associates to an afternoon meeting in the partners' room at 23 Wall Street and announced that the top offer would be $110 million payable in the new trust's stock. This was generous, as the current value of Steel and Wire stood at around $60 million, but Gates demanded a still higher figure and a directorship. The arguments dragged on while Morgan chainsmoked in his private office. At a few minutes past three, his usual time for departure, he sent in a clerk to inform them that he was about to leave for the day. Gary pleaded for another half-hour, which was grudgingly extended while Gates continued to haggle.

When the clock struck five, Morgan burst in with a newly lit cigar jutting from his mouth and the high-crowned derby jammed down on his head. He thumped the board table with his cane and announced coldly, "Gentlemen, I am going to leave this building in ten minutes. If by that time you have not accepted my offer, the

205

matter will be closed. And we will build our own plant." He strode out, grim-faced.

Gates turned to one of his partners and muttered, "I don't know whether the old man means it or not."

"You can depend on it, he does," snapped Judge Gary.

"Then I guess we'll have to give it up," said Gates.

Morgan was called back and told that the deadlock had been broken. He shrugged and irritably declined to stay chatting with Gates and his friends but, as Gary later recalled, "We went up together on the Elevated to Fiftieth Street where his old electric car met him. He was like a boy going home from a football game."

His elation subsided when Gary reminded him that Standard Oil's large iron ore holdings in Minnesota could still have a nuisance value. Pierpont then agreed to Henry Frick's acting as a go-between. The Rockefellers, prompted by Frick who could never resist double-dealing, asked $80 million for their properties, which Gary had valued at $75 million maximum. But Pierpont, impatient to launch the new trust now attracting so much press gossip, agreed to the higher figure.

The banker was already mentally blueprinting plans for a new venture, a huge cartel to be composed of the various competing American, British, and German shipping lines. He had as a nucleus two small American shipping lines, and he had sounded out the German Hamburg-American Company that seemed receptive. His primary targets would be the two leading British operators, White Star and Cunard. The former was in poor shape financially and vulnerable, and he was sanguine that Cunard, whose minions had offended his dignity on that never-forgotten Christmas Eve a score of years ago, would be unable to resist increased competition and, if necessary, a costly fare- and freight-cutting war.

The Commodore of the New York Yacht Club evidently saw himself as All-High Admiral of a fleet whose name he had already penciled in: International Mercantile Marine. It presented no apparent difficulties to the man who dominated America's railroads and was now launching the mightiest merger in history.

On March 3, 1901, the world's leading newspapers announced the birth of the United States Steel Corporation. Registered in

Trenton under New Jersey's benevolent laws, it would have 168,000 workers on its payroll and control over 60 percent of the nation's iron and steel output, plus over one thousand miles of strategic railroads. It was capitalized at a staggering $1,402,-846,817, issued by the Morgan firm in mortgage bonds and stock, common and preferred. Modeled on Standard Oil's original structure, it quickly shot higher than any gusher. James R. Keene, Wall Street's "Silver Fox," Gould's one-time hatchet man, and a veteran of mining and railroad stock manipulation, was entrusted with a sales campaign that unloaded half a million shares in two days and a further million in the following week.

The public in America and abroad rushed headlong to buy into "Big Steel's billion-dollar bonanza." Common stock jumped from 38 to 65, while the preferred put on 20 points almost overnight. As promoter, J. P. Morgan & Co. was paid a fee of nearly $12 million and a share of the subscription profits, which would quadruple the underwriting syndicate's investment. Carnegie deposited his millions of dollars in proceeds in a specially built vault in Hoboken before departing for the Scottish Highlands. Tortured by the thought that he might have sold out too cheaply, he dismissed the bullish frenzy as a Klondike of fool's gold. He predicted to a friend, "Pierpont will make a fizzle of the business and default in payment of interest. He feels that he can do anything because he has got the best of the Jews in Wall Street. But it takes a Yankee to beat a Jew, and it takes a Scot to beat a Yankee." He seemed quite convinced that he would be able to buy back his holdings at a low valuation after the amateurs had burned their fingers in Pittsburgh's blast furnaces.

But U. S. Steel would flourish under Schwab, who had been appointed president and production supremo, while Judge Gary directed policy as chairman of the executive committee. Frick, qualified by his many hard years of practical experience, went on the twenty-four-man board, which also included two Morgan partners, lawyer Charles Steele and Robert Bacon; the Rockefellers, father and son, with Henry Rogers from Standard Oil; Peter Widener, the utilities magnate; and representatives of the leading banks and insurance companies with whom J. P. Morgan's interests were interlocked. Two men were conspicuously excluded from this impressive parade of wealth and influence.

Gates and Harriman paid the price for Morgan's lasting dislike and contempt.

He would never forgive Gates for his attempted "blackmail" over Steel and Wire and enjoyed informing him, "It will be impossible for you to enter the directorate. You have made your own reputation. Good day, sir." He then proceeded to blackball his nominations for both the Union League and the New York Yacht Club. Harriman did not risk rejection by the new steel hierarchy. Instead, he consolidated his grip on the Union and Southern Pacific Railroads and began to push eastward by buying into the Chicago, Burlington, and Quincy line, popularly known as the Burlington.

James J. Hill, who directed the rival Northern Pacific and Great Northern networks after the merger masterminded by the Morgan firm, considered that the Burlington was essential for securing an eastern terminal in Chicago, which Harriman's Union Pacific also coveted. Morgan accordingly sanctioned the purchase of a majority holding in Burlington at well above the market valuation. Later it was disclosed that Harriman would have been satisfied with one-third of the stock and a face-saving appointment to the board, but magnanimity to a defeated opponent, particularly one he despised, was foreign to the banker's nature. Brushing the suggestion aside, he instructed Steele and Bacon to buy as much stock as was needed to squeeze out Harriman altogether.

Morgan's handling of the Burlington affair, though effective in the short term, demonstrated not only his autocratic style but a serious misreading of his opponent's character. Still basking in his Big Steel triumph, he was content to ignore the possibility that Harriman, who did not easily accept his humiliation over Burlington, would choose his own time and ground upon which to launch some counterattack.

In that spring of 1901, Morgan was looking forward feverishly to his trip to Europe. He seemed exhausted and showed his irritation at the often distasteful publicity that had inevitably followed the creation of the steel trust. It had transformed his firm's role as private bankers. For years he had marketed huge pools of stocks and bonds without the slightest personal contact with investors. Millions had ridden on his railroads and used the power generated by General Electric without having more than hearsay knowledge of the activities at 23 Wall Street. Now J. P. Morgan & Co. was out in the open, selling directly to the public instead of pursuing its traditional policy of financing other companies and wielding power through mysterious voting trusts, which even Bryan, Pulitzer, and other probing liberals had had difficulty in exposing.

Pierpont found himself pestered by reporters who published extravagant accounts of his coup. Their flattery was echoed by brokers and jubilant investors, but others saw the chance to poke fun at the reserved old autocrat, who squirmed when vaudeville comics chanted a ditty: "It's Morgan's, it's Morgan's, the great financial Gorgon's." From San Francisco it was reported that a black-bearded former anarchist had celebrated the grant of citizenship by solemnly changing his name from John Bielaski to John Pierpont Morgan. Such vulgarities could be ignored but not the gibe from President Arthur Hadley of Yale, who predicted at a meeting in Boston that, unless trusts were regulated, "there will be an emperor in Washington within 25 years."

It had been irksome enough to see photographs of himself in the newspapers, but far more painful to be confronted by almost daily caricatures, naturally emphasizing his nose. Morgan commented, "Well, it's part of the American business structure and it would be impossible for me to appear in the streets without it."

Morgan had another excellent reason for bringing forward his usual spring visit to Europe. Morland Agnew, the London art dealer, had arrived in America late that March after receiving a cable from Pinkerton's. They had finally tracked down the long-missing Gainsborough portrait of the Duchess of Devonshire. The canvas, still undamaged after several journeys between hiding places in England and the United States, was handed over in a Chicago hotel room by Adam Worth, now a dying man, who wanted police immunity for that theft as well as other crimes.

Before sailing back with the painting, Agnew stopped off at 219 Madison Avenue and left his card with a brief message. Anxious to acquire the picture that his father had so nearly bought for him a quarter of a century earlier, Pierpont took passage on April 4, 1901, in the fast White Star liner *Teutonic* with his sister, Mary

Burns, and arrived ahead of Agnew, whose very reputable firm willingly gave him first refusal. He would neither confirm nor deny the *Morning Post* story that he had paid 20,000 guineas (or $100,000 at the exchange rate of five dollars to the pound).

The picture was cleaned, relined, and remained on exhibition—this time under heavy guard—before taking an honored place in the drawing room of 13 Prince's Gate. In the dining room hung another Gainsborough, a portrait of Mrs. Tennant, with a Romney, a Reynolds group, and several Constable landscapes. Behind his chair at the head of the table was a beautiful Hoppner of three children. This taste for family groups was assumed to reflect his sentimentality toward his own grandchildren. He would indeed spoil them at Christmas and Thanksgiving dinners, but sometimes he behaved with crabby impatience. He had once turned on Juliet, whose noisy offspring irritated him, and growled at her, "Don't ask them what they want to do. *Tell them!*"

London journalists followed him everywhere, but he would not satisfy their curiosity about his plans to establish an international shipping cartel or respond to persistent reports that he was buying heavily into London Underground stock for a takeover when a new franchise extended the system. A frustrated reporter started the rumor that overwork on the Steel Trust had affected his heart. It caused some nervous brokers, heavily involved in American securities, to take out insurance policies against his death. Lloyds quoted a rate of £30 per £1,000 for three months, but he was in fact exceptionally fit and enjoyed being fêted by the Barings and other City magnates. Most of all he liked dining at the hospitable table of Alfred de Rothschild, sharing the honors one night with Kitchener, the hero of Omdurman, and Almina, Countess of Carnarvon, to whom Alfred would bequeath the bulk of his fortune.

He interrupted his negotiations with Bruce Ismay, chairman and chief shareholder of White Star, and departed for Paris with Jack and his family. After receiving art dealers and indulging in the now habitual shopping spree for diamonds and trinkets, he went off alone to Aix, where he installed himself in his $500 a day corner suite at the Grand Hotel and divided his time between sampling the bitter waters and the more appetizing charms of his

French mistress. He seemed quite unaware of the pressures invisibly building up against his steel and railroad hegemony.

Big Steel showed net profits of $85 million in its first nine months. The trust was turning on its axis like a huge scintillating globe of solid steel, but the world remained flat and bleak for miners and millworkers who still toiled a twelve-hour day, often without adequate safety precautions. Their pay had been slightly increased to average eleven dollars a week and they were now allowed to buy company stock at a small discount. Schwab had dangled this carrot of employee stock ownership but unwisely went about boasting that U. S. Steel was paying him a salary of a million dollars a year. Smiling Charlie had carelessly added a zero, Judge Gary told the newspapers. Schwab was not alone in offending Gary's sense of decorum. At board meetings he had to endure the vulgarity of extroverts like Peter Widener and H. H. Rogers who gaily tossed for the twenty-dollar gold pieces in attendance money forfeited by absent colleagues.

The railroad barons and other entrepreneurs of the nineties, who had ransacked Europe to furnish their gaudy Fifth Avenue palaces, were now joined by the steel millionaires, Western ranchers, oil kings, and coal mine owners who multiplied in Society "like germs in a bouillon culture," as Frank Crowningshield later reported. They bought paintings, feverishly endowed universities, and gave bountifully, usually with maximum publicity, to their churches for boxes in a kind of celestial Diamond Horseshoe.

Such a lifestyle, together with reports of nouveau riche Pittsburgh speculators who lit their havanas with ten-dollar bills, supplied fodder for union bosses like Samuel Gompers, who would create the American Federation of Labor. Early in the summer of 1901 the Iron and Steel Workers Association had called for a strike, but this came to nothing after the U. S. Steel directors passed a resolution, "We are unalterably opposed to any extension of union labor and advise subsidiary companies to take a firm position." Gompers' speeches were laughed off as the ravings of "a Jewish anarchist."

The threat to Morgan's railroads was far more dangerous. In

his absence abroad Harriman and Schiff decided to mount a flank attack on the seemingly impregnable Morgan-Hill stronghold of North Pacific. They secretly bought blocks of shares, which soared in price, even tempting at least one associate at 23 Wall Street to unload 35,000 for a fat profit without presumably suspecting that Harriman's nominees had picked them up.

Had he not been overseas, Jupiter might have smelled trouble, but both Bacon and Charles Steele were too busy with other business to take the Northern Pacific's boomlet seriously. By the end of April James J. Hill had become uneasy. He hired a special train to take him from Seattle to New York, where he discovered that nearly $15 million of stock had changed hands, quite a proportion having been sold by Northern Pacific directors. He at once guessed who had masterminded the operation.

On Friday, May 3, he dined with Schiff, who admitted that he had been buying heavily on behalf of Union Pacific and argued that Harriman was more than justified after being so ruthlessly squeezed out of the Burlington takeover. "Morgan may not be as big as he thinks he is," he said tartly, adding that the Harriman group now had a controlling interest in Northern Pacific stock. They had in fact over half the preferred (subject to retirement on New Year's Day) and rather less than a majority of the common. Hill protested that Morgan genuinely wanted peace and hinted that he himself would personally back Harriman's appointment to the board of Burlington if he at once abandoned his tactics.

It was no more than a delaying move, as Schiff shrewdly guessed. Hill then went off to see a very nervous Bob Bacon, who agreed to send a cable to Aix requesting authority to buy another 150,000 of common stock, currently valued at an inflated $15 million, to ensure absolute control of Northern Pacific. Morgan angrily consented, but his cable did not reach Bacon until Sunday.

Informed of Hill's call on Jacob Schiff, Harriman figured that he would need more stock to block the expected countermove. Although ill in bed in his 50-room mansion, he at once rang Kuhn, Loeb and ordered them to buy him another 40,000 shares of common. But as it was the Jewish Sabbath, with Schiff at his devotions in Temple Emanu-El, his deputy hesitated to execute on his own responsibility such a large order, then worth $5

212

million on a still-rising market, although it was possible as the Stock Exchange then operated on Saturdays. Back from the synagogue, Schiff weighed the pros and cons; he may have been misled by Hill's hints of a peace pact, but it is more likely that he had grown nervous at the prospect of some sort of retaliation by Morgan's forces. He finally decided to wait until Monday, the 6th, by which time the inflated market might have settled down, before executing Harriman's order.

Early that morning Jim Keene, working through his well-drilled squad of brokers, began buying 150,000 shares for the Morgan-Hill combine. Kuhn, Loeb then attempted to make up for lost time by scooping up the 40,000 for Harriman. This unprecedented demand at once sent up Northern Pacific stock. It jumped forty points in two hectic days. Many Wall Street operators sold short in the hope of a future killing, but they soon found it impossible to buy back the stock that the two warring groups had by now absorbed between them. By Thursday the market was well and truly cornered, with stock touching $1,000 a share from its $114 quote on the Monday morning. Several bears, unable to escape from the trap, faced ruin, and Wall Street was racked by a slump that crippled many other sound securities. Ironically, even mighty U. S. Steel slipped by almost 50 percent. British investors, who had bought its high-priced shares, naturally became embittered over losses for which they held J. P. Morgan responsible.

During that feverish week he left his mistress's silk sheets for the Paris office. One American reporter asked him sharply, "Don't you think that since you are being blamed for a panic that has ruined thousands of people and disturbed a whole nation, some statement is due to the public?"

"I owe the public nothing," he growled back, almost echoing Billy Vanderbilt's unfortunate response to reporters a decade before. Next day *The New York Times* flayed Wall Street bankers for "behaving like cowboys on a spree . . . shooting wildly at each other in entire disregard of the safety of bystanders." Piqued by criticism he thought wholly unmerited, Pierpont cabled his office to organize a $20 million pool, which helped to steady the market. Several harassed brokers were also rescued from their short-selling fiasco by being allowed to settle for a relatively modest $150 a share.

Harriman only just failed to achieve his majority in Northern Pacific but still planned to oppose the threatened retirement of the company's preferred stock. The moment he came out of the anesthetic after removal of his appendix, he telephoned Kuhn, Loeb to announce his intention to take legal action. Schiff argued strongly for a truce with Morgan. He was backed by William Rockefeller who managed to persuade his brother that Standard Oil had much to gain once the dust had settled.

Both sides were bruised in a conflict that brought them much cash from the artificial boom in Northern Pacific though precious little credit. Schiff righteously assumed the role of peacemaker and convinced James Hill that some plan had now become essential to appease both embittered chieftains. It took considerable effort to sell Morgan on the idea that Harriman's substantial holdings in Northern Pacific entitled him to a place on its board and also of the board of the Burlington.

In a series of letters and coded cables to Bob Bacon, he then elaborated on the plan he had briefly outlined to Hill before sailing for Europe. He proposed setting up a vast new holding company, the Northern Securities Corporation, to acquire all the stock of the Northern Pacific and Great Northern systems and form a transportation complex between the Great Lakes and the Pacific. He envisaged a $400 million capitalization to protect the additional 9,000 miles of track from any possible attack, hinting that he would not be averse to inviting Harriman and the Rockefellers to bring in their Union Pacific holdings.

On May 31, Bob Bacon and Hill cautiously put the embryo scheme to Harriman and Jacob Schiff over a lengthy dinner at the Metropolitan Club. Schiff, quick to scent a brokerage harvest, was enthusiastic but Harriman, not yet recovered from his recent defeat, exhibited the deepest suspicion. After much argument he agreed to reserve judgment until Pierpont Morgan's return from England in July.

The court was still in mourning for the queen's death in January, but the London season had revived a little with the prospect of King Edward's move into Buckingham Palace. Pierpont was fitted for several suits and overcoats by Henry Poole of Saville Row, who noted that his figure had grown far bulkier since the mid-seventies when he had been measured for an angora silk-lined frock coat costing seven sovereigns. He wore a new frock coat with formal silk hat to lead a New York Chamber of Commerce delegation to congratulate the king on his accession. One reporter, recalling his recent purchase of the Gainsborough Duchess and a valuable collection of bronzes and coins, scheduled to go on indefinite loan to the South Kensington Museum, professed alarm that "Mr. Morgan might take a fancy to Windsor Castle and buy it." The king, whom he had already met several times at Alfred de Rothschild's, went out of his way to be agreeable and later insisted that he sit beside him at a dinner given by the American ambassador. Over cigars they talked yacht racing and also compared notes about the relative merits of Aix-les-Bains and Marienbad, the king's favorite spa.

At the end of June 1901 he sailed home on the *Deutschland* to familiarize himself at firsthand with the Hamburg-American Line that he expected to incorporate into his cartel. The liner was met by *Corsair III,* with pennants flying from stern to stem, dominated by his flag as commodore of the New York Yacht Club. He ran down to Cragston with the family but stayed aboard *Corsair* most of the month. He found time to see McKim and approve his early plans for the new library. He was specially enthusiastic over the architect's designs for a majestic West Room, with walls of red brocade to set off his Florentine paintings.

At the office he hammered out the final details of the Northern Securities Corporation due to be launched that November in New Jersey, with or without Harriman's participation, although he imagined that would not be long delayed if Schiff had his way. He remained equally sanguine that the recurrent steel workers' strikes would soon be crushed if the management stayed firm. Like ebullient Charles Schwab, he pooh-poohed solemn warnings from the authorities that anarchists might resort to violence. He had submitted ungraciously to a small police bodyguard and left them stranded ashore when he boarded his yacht to watch the preliminary races for the America's Cup, which would be defended again by *Columbia* against Lipton's new challenger, *Shamrock II.*

One afternoon in mid-September, while he was impatiently

clearing some papers in his office before driving out to the West Thirty-fifth pier to run down to Great Neck, several reporters burst in to announce that McKinley had been seriously wounded by shots fired by a young anarchist in Buffalo. "It's the saddest news I ever heard," he said in a low voice. But he was less apprehensive about Roosevelt than was Mark Hanna, who after the stricken president's death a week later turned bitterly to a friend at the swearing-in and rasped, "I told William McKinley it was a mistake to nominate that wild man and, look, the damned cowboy is president of the United States."

At the end of the month Pierpont traveled on the special train he had hired to take his party of bishops and their wives to the Triennial Convention in San Francisco. All other trains were shunted aside enabling him to make a record run from coast to coast. He installed his party in a rented mansion, where they were wined and dined under Louis Sherry's supervision. He was rather nettled by the city's chief of police insisting on a security corps to protect him but became more cheerful as telegrams arrived daily from New York informing him that *Columbia* had retained the Cup. He celebrated with a banquet. To round off the convention he took Bishop William Lawrence of Massachusetts and other delegates on the special for a sightseeing trip up the coast. The ladies twittered with delight when he personally escorted them around the smartest shops in Seattle, footing the bill for costly furs, gloves, and rugs.

Back in New York he worked on plans for his shipping cartel, optimistic that the new president, staunchly navy-minded, would back a subsidy. He was also encouraged by reports from the London office that White Star, pressured by its Belfast ship-builders, was moving smoothly toward an amalgamation. Cunard remained hostile, but the Hamburg-American group seemed warmly interested.

He turned to the more immediate business of launching Northern Securities. It was unobtrusively incorporated in New Jersey on November 12, 1901, with a capital of $400 million. Morgan, Hill, Bacon, and George Baker of the First National Bank went on the board, but Harriman, who had declined to contribute his hard-won Pacific holdings, was left out.

Morgan celebrated a most festive Christmas with his family,

lately increased by his third grandchild, Mabel Satterlee, who became his special pet, although he was gratified when the dynasty seemed assured with the arrival of Jack's first two children, Junius and Henry. Nothing gave him more pleasure than handing out presents from the giant tree at 219 Madison Avenue. Satterlee records that "when he sat down it was always with a baby on his knee."

That New Year's Eve he went off as usual to The Corner to sign the accounts. It had been a bumper year, with U.S. Steel yielding huge revenues, although heavy criticism was being fired at the trust's increased price for steel rails: over four dollars per ton more than even grasping Andrew Carnegie had charged. Judge Gary was also finding it more difficult to work with Schwab, whose business style and vulgar flamboyance he found almost intolerable. Morgan attempted to mollify him, although he shared his distaste for the publicity that Smiling Charlie was attracting.

At thirty-seven Schwab was in his prime and had exuberantly celebrated his presidency with a business-cum-pleasure junket in Europe. He bought a splendid limousine in Paris and had himself chauffeur driven down to Nice, where he was joined by Henri de Rothschild, a party-giving yachtsman, and convivial Dr. Wittgenstein, head of the Austrian steel cartel. They moved on to Monte Carlo to tipple, dine, and gamble until dawn in the *salons privés,* attended by a retinue of hungry cocottes. Schwab was falsely said to have broken the bank and then lost it all back, plus much more. The New York tabloids at once splashed tales of his irresponsibility in flinging "millions of francs" about while Pittsburgh's workers clamored hopelessly for a living wage.

Andrew Carnegie seized the chance to proclaim his own high morality and punish his one-time protégé. He wrote with unctuous relish to Morgan: "I feel as though a son had disgraced the family. . . . He is unfit to be head of the United States Steel Company, brilliant as his talents are. Of course he could never have fallen so low with us. His resignation would have been called for instanter had he done so."

Pierpont saw through Carnegie's malice but, prompted by Judge Gary, could not overlook the reported shenanigans. When Schwab arrived back after completing several excellent deals with Wittgenstein and other industrialists, he was summoned to 219 Madison Avenue where Jupiter awaited him in the library. Schwab admitted that he might have gone a little wild at Monte Carlo but added with an impish smile, "At least, I didn't do it behind closed doors."

"Well, that's what closed doors are for," Morgan snapped.

They parted amicably, with Schwab puffing on one of his host's best cigars. He appeared to have accepted the rebuke in good part but guessed that in any future brush Morgan would side with prissy Judge Gary. As president of a billion-dollar corporation that he ran with outstanding skill and drive, he very naturally resented having his peccadilloes judged by the same rigid code that Morgan imposed on his clerks. He came away convinced that the crusty old autocrat thought his own social background, wealth, and power immunized him personally from all criticism and entitled him to disregard not only the workers, whose respect Smiling Charlie had kept by a blend of blarney and commonsense, but the feelings of even his most senior associates.

Morgan could not have anticipated that his high-handed treatment of Schwab would prove very costly indeed to United States Steel. He was equally clumsy and ill-advised in his assessment of Theodore Roosevelt who, he imagined, would soon be kneeling to the party machine to win its support for a new term. He was contemptuous but not altogether surprised when the president, apparently playing to the gallery, thundered in Congress at "the malefactors of great wealth . . . the men who seek gain not by genuine work . . . but by gambling . . ." From his Olympian heights of self-regard, Jupiter complacently regarded this rhetoric as directed at the likes of Gates and the unspeakable "two-dollar" broker, Edward H. Harriman, rather than himself.

Roosevelt was in fact loading for bigger game. "When I became President," he recalled in his autobiography, "the question as to the *method* by which the U.S. Government was to control the corporations was not yet important. The absolutely vital question was whether the Government had power to control them at all." For his first target he chose the great railroad merger of Northern Securities, which the courts would be invited to dissolve as a monopoly and an illegal restraint of trade.

It was a daring challenge to a man whose sovereign power was already unique in American history and only comparable to that of Europe's Rothschilds in the palmy seventies. Morgan had won a dominant position in the Wall Street hierarchy and successfully used banking pressure to outflank even mighty captains of industry like Carnegie and the Rockefellers. He had salvaged the nation's credit in the gold crisis, amalgamated the unwieldy steel industry, and, by concentrating massed capital on weak spots, had triumphantly restored order to the railroads. His firm and affiliates now had interests in 55,000 miles of track. There seemed no valid reason why his technique should be less successful in dominating the world's shipping lines.

Morgan's bullish euphoria led him to see himself as a one-man super state, free from moral, legal, and political restraints, ruling lesser men by Divine Right. In this context he could afford little misjudgments such as allowing Ned Harriman to capture Union Pacific and supporting a prim mediocrity like Judge Gary against the infinitely more valuable Schwab.

The new president of the United States had as yet no means of fully assessing Morgan's mounting egomania, nourished by courtesans, self-indulgent bishops, wheedling art dealers, and above all associates from whom he demanded the devotion that had helped to kill Coster, shortened the life of Walter Burns and would soon crush his beloved deputy, Robert Bacon. When one client, white-faced and still shaken after a typically curt interview, emerged from the Drexel Building, a passing friend had asked why he was looking so gloomy. The half-stunned victim replied, "I have just been subjected to the unconscious arrogance of conscious power."

That arrogance misled him into taking Roosevelt's "radicalism" far too lightly. It also held other built-in dangers. Since he now tended to regard all opposition to his views as stupid and unpatriotic, if not blasphemous, he was vulnerable to a man like Jacob Schiff, who ventured to use flattery while the Northern Securities plan was maturing. In a letter outstanding for its servile hypocrisy, Schiff gushed, "I trust you will accept my assurance that, as far as my partners and I are concerned, we have at all times wished, as we continue to do, to be permitted to aid in maintaining your personal prestige, so well deserved."

Morgan was supremely self-confident and expansive when,

early in February 1902, he welcomed Prince Henry of Prussia, brother of the kaiser, who was having a yacht specially built in an American shipyard for the New York to Kiel race. He hosted a banquet in the prince's honor at Louis Sherry's new establishment on Fifth Avenue, followed by a more intimate dinner at the University Club with Harry Burleigh rendering Negro spirituals as a "cabaret." After the *Meteor* had been launched by Alice Roosevelt, her father gave Prince Henry a state dinner at the White House. He did so with some reluctance as he remained deeply suspicious of German expansionism in Venezuela. J. P. Morgan had been invited as America's leading financier.

A few days later, on February 19, while dining at home with his wife and a few friends, he was called to the telephone by a newspaper editor who informed him that next morning Attorney General Philander C. Knox would announce a suit to dissolve Northern Securities under the Sherman Antitrust Act. Flushed and with hands shaking, he turned to his guests and angrily denounced Roosevelt for not giving him the opportunity to work out some compromise before charging in with this public challenge. "And I regarded him as a gentleman," he said bitterly.

The announcement at once hit stocks, with U.S. Steel prominent among the casualties. Wall Street denounced Roosevelt for betraying his party and shamelessly wooing Democratic support for his next term, but it was noted that the messages of approval were by no means limited to the liberal followers of Eugene Debs or William Jennings Bryan. Quite a sprinkling of rival businessmen, who had tired of seeing J. P. Morgan arrogantly riding through the land in his princely howdah, rejoiced that the elephantine Northern Securities Corporation had stepped into a hole and might soon come crashing down in the mud. Harriman, always the opportunist, now began to dream again of extending his railroads and perhaps even dissolving the hated merger of Northern Pacific with Great Northern once the holding company was destroyed. He even felt confident enough to put out feelers to certain lobbyists with the hope of getting himself elected to the Senate!

Morgan had bustled off to Washington and demanded an audience with the president. He protested at being denied the courtesy of previous consultation.

"That's exactly what we didn't want to do," Roosevelt rejoined coolly.

"If we have done anything wrong," growled Morgan, "send your man," he pointed his cigar at Knox, "to see my man, and they will fix it up."

Roosevelt shook his head in disbelief, while Knox interjected furiously, "We don't *want* to fix it up. We want to *stop* it."

Morgan ignored him and said to the president, "Are you going to attack my other interests, the steel corporation and the others?"

"Certainly not," said Roosevelt, adding almost as an afterthought, "unless we find that they have done something we regard as wrong." According to Roosevelt's biographer, Joseph B. Bishop, the president commented afterward to Knox, "He could not help regarding me as a big-time operator, who either intended to ruin all his interests or else could be induced to come to an agreement to ruin none."

The shock to Pierpont's pride from the Northern Securities suit was cushioned by a series of coups that demonstrated both his contempt for Washington's antitrust noises and 23 Wall Street's intention to pursue its chosen path. The new partner, George W. Perkins, had confirmed his early promise by skillfully floating International Harvester with a capital of $120 million, absorbing the interests of the McCormicks, whose pioneer Reaper Company had been financed by Junius during his first days with Peabody. With Gary on the board and Perkins as a voting trustee, the firm moved swiftly into a near-monopoly of agricultural machinery.

A far more difficult challenge, however, had surfaced through Bet-a-Million Gates and Barney Baruch. Having forged close links with Harriman, Jacob Schiff, and astute James R. Keene, the pair began juggling the market for a majority holding in the Louisville & Nashville Railroad. This was a plain threat to the southern network in which Morgan had invested heavily. The banker decided to buy an option in their stocks but Gates, welcoming the chance to pay off several old scores, kept Perkins dangling while the Louisville share continued to rise. One day, after Perkins and his assistant had been wearily chasing him for several hours, they finally ran him to earth at 3 A.M. in the Waldorf-Astoria where he was carousing. Perkins impatiently demanded a yea or nay. Gates still refused to part with an option but at last chortled, "Okay, you fellers can have the road, but you gotta pay me and my friends a bonus of ten million bucks." To the astonishment of his partners, Morgan agreed without hesitation and rapidly drafted details for a merger between the Louisville and the Atlantic Coast Line.

Morgan sternly insisted, before embarking on his annual European tour, that he be kept informed of every stage of the operation in case Gates, Baruch, and Schiff attempted some last-minute ploy. He also told Bacon and Perkins to maintain a close but discreet watch on Schwab, whose recent maneuvers were very odd.

Smarting over Morgan's rebuke and now barely on speaking terms with Judge Gary, Smiling Charlie had won himself control of Bethlehem Steel, a small but thriving concern established in Pennsylvania before the Civil War. He secretly planned to expand it and then sell out for a big profit to the mammoth trust. With typical impudence he cajoled 23 Wall Street into advancing him seven million dollars, on favorable terms, to secure a majority interest. Pierpont became uneasy, summoned him to his office, and charged him with abusing his position in U. S. Steel. The trust was not interested in buying Bethlehem, he declared brusquely. Schwab was ordered to sell his holdings or resign the presidency. Retaining his embalmed smile, Schwab agreed to seek a suitable purchaser and pay off the loan.

Pierpont, meanwhile, seemed blindly insensitive to Robert Bacon's health, which was cracking under the cumulative strains of the U. S. Steel launch, the tussle with Harriman over Northern Pacific, and Roosevelt's open declaration of war on the trusts. He was torn between deep loyalty to Morgan and hero-worship of his old classmate, Roosevelt, whose patriotism and sincerity he never questioned. With Morgan charging full-steam into his grandiose shipping cartel, and Judge Gary continuing to feud openly with Schwab at every board meeting, Bacon was heading for a nervous breakdown, or worse, unless he took his doctor's urgent counsel and went on prolonged sick leave.

Morgan himself sailed on April 2, 1902, for a trip that promised, most agreeably, to combine business with pleasure. He expected to finalize the flotation of International Mercantile Marine, take the London Underground franchise in his stride, and buy more art treasures. He planned to see the races at Kiel to celebrate the opening of the Canal, followed by a leisurely Mediterranean cruise aboard *Corsair III,* which had been sent on ahead. Although a good sailor, he was not prepared to expose himself or his guests to the possible hazards and discomforts of a rough Atlantic crossing (a wise precaution, as it turned out, since *Corsair*'s maiden voyage proved anything but smooth). He had decided to travel by White Star liner. As the prospective new owner he would be, if possible, more pampered than usual.

The highlight of his London visit would, of course, be the forthcoming coronation of King Edward VII in Westminster Abbey, to which he and his daughter Anne had been invited. Anne would replace Louisa, his companion on many trips to Europe but now busy with her husband and baby. Before long the Satterlees would move into the house he was building for them on Thirty-sixth Street, where they would be at his beck and call. Anne was livelier than her sister and could be pertly amusing until she started prating about slum clearance and the suffragette cause. Now nearing thirty, she looked set to become a cranky spinster and had once or twice angered him by equating tenement land-lords and sweatshop bosses with Wall Street plungers. However, she was always sympathetic during spells of ill health and suf-fered with him when the gutter press caricatured his monstrous nose or viciously stigmatized him as a hymn-singing hypocrite. She was also a capable hostess, and, with Fanny choosing to spend the summer months placidly at Cragston rather than face an exhausting London season, she could be relied upon to pour tea for duchesses with the unaffected charm so long enjoyed by the derelicts in her Bowery soup kitchens.

Jack was looking forward more eagerly than his sister to the coronation festivities, thanks to a touch of machiavellian diplo-macy by President Roosevelt, who had asked him to act as a special government attaché at the embassy. He would have his own office and the congenial task of steering American V.I.P.s through a round of social and official functions.

It did not blunt Pierpont's resentment of the forthcoming Northern Securities suit, but he was gratified, as Roosevelt had anticipated, by what seemed to be both a gesture of appeasement from the White House and an accolade for America's leading banking family.

CHAPTER TWELVE

Pierpont settled cheerfully into the London mansion with Jack and his family. In the weeks before the coronation, scarcely a night passed without some elaborate ball or reception at Stafford House, Grosvenor House, and other ducal palaces. The Morgans mounted soaring marble staircases, lined by powdered footmen in full livery, and filed past the glittering tiaras and lorgnettes to greet City bankers and some of the American dignitaries whom Jack had winnowed from his list of new arrivals.

When Pierpont was sated with the quails in aspic and the endless waltz music, he supped quietly with Alfred de Rothschild in Seamore Place or stayed with his other close friend, Lord "Algy" Gordon-Lennox, whose country house, Broughton Castle, was always open to him. He also enjoyed visiting his niece, May Burns's daughter, who had married Lewis, son of Sir William Harcourt, Rosebery's Chancellor. They owned a London house in Brook Street and a magnificent Oxfordshire property, Nuneham Park, with furnishings and paintings reflecting the connoisseur taste of Lewis Harcourt.

His sister, May Burns, now widowed, often welcomed Pierpont to her charming Jacobean mansion and estate, North Mymms Park, near Hatfield, Herts, which Walter Burns had bought in anticipation of a peaceful retirement after his many grueling years of partnership with Junius Morgan and his even more demanding successor. The house, run by a score of servants, was stuffed with the fruits of many continental forays by May Burns and her brother over the past decade. The elegant drawing room, glowing in crimson damask and velvet, was adorned with exquisite Chinese mirror paintings that Pierpont had recommended to her to buy. A splendid Algardi bust at the head of the staircase also typified his own taste, while his enthusiasm for Napoleon, dating back to his schooldays, had inspired her to start a special Napoleonic library that would grow to a thousand handsomely bound volumes. Her paintings could not rival Pierpont's collection but they included a fine Canaletto view of Greenwich, and so far he had nothing to outshine her 200-piece Meissen dinner service with its rare *Alter Gelber Loewe* pattern.

Most of all she envied his recent purchase of the celebrated Mazarin tapestry, which had once belonged to the Spanish Royal Family. He had paid the Duveens $500,000 and was well pleased until he heard rumors that they had acquired the treasure for only 300,000 francs (then about $60,000) at a Paris auction. He accused the dealers of making an exorbitant profit and bluntly asked what they had paid. "Uncle Henry" refused this information and instead offered to scrap the deal. Pierpont puffed on his cigar and then announced with a shrug that he would not go back on his word. Duveen bowed politely, quite aware that his client could neither bring himself to relinquish the prize nor admit openly that he might have overpaid.

He had one consolation when the Lord Chamberlain's office hinted that he might care to loan his Mazarin for the coronation in the Abbey. But to his lasting regret the idea was abandoned and it went on display instead at the South Kensington Museum.

The social colunmists also noted that he, Jack, and Jessie attended the last court of the season at Buckingham Palace in mid-June, and they were guests at the American embassy in Dorchester House at a banquet and musicale in honor of the king and queen. The City applauded when, together with the Rothschilds and the Barings, his firm subscribed half of a £32 million British Government issue of Consols. The flattering publicity was echoed by Maurice Low, Washington correspondent of *The Independent,* who enthused, "Great is Mr. Morgan's power, greater in some respects than that of Presidents or Kings." It was some consolation for his quite unexpected failure to secure the London Underground Railway franchise. This went instead to the banking firm of Speyer & Co., fronting for Charles T. Yerkes, the shady Chicago electric railroad operator who had often boasted, "The secret of my success in business is to buy old junk, fix it up a little, and unload it upon other fellows."

But his failure to obtain the franchise seemed only a pinprick when set against his triumphant takeover of White Star, following his acquisition of the smaller British lines, Leyland and Dominion. He offered ten times the company's gross earnings for 1900, an exceptionally good year, but Bruce Ismay's opposition to American ownership was only overcome by pressure from his shareholders and the Belfast shipbuilders, Harland & Wolff, who were anxious for an infusion of new capital to fill their order books. Ismay also found it difficult to resist the banker's high-sounding plans for a huge cartel, which would include Morgan's two New York-based companies, the American and Atlantic Transport Lines, and might soon be reinforced by a takeover of Cunard and Hamburg-American.

Ismay finally agreed to accept part payment in the stock of International Mercantile Marine. He would remain as chairman and chief executive of White Star, whose head offices would remain in London, and he stipulated that its ships would be held at the disposal of the Royal Navy "in case of emergency."

Cunard was far less receptive to Morgan's overtures. It was in better financial shape and had a bigger share of the Atlantic traffic than its main competitor. Backed by a parliamentary group bubbling with Boer War jingoism, the board remained hostile to any suggestion of hauling down the flag for an American invader. Nevertheless, Pierpont remained sanguine that, with White Star already conquered and the Hamburg line still making friendly noises, Cunard would quickly see reason. To the man who had crushed so much powerful opposition to dominate his country's steel and railroad industries, this setback could only have seemed insignificant and temporary. It would certainly not interrupt a busy social program, although the June coronation had had to be postponed when King Edward suffered an attack of appendicitis that needed surgery.

Pierpont decided to see the races at Kiel and sailed off in *Corsair* on the first of July. Maxine Elliott was prominent among his guests, and Anne tactfully decided to remain behind in London. This prevented her from meeting the kaiser but spared her the experience of his unnerving habits. The kaiser, who came aboard for luncheon from his 4,000-ton white and gold *Hohenzollern,* liked to stress the power of his good right hand with its abnormally strong grip. As he wore his rings turned inward on the fingers, Maxine and the other ladies discovered that shaking hands with him could be a bruising encounter even though they were wearing gloves. They joined politely in his hearty roars of laughter at his own coarse jokes in German, which only he and his entourage understood. It was less easy to keep one's eyes off his withered left hand while a servant was cutting his meat for him. After lunch he and Morgan took a turn on the quarter-deck and sat down in the wicker chairs for a private talk. Asked later by reporters for his view of the emperor, Pierpont said curtly, "I like him."

They had discussed more serious matters than the yacht races. Morgan and his guests went to Hamburg where they were taken on to Berlin in the imperial private railway car. Albert Ballin, head of the Hamburg-American Line, entertained them before detaching Pierpont to examine his proposed cartel. He still showed interest but would not yet commit himself and his codirectors on the terms for German participation.

In the London office, Pierpont studied disquieting reports from 23 Wall Street that U.S. Steel was feeling the effects of a Pennsylvania coal strike that had come to a head in April after several months of seething labor discontent. The 150,000 anthracite miners involved showed no sign of yielding to lockouts by coal mine owners, with the support of equally reactionary railroad bosses led by George F. Baer, president of the Morgan-controlled Philadelphia & Reading. Like other eastern lines it was being hit by low coal stocks and chaotic running schedules.

Pierpont was also troubled by another problem that had developed during his absence abroad. As agreed, Charles Schwab had duly sold his Bethlehem Steel stock, part of which Morgan's firm held as collateral for their loan. Unhappily for them, though not for Schwab, the buyer was the recently formed United States Shipbuilding Company, which had ambitious plans to merge several shipyards into a trust. It was launched with glowing prospectuses, concocted by Gates, James R. Keene, and other sharepushers, who boasted without any foundation that a huge government subsidy was in the offing. Schwab had parted with his Bethlehem holdings for $10 million of shipbuilding trust stock and an equivalent amount in bonds with voting power.

But apart from Bethlehem Steel, the trust had few assets of true worth to justify its gross overcapitalization. By July it was in the hands of a receiver who condemned "an artistic swindle." The hapless investors, many of them ruined, were not comforted by discovering that Schwab had got out from under with millions of dollars by a prior arrangement to have his stock redeemed ahead of all other creditors and debenture-holders.

Pierpont was angered by New York reports hinting at his alleged complicity, but not until his return in the fall would he reluctantly authorize a press release flatly denying that J. P. Morgan & Co. had engineered the sale of Bethlehem or had profited in any way from the doomed shipbuilding trust. He would always insist that its role had been limited to holding Bethlehem stock as collateral for the loan to Charles Schwab. This failed to stem malicious gossip. He had not only misread public opinion but was inept in first financing Schwab's purchase of Bethlehem, without anticipating the risks, and then high-handedly dictating its sale. It would soon result in U. S. Steel's loss of its most capable executive and the birth of a dangerous competitor.

Pierpont put these nagging anxieties aside to enjoy the coronation in Westminster Abbey on August 9. Dressed in full court regalia of knee breeches, silk stockings, buckled shoes, and sword, he escorted Anne to their prominent seats in the Abbey, among the crimson velvet and ermine robes of England's peers and their ladies. On their way back to Prince's Gate for a belated luncheon with the family, now joined by the Satterlees who had sailed over from New York, a photographer attempted to snatch a snapshot of the great American banker, but he stepped nimbly from his brougham and was out of range before the man could click his camera.

By the time the White Star liner *Oceanic* had docked on August 20 (Morgan's yacht had been sent on ahead), the miners' strike had spread. Several railroad chiefs called at 23 Wall Street and pleaded with Morgan to protect their interests if the price of coal soared, as seemed likely, with the approach of winter. He declined to intervene in the dispute, insisting that this was a matter for the government, but he drafted plans to import 50,000 tons of British coal in his fleet of vessels if the emergency continued. He also contributed $20,000 to an emergency depot in Grand Street on the East Side where the poor could buy basketfuls of coal at wholesale prices.

This gesture did not impress the strike committees who had good reason to infer that, without the backing of the railroads, the Pennsylvania employers might have been more receptive to their grievances. George F. Baer, whom they identified as Morgan's mouthpiece, had become violently hostile to any recognition of the miners' union, and the banker himself soon emerged as a prime target for those seeking a compromise. On September 10 he was asked by a reporter to comment, for the railroad interests, on the governor of Pennsylvania's appeal to the coal owners to show more flexibility. "Tell the miners to go back to work," he replied bluntly. "Then, and not till then, will we agree to talk about concessions." It prompted a group of Pittsburgh businessmen, already bruised by the dispute, to issue a public statement through *The New York Times* in which they called on Washington to break the deadlock by arbitration. It ended, "Is J. Pierpont Morgan greater than the people? Is he mightier than the government? We appeal from the king of the trusts to the President of the people."

Roosevelt had not been idle. After summoning Senator Hanna to Oyster Bay and tactfully suggesting that he should persuade Morgan to modify Baer's intransigence, he arranged a meeting in Washington on October 3 among the union chiefs, the coal mine owners, and the railroad presidents most directly affected. John Mitchell, president of the mine workers union, restated his members' demands but in a surprisingly moderate tone, hinting that he would not oppose arbitration by an impartial body appointed by the president. Baer pooh-poohed any such action and insisted that he and his associates did not recognize the legal existence of Mitchell's union and would never parley with such rabble. The meeting broke up in acrimony, with both sides more bitterly entrenched and Roosevelt's prestige diminished.

The president now made a further bid to enlist Pierpont Morgan, whose authority might yet prove a decisive factor in bringing Baer's bullying claque to heel. On Sunday morning, October 12, Elihu Root, Secretary of War and long-time adviser to the Morgan firm, went aboard *Corsair,* then lying off the West Thirty-fifth Street pier. Over lunch and throughout that afternoon they discussed provisional terms of reference for arbitration.

Morgan did not seem overly impressed by Root's announcement that the president had made contingency plans to send in troops to keep the mines open and prevent violence. It seemed a typical histrionic ploy by the Rough Rider, but he could no longer ignore the serious potential damage to the economy without a swift settlement. The stock market was already depressed by a glut of unsold securities, with several banks, both rural and metropolitan, under strain from a shortage of liquid cash. A continuing strike would not only cause much hardship and cripple transport but might lead to nationwide disruption.

After Root's departure, he at once summoned the two leading mine owners to the Union Club and told them that he supported the plan for a presidential commission, subject to the miners' returning to work as soon as it was appointed. They were joined next day on *Corsair* by Baer, who could not remain odd man out after the others had accepted Morgan's advice.

On Tuesday the 14th, Pierpont and Bob Bacon went to Washington by special train and joined Root for a meeting with the president in Lafayette Place, the presidential temporary home while the White House was being renovated. Roosevelt was delighted by the coal owners' acceptance of arbitration, although they would still have to approve the six-man commission. Bacon stayed on to hammer out these and other details and would be joined by Perkins after Pierpont returned to New York. John Mitchell had meantime expressed his willingness to cooperate fully and surprised an interviewer by paying tribute to Morgon's peacemaking: "I am credibly informed that he is friendly to organized labor."

The strike ended, more or less amicably, with both sides

231

accepting the commission's ruling of a 10 percent pay increase for the miners and the guarantee of equal treatment for union and nonunion labor. Roosevelt seemed to appreciate that the compromise would have been impossible without Morgan's firm action, notably in applying irresistible pressure on Baer, and acknowledged his efforts in a personal letter of thanks. But he was enough of a politician, with a second term impending, to accept popular acclaim for breaking the strike. The Democrats, finding it difficult to deingrate him, preferred to accuse Morgan of having acted solely to protect his railroads and the coal owners' profits.

He shrugged off such now-familiar abuse, but he was far more disturbed by continuing British hostility to his plans for expanding International Mercantile Marine. During the previous summer, while negotiations for the White Star takeover were an open secret, Mr. Balfour, Lord Salisbury's successor as prime minister, had faced awkward questions in the House of Commons about this impudent challenge to Britannia's right to rule the waves. He praised Morgan's long record in Anglo-American finance and attempted to reassure members that his combine would benefit the country's shipping interests. But the Cunard board still remained confident enough to reject all proposals for a merger, however tempting the terms. Morgan's cause was not helped by a press campaign jibing at his "plunder" of England's finest libraries and art collections. Penny broadsheets began to appear on the London streets offering "A License to stay on the earth, signed J. Pierpont Morgan."

His cartel was soon running into heavy seas. Overcapitalized at $170 million, it had been launched in the winter of 1902 while the purchase of the Cunard and Hamburg Lines remained in limbo. His concept of an international Atlantic fleet, aiming at improved efficiency through better management and centralized control, had seemed valid enough after the spectacular amalgamation of his country's steel and major railroads, but he now confronted forces beyond his power to control. He had simply failed to anticipate the hostility to an American-run shipping combine that two imperialistic countries, suspicious of each other's growing naval power, would feel.

The cartel's stock issue failed to attract City of London support

232

once the government, anxious to win popularity, granted Cunard two million sterling to build bigger ships for the Atlantic market. And the kaiser's personal regard for Morgan could not blind him to the unpleasant prospect of a leading German shipping line sailing under a foreign flag. The Hamburg Line could not resist imperial pressure and a fat subsidy. It abruptly withdrew from negotiations with International Mercantile Marine.

Now, instead of a virtual monopoly, the cartel's share of Atlantic traffic would be barely 40 percent and this might easily be diminished by vigorous price cutting by its state-aided competitors. The Morgan firm found itself marooned with almost $150 million worth of unsold securities. American investors, still sensitive to the shipbuilding trust bankruptcy, had shown understandable reluctance, and few of Wall Street's pundits imagined that the antitrust president would rush to bale out the stricken combine with government funds.

There would be no quick dividends for those who had been dazzled by the Morgan name and expected another U. S. Steel bonanza. The board was headed by Pierpont, with his partners, Charles Steele and Perkins, George F. Baker of the First National Bank, and Peter Widener, but he was the undisputed architect of the enterprise with a heavy responsibility for its disastrous history. Apart from the overoptimism that had led him to pay uneconomic prices for White Star and the smaller British and American lines, he had exposed a startling ignorance of foreign affairs. It soon became apparent, although not to himself, that he was at a disadvantage with bred-in-the-bone cosmopolites like Belmont, Schiff, Otto Kahn, the Warburgs, and Guggenheims.

He had traveled widely on the Continent without arriving at any true perception of its diplomatic shifts and undercurrents. His relationships with King Edward and the kaiser were essentially social, and his horizons were not broadened by European contacts largely confined to fellow bankers, yachtsmen, and art dealers. Worse, the firm's monolithic structure had made him too satisfied with his own judgments. Not until his last years of semiretirement did The Corner benefit from the arrival of Tom Lamont, whose specialist grasp of world affairs would later be supplemented by the expertise of Dwight Morrow, Edward R. Stettinius, and others.

He remained stubbornly confident of the cartel's long-term prospects. Thanks mainly to the Steel Trust revenues, his firm's turnover for 1902 was the highest in its history, with the partners sharing bumper profits, according to seniority, after he had taken his 51 percent. His Christmas was only soured by the departure of Bob Bacon, whose health had finally crumbled after the strain of the bitter coal strike. He took a year's absence on full pay. Physically he recovered quickly and rode to hounds five days a week while in England, but his wife and doctors wisely persuaded him not to resume his duties at 23 Wall Street.

George Perkins had stepped smoothly into Bacon's shoes and consolidated his position with a little flattery. Backed by his fellow partners, he persuaded "Senior" (the name by which, within the company, he was distinguished from his son), to sit for a portrait that would be hung in the board room. Pierpont, always disinclined to pose for any artist or photographer who might be tempted to stress the Nose, had at last agreed to sit for the fashionable German painter, Fedor Encke, but he could not be persuaded to give regular sittings, and after a few minutes he would become so restless that Encke finally proposed finishing the portrait from a photograph. Edward Steichen, whose studies of Rodin and of other celebrities had won acclaim, was selected.

Pierpont arrived one morning at the small studio in 291 Fifth Avenue with Encke anxiously in tow. He took off his hat, "laid a foot-long cigar on the edge of a table," and adopted the same pose as in the unfinished portrait. He looked tense and ill-at-ease. "Meeting his blazing dark eyes," Steichen would recall, "was like confronting the headlights of an express train bearing down on you." The stiff pose dictated by Encke and the subject's obvious disdain for the camera severely tested even Steichen's art. The session lasted only three minutes. Then Pierpont picked up his smoldering cigar, nodded to the photographer, and left with the totally unexpected remark, "I like you." As he stepped into the elevator he took out a wad of $100 bills, and peeled off two which he instructed Encke to pass on to "the young man."

In the darkroom Steichen was horrified by what he described afterward as "that huge, more or less deformed, sick, bulbous nose." He retouched the monstrous organ very gently on the negative and by the skillful use of shadow achieved an impressive likeness without giving offense to Morgan, who expressed a grudging approval and ordered a dozen prints.

The banker was preoccupied in 1903 with a circuit court's ruling upholding the government's decision to dissolve Northern Securities. The Northern Securities board gave notice of appeal to the Supreme Court, but confidence in railroad shares was severely shaken and infected every other section of the market. Money became tighter as the banks called in their loans, and this drove many clients to bankruptcy. Even U. S. Steel became vulnerable to heavy selling and had to suspend dividend payments, which prompted Carnegie to sneer that its common stock was "water, and the preferred, air."

Pierpont grimly set about reorganizing the Steel Trust's finances, fully convinced that the harsh price agreements he had imposed on Europe's industrialists would soon restore its profit margins. Against all the evidence, he regarded his shipping combine's abortive start as no more then a temporary setback and prophesied Roosevelt would have to change his tune over Northern Securities if he hoped to remain in the White House.

The continuing slide in U. S. Steel together with the misfortunes of International Mercantile Marine spawned fresh attacks on Morgan's personal integrity, but he was not the only victim of popular abuse. With so much mud flying about, the climate suited blackmailers like Colonel William d'Alton Mann, a con man who sported a patriarchal beard, never appeared without a silk hat, and claimed to have fought beside Custer at Gettysburg. From the early nineties he had owned and edited a scandal sheet called *Town Topics* that seethed with reports of orgies and adultery supplied by sundry waiters, chauffeurs, valets, and some of Western Union's night clerks in Newport.

By the time he died in 1920, he had amassed a comfortable fortune from the so-called loans made by Pierpont Morgan, Schwab, H. E. Huntington, Thomas Fortune Ryan, and others listed among his papers. To keep his own name and Maxine Elliott's out of *Town Topics,* Morgan had paid over various sums and also contributed $2,000 to appear in a de luxe collection of potted biographies, *Facts and Fancies,* which eulogized its subjects' wealth, achievements, and philanthropy. J. J. Astor, William C. Whitney, and James R. Keene all subscribed to it rather than face the vicious attentions of *Town Topics.*

This blackmail was only partially countered by a revival of the sycophantic ancestor hunting that attended the first bloom of the great American fortunes. Pierpont had for years encouraged the New England Historical Genealogical Society to shed more light on his origins, but he saw through an imaginative cleric, one Dr. Nicholson, who rushed hotly into print to claim that the Morgans of Llandaff could claim descent from "a dynasty founded by Gwynned Cymric, King of All Wales, 605 A.D."

Andrew Carnegie chanced to be on the passenger list when Morgan sailed for Liverpool with Anne at the end of April 1903, hoping to drum up City support for International Mercantile Marine and also escape the unpleasant aftermath of the shipbuilding trust scandal. He felt in no mood to encourage Carnegie's brash attempts to socialize. He was taking a turn on deck one morning when the little Scot caught up with him and remarked, "I made one mistake, *Pierpont,* when I sold out to you."

"What was that?"

"I should have asked you for a hundred million more than I did."

"Well," growled Morgan, "you would have got it if you had." He turned on his heel and, according to one of his party, added in a gritty stage whisper, "if only to be rid of you."

Carnegie had some satisfaction when, that July, Schwab ended an intolerable situation by formally resigning from the presidency of U. S. Steel. His successor, a former Carnegie plant supervisor, William E. Corey, was much less competent and, ironically, soon brought disrepute to the trust's fair name. He callously divorced a devoted wife to marry his mistress, a fluffy soubrette with madly expensive tastes. He spent $6,000 on flowers for the wedding breakfast at the Gotham and boasted to reporters that the honeymoon would cost a further $200,000. His wedding gift to the unblushing bride was a French château. She divorced him after a few stormy years, giving the yellow press far more column inches than Smiling Charlie's little fling in Monte Carlo.

Pierpont's prim reproof had turned out most costly for U.S. Steel. By using his voting bonds in the shipbuilding trust and skillfully stripping its few viable assets, Schwab was able to take back Bethlehem. In 1905 he formed a new corporation, which he transformed into one of the world's largest steel producers, second only to Morgan's combine. Over the next decade he would raise huge sums in investment capital to finance more plants and the latest technical processes for such profitable outlets as steel-framed skyscrapers.

Pierpont continued to minimize any real threat from upstart Bethlehem and preferred to concentrate on his self-imposed crusade to rescue Big Business from Theodore Roosevelt, about whom he had become almost paranoid as his first term neared its end. He brooded darkly on forming an alliance with Standard Oil to support Mark Hanna for nomination and confided to a friend, "I'd even vote the Democratic ticket to get that fellow out of the White House. If he had his way we'd all do business with glass pockets." Irritated by similar gibes, Rainsford, the rector of St. George's, once lost his temper and burst out angrily, "The time will come when you will get down on your knees and bless Providence for having given us Theodore Roosevelt as President."

As a lifelong compassionate radical, he foresaw the danger from extremism if the banking oligarchy failed to seek a just compromise. Still thinking back sentimentally to many amiable breakfasts on Madison Avenue, he was touchingly hopeful that Pierpont would come to accept the painful logic of the Northern Securities suit and view Roosevelt as a true fellow patriot with the nation's best interests at heart. The good doctor also deceived himself into imagining Morgan would soon retire gracefully, occupying himself with church affairs and spending his hours in the great marble library that was now taking shape on East Thirty-sixth.

Rainsford failed to understand that, far from mellowing him, his domination of the country's steel and railroads had barnacled him against all opposition. Even Anne, who had drawn closer to him during their travels, did not escape his cruel mockery when she joined various feminist enthusiasts, including Mrs. Rainsford, in founding the Colony Club. He soon pompously reminded its committee that "a woman's best and safest club is her own home."

His misunderstanding of Roosevelt's motivation was of course far more serious, but just as explicable. He had grown up in conservative New England and been educated in a strongly class-ridden Europe. Britain would often color his outlook rather more than his own country, whose growth and aspirations he tended to filter through the crisp balance sheets at 23 Wall Street. Unlike Roosevelt, whose showmanship was underpinned by a sure instinct for public opinion, he remained quite out of touch with changing social trends. Apart from trips to Washington or Boston, his landscape was largely restricted to the office, Cragston, the Episcopal conventions, *Corsair III,* and his nineteen exclusive clubs.

One of his few visits to Chicago in years was made aboard the new all-Pullman Twentieth Century on which he could wallow in a bath, have his moustache trimmed in the barber's shop, and study the latest Stock Exchange quotes. Morgan kept to himself and shrugged off excited porters who mentioned that Caruso or Melba happened to be on the train. He was more concerned to work his way through the celebrated $1.50 menu, well up to the standards of Delmonico's and Sherry's and featuring his favorite Terrapin Maryland and Maine Lobster Newburg on toasted corn bread, with a superb watermelon relish specially made in Cambridge, Massachusetts. He often repeated the trip and always rewarded attentive service with $100 tips, though he would disembark irritably without giving a cent if his needs were not fully anticipated.

As the election year approached he was disappointed to find that the Rockefellers did not share his enthusiasm for supporting Hanna, who was now an ailing man. Together with many on Wall Street they believed that "the damned cowboy" was still at heart a middle-of-the-road Republican, who would soothe the liberal hotheads without disturbing the financial status quo. They could not hope for a return to the halcyon days of McKinley when not a single indictment had been filed under the Sherman Act of 1890, but apart from Northern Securities Roosevelt had instituted relatively few suits. They were of no great significance and he once sadly admitted to a colleague that his antitrust legislation seemed "about as effective as a papal bull against a comet."

Pierpont discovered common ground with his enemy before the

238

end of 1903. The French Panama Canal Company owned a concession, due to expire the following year, to build a waterway through Colombia. However, it was now almost bankrupt, and American shareholders, disturbed by well-founded stories of fraud and corruption, began pressuring Congress to intervene. As Colombia demanded exorbitant terms for handing over its strategic strip, a Panamanian junta had seized the chance to declare an "independent" republic. The U. S. cruiser *Nashville* arrived opportunely at Colon during the rioting and stopped troops from dispersing the mobs. Washington speedily recognized the new Republic of Panama, which then signed a treaty leasing the Canal Zone to the United States in perpetuity for $10 million.

With Roosevelt's approval, J. P. Morgan and Co. was appointed in March 1904 as fiscal agent for the transfer of the $10 million to Panama and a further $40 million for the purchase of the French Panama Company's stock. This seemed excessive for a rundown concern whose main asset was a concession valid for only a few more months, but Roosevelt was feverishly anxious to settle the affair, which was already arousing hostility among Democrats at home and foreign governments, notably the British, who suspected America's policy of territorial expansion.

Morgan's role was limited to the difficult task of transferring the huge sum in gold and securities to the Banque de France without dislocating the international money market. He needed the cooperation of Lazard Frères and other leading houses to execute the transfer, which had been made on the insistence of William Nelson Cromwell, who was acting for the French shareholders and seized his chance to make a quick killing. As George Jay Gould's attorney and a specialist in bankruptcy problems, he had the ideal background. He lost no time in dissolving the old company by splitting its assets between two swiftly formed corporations, New Panama and American Panama, whose boards included several of his appointees.

The final disposition of the $40 million has always remained blurred, but Cromwell undoubtedly made a handsome profit, far exceeding that of 23 Wall Street, which only benefited by the normal commission and service fees for efforts involving several trips to Europe on Morgan's part. It did not save him from accusations in Pulitzer's *New York World* and other anti-

239

Republican papers of having taken part in a shabby and "collusive" transaction with Roosevelt and Cromwell.

As usual, Pierpont ignored the press attacks and saw no reason to justify himself to the wild men of the Populist Party. He was more exasperated by British politicians who continued for years to trumpet sympathy for Colombia. For once he found himself in the novel situation of siding with Roosevelt who would bluntly declare "I took the Canal Zone and let the Congress debate, and while the debate goes on, the Canal does also."

But it still took much heart searching to support Roosevelt's nomination for a second term. In March 1904, while the Panama Canal wrangle continued, the Supreme Court declared Northern Securities "an illegal combination or conspiracy in restraint of trade." It was expected and, though unpalatable, inflicted little financial loss on Morgan, Standard Oil, and the others whose stock was sold on a pro-rata basis. Moreover, instead of the expected cavalry charge from Washington, Wall Street's listening posts picked up a dovelike cooing that scarcely rustled a strip of ticker tape. Nomination day was looming, and Attorney General Knox assured *The New York Times* that there would be no "running amuck" on corporation control. It was enough to release over $2 million for the presidential campaign.

Already conscious of Gary's strong pro-Roosevelt stance, Pierpont was further influenced by Bob Bacon, who announced his intention to enter government service, in any capacity, if his old Harvard hero was reelected. The firm contributed $150,000, topping Standard Oil's $100,000 but short of George Jay Gould's munificent half-million. Harriman, nursing a fantasy of entering the Senate, had parted with $250,000. Roosevelt stoutly denied all knowledge of these subsidies from "the malefactors of great wealth," but his claim seems no more credible than Harriman's subsequent assertion that the candidate had "practically gone down on his knees" to him for funds.

Roosevelt was unanimously nominated at the Republican Convention in Chicago and won a landslide victory over Judge Alton B. Parker in November 1904. Meantime, his Bureau of Corporations, set up to investigate interstate trusts, had remained so inert that Pulitzer's *New York World* echoed a widespread suspicion that the cartel barons had bought themselves protection by "pouring money into the campaign chest."

Pierpont remained unruffled throughout that summer. He spent it cruising with guests in *Corsair*. During these months he also settled last-minute plans for his library with McKim and asked his advice about the house he had bought for Jack and his family on the corner of Madison Avenue and Thirty-seventh. It would be a severe wrench for his son to leave London, but the City office had long become secondary to 23 Wall, particularly after the launching of U. S. Steel. More Anglicized than the tweediest of Henry James's expatriates, Jack would miss the grouse shooting and country houseparties, but he was needed in New York to fill part of the gap left by Bacon's departure. He would also act as his father's stand-in at some meetings, with Charles Steele and Perkins providing the initiative and business flair he had so far failed to demonstrate. And it was none too soon to arrange for the education of his two boys, who would naturally be sent to Groton and Harvard.

At Bar Harbor, Pierpont received his friends Bishops Lawrence and Doane to discuss arrangements for the Archbishop of Canterbury's forthcoming visit to the Triennial Convention in Boston. He mapped out the full itinerary for a program of entertainment lasting several weeks, generously agreeing to provide special trains and bear most of the other expenses. He hoped to show the visitors his treasury of rare Bibles and hymnals, as well as one of his latest finds, a beautiful gold-embroidered vestment presented by Pope Nicholas IV to the Cathedral of Ascoli. Unfortunately, the cope, which he had bought from a dealer for a reported $15,000, was back in Ascoli by the time the archbishop and his entourage arrived in America.

Morgan had placed it on exhibition at the South Kensington Museum, but the Italian Embassy in London quickly confirmed that it had been stolen two years earlier while the cathedral was undergoing repairs. Further enquiries led to the arrest of the thief. He confessed, implicating five priests and a photographer who hanged himself in his cell while awaiting trial. A national subscription was started in Italy to reimburse Morgan. But he waived all offers of payment and arranged for the relic to be restored to its honored place in the cathedral.

He took charge of the Archbishop of Canterbury's party some weeks before the opening of the Convention in early October. He entertained them aboard *Corsair* and then brought them up to

Cragston where the archbishop, Randall Davidson, admired his pedigreed cattle and blue-ribbon collies. Special trains carried them to Niagara Falls, Montreal, and Quebec, then back for a week's break at Cragston, with a special parade by the West Point cadets. At a White House banquet in their honor Morgan ceremoniously presented the distinguished visitors to President Roosevelt. Another special transported them to Boston for the Triennial, preceded by a mammoth reception that he had organized for the eighty American bishops and four hundred other delegates. Throughout the Convention the Randall Davidsons stayed at an imposing house he had rented, with Louis Sherry catering to all their temporal needs.

Bidding his host a grateful farewell, the Primate had smilingly addressed him as Pierpontifex Maximus. The flattering witticism may have been gently ironic, but it remained a tribute to a *grand seigneur* whose generosity and banking eminence had recently won him the accolade of president of the Metropolitan Museum of Art. He held the office for the rest of his life and during that period the museum enjoyed unprecedented solvency and expansion. He was remarkably open-handed but the trustees would be required, like his own employees, to submit to his imperial thumb.

Part Three

THE STUBBLE

CHAPTER THIRTEEN

As soon as he became its president, Pierpont bought more treasures on behalf of the Metropolitan while continuing to make good its annual deficit with the help of Frick, George F. Baker, and Edward Harkness, whom he soon enrolled as trustees. He relied greatly on the personable secretary, Robert de Forest, one-time attorney to the Central Railroad of New Jersey. Early in 1905 one of his first decisions, backed by de Forest, was to appoint Sir Purdon Clarke, the distinguished head of the South Kensington Museum, as director, although many thought that Edward Robinson of the Boston Museum of Fine Arts should have been chosen rather than "a foreigner." London art circles chuckled over the report that Purdon's deputy had first heard the news on returning from a vacation. Before leaving on his holiday he had put in a bid for some Chinese pieces at a Paris auction.

"What happened to the porcelain?" he asked his assistant.

"J. P. Morgan bought them."

"And the tapestries?"

"Mr. Morgan got them."

"Good God, I must talk to Sir Purdon!"

"Sorry, Sir, Mr. Morgan bought him also."

Within a few months Clarke persuaded Pierpont to recruit Roger Fry, a snobbish English esthete, painter, and art critic, who had grown impatient waiting for the National Gallery in London to appoint him director. After Morgan had bribed him with a contribution of £1,000 to the *Burlington Magazine* he edited, Fry condescended to act as part-time curator of paintings. This allowed him to spend several months of the year in Europe buying first-class paintings for the museum.

For years Fry had haughtily represented Altman, Frick, H. E. Huntington, and other American magnates at the London sales, but he soon learned that J. P. Morgan was far less easy to patronize. After their very first meeting he reported to his wife, Helen, "He is most repulsively ugly, with a great strawberry nose. . . . The man is so swollen with pride and a sense of his own power that it never occurs to him that other people have any rights."

Influenced by her anxiety for him to keep his well-paid and not too arduous post, he somehow managed a show of politeness whenever he met Morgan on museum affairs. He had started off well enough by weeding out much mediocre stuff and soon purchased several da Vinci drawings and paintings by Goya and Murillo at lower prices than the owners might have secured in the open market. But the trustees still chided him for spending a large sum on having a Rubens cleaned, and they turned even sourer after he paid $20,000 for a Renoir, then as unfashionable as the other French Impressionists whose praises he continuously sang.

He resented Morgan's high-handed practice of buying pictures for the museum without troubling to consult him, but most of all despised Clarke and Robert de Forest, who he felt toadied to the great banker in return for his large checks and his gifts of paintings, porcelains, and tapestries. Except for a small number of Americans like Mark Twain with whom he enjoyed dining, he had no use at all for a society which, he assured his father, was "drifting back to sheer barbarism. . . . The trouble is that no one really *knows* anything or has any true standard."

Accustomed to the more traditional and less impatient attitudes toward art found in a Europe that possessed art in abundance, Fry could not understand that self-made business magnates like Frick and Altman would naturally retain their suspiciousness and their taste for haggling. It was easy enough to ridicule Frick, who had suffered agonies on learning that his Velasquez portrait of Philip IV, bought for $400,000, had been commissioned from the artist for the equivalent of $600. According to Berenson, his self-torment only ended when he had figured out that, if that modest sum had been invested at 6 percent compound interest from 1645 onward, the masterpiece would have cost him nothing! Frick was undoubtedly tight-fisted, but no philistine could have assembled the treasures that he did in the two decades before his death in 1919. The astonishing Frick Collection in New York is a monument to good, if traditional, taste.

Fry also did Pierpont Morgan less than justice in sneering at his "crude historical imagination . . . the only flaw in his otherwise perfect insensibility toward art." The banker had obvious faults. He was never known to relieve any living painter or writer from need. His acquisitions, on which he spent altogether over half his enormous fortune, were confined to artifacts sanctified by age and the academic consensus of "safe" experts. At times he rampaged like a bull elephant in his lust for Old Masters, rare manuscripts, snuffboxes, coins, and miniatures. He preferred to snap up whole collections ready-made, justifying himself by remarking testily, "What's the use of bothering about one little piece when I might get them all?" He instructed his London agent to buy an entire library of seven hundred manuscripts simply to secure a *Roman de la Rose* from the fourteenth century and some *Books of Hours* he had long coveted.

He could be criticized for greed and a brutal insensitivity to the feelings of the dealers who represented him or to rivals who dared to bid against him, but he did not merit Dos Passos's curt verdict: "His collectors bought anything that was expensive or rare or had the glint of empire on it. He had it brought to him and stared hard at it with his magpie's eyes. Then it was put in a glass case." That may have been true of his last years when the almost megalomaniac trust to dominate the financial scene was paralleled by the bullying of art dealers and museum authorities, including his fellow trustees at the Metropolitan, but it still ignored his many generous gifts and the absence of the sort of vulgar ostentation that motivated a number of his parvenu contemporaries who found some difficulty in not confusing Canaletto with canelloni.

His passion for art was no sudden fever induced by overnight riches. It began almost inconspicuously and developed, together with improving taste and discrimination, from the late eighties, when he had bought a few dull pictures by French Salon painters, until he died. Junius's death had brought him his first Old Mas-ters together with the means for adding to them. Throughout the nineties he steadily built up a small but well-chosen collection of pictures and antiquities, while continuing to spend rather more on books and autographed letters. He paid £8,000 for a Gutenberg Bible and £5,000 for the only small fragment of *Paradise Lost* still extant. On his behalf Sotheby's of London successfully bid £200,000, then a record sum, for Richard Bennett's magnificent library, which included William Morris first editions and over thirty rare Caxtons.

From the turn of the century on, his expenditure soared without overtaxing his multiplying revenues from railroads, bond sales, U. S. Steel, and the numerous other trusts organized by him. Not long after buying the Mazarin tapestry he interrupted his London Coronation visit to slip over to Paris where he acquired the Mannheim collection of rare objets d'art. It was shipped over to England and loaned for exhibition to the South Kensington Museum.

Before sailing for England he had seen and envied the magnificent James A. Garland collection of Oriental ceramics on display at the Metropolitan Museum. After Garland's sudden death later that year, the Duveens bought the collection from the estate for half a million dollars and planned to split it among British connoisseurs. But Uncle Henry then decided to give Pierpont first refusal for 15 percent above the half-million, hinting broadly that the firm could make a bigger profit from W. H. Lever (later, Lord Leverhulme), the soap magnate, who had shown strong interest. Morgan at once closed the deal and added other pieces of the period, amounting in all to 1,500 items, which he lent to the Metropolitan.

He was gratified by the splendid exhibition, mounted at his expense, but became irritated by sneers from the art world that he was showing a blind faith in the Duveens, whose rivals denied that old Joseph was the only worthwhile expert on Chinese porcelain. Pierpont thought it time to make a little experiment. On his next visit to London he summoned Joseph Duveen to Prince's Gate, where he had laid out five Oriental vases in the drawing room. "Only three of them are genuine," he said. "Now tell me which they are." The dealer examined them minutely for a few minutes before smashing the two fakes with his cane.

After that episode and the firm's generosity over the Garland deal, the Duveens ranked even higher in his esteem. They would enjoy a major share in his vastly increased outlay following his election to the presidency of the Metropolitan. But they had to wait until after his death before acquiring some of the much-prized Fragonard panels he had bought from Agnew's in 1905. The superb murals, entitled *Le Roman d'Amour et de la Jeunesse,* had been commissioned by Madame du Barry but capriciously rejected by her. To escape the Terror, Fragonard had fled to Grasse where he gave the paintings to a friend. A century later the owner's grandson sold them to Agnew's. Pierpont paid the asking price of $325,000 and planned to place them in a special gallery in the house he had bought next door to 13 Prince's Gate for his expanding art collection. Meantime he lent the Fragonards to London's Guildhall for an exhibition.

His relations with Henry Duveen remained most cordial but were far less so toward Joseph's son, who succeeded his father as a partner. He was astute, aggressive, and less tactful than his uncle in dealing with clients like the prickly banker. He once assembled thirty miniatures, only a few of the highest quality, and brashly offered them to Morgan, quoting for the whole collection. Making up his mind with a tantalizing slowness, the banker culled the best half dozen. He then divided the price by thirty, multiplied it by six, and agreed to buy his selected items at that figure. Young Duveen flushed angrily but had to accept. His uncle much enjoyed his discomfiture and jeered, "You're only a boy, Joe. It takes a man to deal with him."

Joseph would often argue with Uncle Henry over the firm's preferential treatment of Morgan, who acquired pictures on what was virtually long-term approval by withholding payment until his next financial year if he had exceeded his average million-dollar allocation for the Duveens. Although they were often heavily overdrawn and occasionally almost bankrupted themselves with interest charges, while Pierpont Morgan might be holding two million dollars' worth of unpaid-for pictures, Uncle Henry warned Joseph, "Never, never ask him for money." It was shrewd advice. Apart from ensuring Morgan's continued goodwill and patronage, it did the Duveens's prestige no harm to boast of a credit account at 23 Wall Street.

Young Joseph conspicuously lacked his uncle's warmth and charm. He was far too slick and he gave himself such airs that Pierpont delighted in treating him like an uppity office boy. It left a scar. Years later, when he had become Lord Duveen of Millbank and rode arrogantly in tandem with Berenson across the art world, he engaged as a secretary one H. W. Morgan so that he could relish the sadistic pleasure of pressing a button and barking his orders at him.

Reports of Pierpont's enormous budget of course attracted swarms of smooth-talking dealers. One of them offered him a portrait of a young maid of honor and suggested that it would make a suitable companion to Velasquez's *The Infanta Maria Teresa,* which already graced a wall at Prince's Gate. He asked the current market price for what he implied was a Velasquez. Pierpont delayed his decision until various experts had examined the painting. They confirmed that it was almost certainly the work of some gifted contemporary of the Spanish master. Informed of their verdict, the dealer started angrily to remove the painting but Pierpont stopped him. According to Satterlee, he had become attached to the portrait and decided to retain it, "no matter who was the artist." The painting duly took its place beside the authentic Velasquez after the vendor, now much deflated, agreed to accept a sharp reduction in his first price. Another London dealer, knowing his weakness for flattery, was more successful. He offered him a painting said to be "adapted" from a Ghirlandaio, murmuring, "All the critics say this is not a Raphael, but *you* know it is." Morgan pondered then grunted, "I'll take it."

The bulk of his buying was from reputable sources like Agnew's, Duveen, and Jacques Seligman of Paris, who sold him magnificent Rouen faience and for years advised him on antiquities and manuscripts. He also had much faith in George S. Hellman, who once submitted Vermeer's *A Lady Writing* to him. Morgan liked the charming small canvas but thought the price of $100,000 preposterous for an artist whose name was obviously quite unknown to him. Hellman calmly delivered a short lecture on the Little Master from Delft, assuring him that the best judges valued his work far above that of many better-known artists. Morgan cut him short to cover his own embarrassment. "I'll have it," he said gruffly.

So many touts plagued him that he made it a rule never to receive a dealer except by appointment. On one occasion, however, he was sitting down to a solitary dinner in Prince's Gate when his butler whispered that "an individual" had called with a brown paper parcel and stubbornly refused to leave though threatened with the constabulary. The banker kept him waiting for a good hour and then fidgeted while the fellow carefully unpacked a piece of Sèvres. His price was very modest for an item that Morgan's agents had vainly hunted for months to complete an exquisite set that stood on the mantelpiece in his library. Writing out the check, he asked the visitor, "What made you bring this to me?"

"Well, sir, I read in the newspaper that you liked pottery, and this seemed rather good."

The episode was bettered some months later when a shabby old woman arrived at the back door with a china object in her shopping basket. The butler fingered it with much distaste and informed his master that, since it was only a "rubbishy" figurine of a sailor with ribbons down his back, he had sent her packing. Morgan jumped to his feet, rushed out, and caught up with the bewildered woman. He sat her down comfortably while he studied the figure, which was still in good condition and the exact companion of another in his possession. She explained in a thick Welsh accent that a lady of title, whom she had served as a parlormaid, had bequeathed a pair of porcelain sailors to her. Years before she had sold one of them to a peddler but now, since she was almost destitute, she hoped the remaining piece might be worth a sovereign or two. Morgan not only handed over a tidy sum for the piece but arranged through his London solicitors to find her a pleasant cottage in Wales with a modest pension to keep her from want.

He sometimes surprised bibliophiles and collectors with a courtesy recalling Old Boston, but he could be ruthless when anyone rashly abused his code of business ethics. While in Paris early in the spring of 1905 he decided to buy three ancient tapestries on behalf of the Metropolitan, but had gracefully withdrawn when the Louvre, to which he had recently presented some rare Byzantine enamels, asked for an option. When this had expired the directors requested a further three weeks' grace, to which he readily agreed. They then demanded another week, backed by a shrill newspaper campaign insisting that France should on no account sacrifice her heritage. After the museum announced that the price was still too high for its budget, Morgan at once bought the three tapestries. He would not yield when the director, to soothe his critics, offered to buy back one of the tapestries. "Too late," Morgan said stiffly.

That visit had been so soured by his brush with the Louvre that although he usually treated servants with consideration, he lost his temper while waiting impatiently for a carriage that had been hired to take him around Paris. He paced the balcony of his suite at the Hotel Bristol, becoming angrier by the minute until it drew up at last. Then he rushed downstairs, picked up a pineapple from a basket in the restaurant, and hurled it with all his force, dislodging the coachman's hat.

He had recovered his spirits when he joined the *Corsair* in Monte Carlo toward the end of March for a fortnight's relaxed cruising. At Catania a telegram was handed to him from Salvatore Cortesi, the Associated Press correspondent in Rome, inviting him to sit for a photograph in profile for a gold medal that the grateful Italian Government had decided to strike in his honor for returning the Ascoli Cope. He had ignored the request but changed his mind on arriving in Rome. Cortesi nervously presented himself at the large $500-a-day corner suite at the Grand Hotel. He found the banker sprawled on a sofa playing solitaire while Chum, his pet pekingese, snapped suspiciously. Morgan asked a few questions, then agreed with a grunt to visit a photographer's studio in the Via Nazionale.

In view of his notorious suspicion of journalists, the acquaintance ripened surprisingly. Cortesi was bilingual and quiet mannered. He could obviously be helpful to Morgan, who did not speak Italian and wanted protection from the dealers and the hard-up noblemen who converged on the hotel every morning. He enjoyed dining informally at small *trattorie* with Cortesi and his wife, a young Boston woman, and welcomed their services as

252

guides to the Eternal City, whose splendors he now saw as an anonymous and relaxed visitor instead of the world-famed financier, with a pack of reporters always at his heels. Cortesi was flattered but not overawed. One day, after Morgan had walked out of a shop on the Corso because the owner refused to take ten dollars less than his asking price for a coral necklace, he said teasingly, "Why, you are no richer than I am! You haggle over ten bucks just as I do over one!" Pierpont laughed but could not be persuaded to go back and pay a cent above his offer.

The young journalist earned his gratitude by arranging an audience with Pope Pius X in April 1905. This had first to be approved by Merry del Val, the Vatican's Secretary of State, who kept them waiting in an anteroom with a vaulted ceiling and magnificent Pinturicchio frescoes, but graciously sent out a message of apology for the delay. "Tell the Cardinal not to worry," Morgan said quietly. "I am happy here and only wish I could have a bed so that I could lie on my back for hours and just look at this ceiling."

The papal audience had opened rather formally, but it thawed when Cortesi mentioned that the visitor would shortly be celebrating his sixty-eighth birthday in Rome. The Pontiff congratulated him and remarked with a twinkling smile that he himself was exactly two years older. He then questioned Pierpont about the religious books and paintings that, he understood, would adorn his great library in New York. A week later, when Cortesi had occasion to pay another call at the Vatican, His Holiness thanked him for contributing to such a pleasant meeting and added wryly "What a pity I did not think of asking Mr. Morgan to give us some advice about our finances!"

Leopold II of Belgium warmly echoed that sentiment when he met the banker for an urgent talk that July. For years Morgan had recommended the Congo's investment potential to entrepreneurs like the Guggenheims, but he now opposed the king's plan to seize China's railroads as a shortcut that would permit him to practice the wholesale exploitation he had so ruthlessly pursued in Africa. The stumbling block was the American China Development Co. which held the franchise to build a railroad from Canton to Hankow. It happened to be dominated by Standard Oil and J. P. Morgan.

Leopold bought heavily into the company but, finding it difficult to secure a majority, formed a consortium with some French financiers. All their efforts to infiltrate were countered by 23 Wall, which kept on paying irresistibly high prices to keep stock control. Pierpont's reasoning was sound. With only a few miles of the Canton-Hankow line completed after so many years, Peking threatened to cancel the concession and had simultaneously launched a violent campaign against all "foreign devils," starting with a boycott of American goods. Morgan decided that it would be in the best interests of the United States—and his own firm— to sell the company to the Peking authorities before the situation deteriorated.

As this move would rob Leopold of his foothold, he invited his long-time adviser to discuss some compromise. The royal yacht docked unobtrusively at Dover, where Morgan went on board for luncheon after traveling down from London. They met rather like two fairy-tale ogres incongruously playing with toy trains. Morgan, though massive and grizzled, seemed almost dwarfed by the king, now an obscenely gross 300 pounds, his evil face hidden by a grotesque Santa Claus beard while he detailed persuasive arguments for enslaving China to their mutual benefit.

They parted amiably, but both knew that their relationship was over. Morgan had refused to reconsider selling the American Development Co. As Leopold, even with his French allies, still commanded less than one-third of the voting stock, he appealed desperately to Senator Henry Cabot Lodge, then visiting Europe, to try and enlist congressional support for keeping the company out of Peking's hands. For a while Roosevelt seemed fairly sympathetic, imagining that public opinion would support him in defending American "commerce and prestige" against the huge investment capital still pouring into China from Britain, Germany, and France. Pierpont took the opposite view. Shortly after returning from Europe, he sailed in *Corsair* to Oyster Bay and lunched with the president at Sagamore Hill. He argued firmly that it would be a costly and unacceptable risk to retain the railroad concession. He was still confident of securing a most generous indemnity but stressed that, in Peking's present mood, further delay might be fatal.

He again visited Roosevelt a fortnight later and announced that the Chinese had agreed to pay $6.75 million, plus five times the nominal value of the shares. J. P. Morgan & Co. cleared $3 million on the transaction, which also brought a handsome profit to the other stockholders, including the defeated Franco-Belgian consortium. Leopold was not consoled by these few crumbs or by the president's bland press announcement: "Mr. Morgan has consulted with the administration and shown every desire to do what American interests in the Orient demanded."*

Settling the future of the Hankow railroad was far simpler than bringing the Russo-Japanese War to an end, but Roosevelt's diplomacy, which won him the Nobel Peace Prize, proved successful. It even gained support from Republicans who had suffered from his antitrust policies. Jacob Schiff had never quite forgotten the atrocity stories relating to the czar's pogroms that he had heard as a child. He initiated huge loans to the Japanese in association with J. P. Morgan, Harriman, and the First National Bank. He would later be invited to Tokyo to receive the well-named Order of the Sacred Treasure from the Mikado himself.

Harriman was rather less fortunate. Now that Morgan was out of China, he saw himself as the financial overlord of the Far East. No doubt the State Department would back his plan to run the South Manchurian Railway with the full approval of the Japanese. After that he intended to organize a monopoly of Pacific merchant shipping, making full use of the Panama Canal.

Pierpont had little confidence that the victorious Japanese would share the spoils of war with Harriman or any other Western financiers except on their own terms. He preferred to play only a social role in the peace conference over which Roosevelt presided at Portsmouth, New Hampshire. He found it specially congenial to welcome Bob Bacon, newly appointed Assistant Secretary to Elihu Root, aboard *Corsair*. With Baron Rosen, the Russian Ambassador, they sailed up to West Point for luncheon and a full-dress review.

---

*Within a few months the unveiling of Leopold's horrific atrocities in the Congo ignited world-wide indignation. A Memorial sent to Secretary of State Root was signed by Mark Twain, by clergy of all denominations, and even by J. P. Morgan, who had at last seen the light. Roosevelt then agreed to cooperate with Britain in condemning the brutal régime. It led to Belgium formally annexing the Congo Free State and inaugurating long-overdue reforms.

Morgan's temporary accord with the president did not extend beyond foreign affairs. He and others who had contributed to the campaign fund had shifted uncomfortably while Roosevelt harangued the Union League Club in Philadelphia: "The great development of industrialism means that there must be an increase in the supervision exercised by the Government over business enterprise. . . . Neither this people nor any other free people will permanently tolerate the use of the vast power conferred by vast wealth." Even his long-time enemy William Jennings Bryan had welcomed his pledge to curb the railroads' sovereignty over rates and rebates.

Wall Street ruefully recalled that it had failed to support J. P. Morgan's threat to vote the Democratic ticket rather than see Roosevelt back in the White House. Now even the staunchest Republicans were openly apprehensive or resentful. Chauncey Depew was not appointed ambassador to France, as he had expected. Harriman, who had tactlessly hinted that he had the White House and even the Supreme Court in his pocket, paid heavily for his lack of discretion. Few listened to him with any sympathy after the Legislative Investigating Committee opened its hearings in September 1905.

For the next three months the committee inflicted far more damage on the trusts than Roosevelt had by his dissolution of Northern Securities. Charles Evans Hughes, the committee's chief counsel, focused on the affairs of the three largest insurance companies, Equitable, Mutual, and New York Life, alleging that they had improperly used their funds to finance the overcapitalized promotions of Standard Oil, Harriman, J. P. Morgan & Co., and Kuhn, Loeb. He insisted that the insurance chiefs had tempted long-term investors with high-interest yields and had an advantage over the national banks who were bound by federal laws to keep at least 25 percent of their deposits in cash. Benefiting from very slack auditing, they had funneled the bulk of their assets into speculative trusts and inflated bonds.

Pierpont was not called to testify, but George W. Perkins had to admit that New York Life, of which he had remained a vice-president while serving as a partner at 23 Wall, had bought almost $40 million in securities from J. P. Morgan & Co. The firm had also benefited handsomely from the sale of bonds to Equita-

256

ble Life. These operations were legal, but Perkins had not impressed the committee by coolly fending off all insinuations of sharp practice and mismanagement. Harriman cut a still worse figure on the stand. He ignored the anxious warnings of his good friend, Otto Kahn, and answered counsel's questions with an impatience bordering on contempt. Hughes prodded him mercilessly, revealing that Equitable Life had loaned Kuhn, Loeb millions of dollars, which soon found their way into Union Pacific stock.

The committee's report disclosed that "enormous sums had been expended in a surreptitious manner" by Equitable Life, in particular, whose "legal expenses" included contributions to political party funds, both national and state, and the highly paid services of Washington lobbyists. These revelations shocked the public but, paradoxically, had no effect upon the good name of the president whose campaign had so obviously benefited from this generosity. He was even given credit for courageously exposing the insurance scandals and the complicity of highly placed Republicans.

Harriman remained the chief scapegoat. He was savagely attacked by the press, the Democrats, and the church, while Roosevelt referred to him as "an undesirable citizen." Within a few months his holdings were being investigated by the Interstate Commerce Commission, which had to admit that his railroads were properly managed and gave no grounds for criminal prosecution. However, they condemned his freewheeling use of Union Pacific funds as "not in the public interest." He reacted by implying that his patriotism had been questioned by an ungrateful politician who had taken his cash and then betrayed him. "I would hate to tell you whom I think you ought to go to for an explanation of all this," he angrily reminded reporters after the new Hepburn Act fixing railroad rates hit Union Pacific shares.

Pierpont Morgan did not of course grant any interviews, but he considered it prudent for Perkins to give up his vice-presidency of New York Life. He thought the insurance probe merely distasteful and unlikely to have the damaging results that some of his fellow bankers feared. His optimism was justified when the committee's very critical findings fizzled into the dismissal of a selected few corrupt officers and an overhaul of loose investment procedures such as sharing in syndicates. The expected large-scale purge failed to materialize, but policyholders were at least assured that company assets would be more closely supervised in future. It did not scare off smooth operators like Thomas Fortune Ryan, who had made his fortune from public utilities and the American Tobacco monopoly. He became a dominant figure on the Equitable Life board by heavy buying and by campaigning for a series of high-sounding, if rather vague, reforms. He also won Morgan's support by pledging himself to oppose any counter-moves by Harriman, who still had considerable holdings of stock.

Wall Street recovered its balance. Thanks to heavy grain and cotton surpluses, shady promoters and sharepushers once again tempted greedy investors with unrealistic dividends. Jacob Schiff won little response from the New York Chamber of Commerce when he gloomily forecast a disastrous slump unless members practiced self-discipline. Morgan took the same view, but he limited himself to warning clients that the market could not absorb too many "undigested" securities. He naturally recommended selective buying of "safe" stocks like his railroads and U. S. Steel but still found it impossible to arouse International Mercantile Marine from its long coma.

During the last few months of 1905 Morgan was concerned with the transfer of thousands of books and manuscripts to his new library, now completed after almost six years and the expenditure of several million dollars. Crates were removed from the basement of his house, the warehouse on East Forty-second Street, and a vault in the firm's offices. He also called in various collections lent to colleges or museums and arranged for dealers to release valuable first editions and other treasures that he had left in their custody until Charles McKim's marble pavilion could be unveiled.

A chimney caught alight at 219 Madison Avenue just after Christmas, 1905. It was quickly put out but Pierpont could congratulate himself on having made his library fully fireproof. He seemed oblivious to the havoc that some bomber or berserk axman might cause before being overpowered by the security patrols. For years he had shrugged off cranky death threats, but recent stories acclaiming McKim's creation as "one of the Seven Wonders of the New World" were an obvious provocation to those who found *Das Kapital* more rewarding than the Gutenberg Bible on vellum or a costly fragment from Spenser's *Faerie Queene*.

Morgan could enter the marble palace by a stone walk that went from his house across a green lawn. Massive bronze doors imported from Italy opened into the lofty, vaulted entrance hall gracefully sectioned by greenish Cipolino columns. The vast octagonal skylight was fringed by paintings of the Muses. The library itself was divided between an East and West Room. The former was of "double-cube" design and was elegantly furnished in the Florentine style and adorned with magnificent statuary. Its lofty walls surmounted by medallion portraits were tiered by Circassian walnut shelves glowing with volumes bound in gold, enamel, and ivory. Several of them were gem encrusted. Lapis lazuli columns framed the monumental fireplace.

The West or Red Room was the banker's special retreat; it served as a study and on occasion a salon where he received friends, business associates, and a few privileged art dealers or bibliophiles. Its walls of crimson damask from the Chigi Palace in Rome, embellished by that aristocratic family's crest, set off masterpieces from the hands of Raphael, Perugino, and Botticelli. Among the bookshelves stood a bust by Michelangelo and a rock crystal bowl mounted for Queen Christina. The gilded sixteenth century ceiling from a cardinal's palace in Lucca was complemented by a fireplace of carved marble surmounted by his father's portrait removed from the house next door.

Here he could lounge in a red plush armchair, smoking or playing solitaire at his folding table. Beyond the door was the huge vault with its priceless cache of treasures, including a five-page letter in Washington's hand, four Shakespeare Folios, and a seventy-two-page volume of Leonardo's notebooks. At his large square-topped desk he faced a Fra Filippo Lippi altarpiece, with a Pinturicchio Madonna and Child behind him. He could turn to gaze on the bejeweled Ashburnham Bible in its crystal showcase; a bronze statuette of Eros unearthed near Pompeii; and a special favorite of his, a ruby-colored vase of the K'ang Hsi period.

Separating the two magnificent chambers was a small room reserved for the librarian whom he had appointed to catalogue his books and manuscripts. She was Belle de Costa Greene, recommended to him by the nephew who had first stimulated his interest in collecting books. She was a young woman from Virginia who had endured years of genteel poverty since her parents' separation. Her mother had given music lessons to support her children, but they had been denied a college education. Belle had worked in the library at Princeton and quickly made her mark cataloguing its rare books. Junius Spencer Morgan, himself a Princeton man, had made her acquaintance and arranged a meeting with his uncle. Then barely twenty-one, she was an attractive, witty girl who soon impressed Pierpont with her orderly mind and capacity for work.

By the summer of 1906, after only a few months on the job, she was supervising a staff of assistants, most of them older than herself. Their efficiency enabled Pierpont to organize in 1907 the first of his series of exquisite catalogues, starting with his paintings. They were lavishly bound and restricted to close friends and distinguished savants after the first two copies had been sent *ex officio* to the president of the United States and the king of England. This was entirely dictated by his sense of protocol. Not even his harshest critics would ever accuse him of playing the courtier.

In the spring of 1906 he paid his usual visit to London, leaving Jack behind to act as his deputy. The young Morgans had settled into their new house on the corner of Thirty-seventh Street and Madison Avenue, where Jack had speedily converted a stable into a squash court. Before breakfast he played a strenuous game with a professional from the Racquet Club. He also introduced English afternoon tea at the office. Otherwise, he made little impact. One or two of his colleagues found his Anglo-Harvard superiority a touch irritating, but he was always urbane and easygoing until someone offended his dignity or dared to murmur criticism of his father.

In May, Pierpont had another audience with the pope and was also received by King Victor Emmanuel. In Rome, Paris, and Venice he spent liberally on paintings, books, and objets d'art that were shipped to the two houses in Prince's Gate. He heard in London that Velasquez's *Venus with a Mirror* was for sale and quickly made an offer, but this caused such an uproar that a public subscription was started to keep it in England. He promptly withdrew his offer and contributed generously to the fund. The National Gallery acquired the painting.

In addition to the superb Fragonard panels, Morgan's first catalogue included three Rembrandts, several Gainsboroughs, Romneys, Hoppners, the Velasquez *Infanta,* a Hogarth, and Constable's *The White Horse.* In the drawing room at Prince's Gate he had several cabinets with trays containing scores of exquisite miniatures, so rare and beautiful that he commissioned his expert friend Dr. George C. Williamson to compile a separate catalogue for them.

That summer he stayed at Dover House with the Satterlees and drove to Old Broad Street most days for business meetings. In mid-July he received King Edward, who had expressed a wish to see the paintings and miniatures at Prince's Gate. During the tour of inspection the King pointed jovially to various paintings that he had seen "elsewhere" before they were netted by his host. He admired the magnificent collection but thought the full-length Lawrence portrait of Nellie Farren (Countess of Derby) seemed rather out of place in a low-ceilinged room. "Why on earth do you hang it there?" he asked. Pierpont studied the picture from several angles and replied firmly, "Because I like it there, sir."

His sensitivity to any criticism, expressed or implied, resulted in his giving up breeding altogether when his collies failed to win all the blue ribbons at kennel club shows, as they had done so regularly in the past. He was particularly incensed to hear that his estate manager at Cragston had allowed himself to be outbid for a pedigreed dog by a Jewish attorney, Samuel Untermyer, whose name meant nothing to him at the time.

During the winter of 1906–7 he suffered a succession of colds and became very short-tempered after his acne rosacea failed to respond to a series of wax treatments in Europe. If anything, the nose was still more hideously inflamed. He spent fewer hours at the office and often summoned his partners to the Red Room for business consultations. He cut down on his social engagements but did attend a dinner at the Gridiron Club in Washington, where the president was scheduled to announce his policy on banking, future trust controls, and possibly further curbs on railroad charges.

Roosevelt was at his most aggressive on that evening of January 27. He started off by attacking the previous speaker, Senator Joseph Foraker of Ohio, whose impartiality on various senate committees had become suspect through his rumored support of Standard Oil. Blazing with anger, he went on to indict the money barons for blocking his reasonable program of reforms. Suddenly he pointed at Henry H. Rogers of Standard Oil, who was sitting beside Pierpont Morgan, and shouted, "If you don't let us do these things, those who come after us will rise and bring you to ruin." In the shocked silence that followed Morgan did not betray the slightest emotion, but Rogers, who felt, no doubt correctly, that he had been singled out as the Rockefellers' representative, squirmed in his chair. Next morning most of the newspapers preferred to identify Morgan as Roosevelt's selected target but he refused to take the bait.

Morgan's self-restraint helped to strengthen his role of "honest broker" when relations between the railroads and the White House deteriorated. Within a week or two of the Gridiron Club speech interest rates had climbed and several corporations began borrowing heavily. Railroad stock was the hardest hit as bearish investors sold short and congressional lobbyists, canvassing the farm vote, agitated noisily for lower freight rates.

Several rail magnates now asked Morgan to postpone his imminent annual visit to Europe and attempt to persuade the government not to take hasty action without hearing their case. On March 12 he reluctantly went to the White House and asked Roosevelt to receive a deputation of three railroad presidents "to allay public anxiety." Roosevelt was genial and gave a half-promise but decided instead to issue a statement that he would be pleased to see "any of them at any time." It failed to mollify them or encourage investment.

Pierpont sailed off on the 13th in the *Baltic* for a trip lasting until mid-August. He spent much of his time buying for his library and the Metropolitan Museum, with pleasant interludes in Paris and Aix-les-Bains, where he saw his French mistress, took the waters, and endowed a wing at the local hospital before departing for Italy. At Ancona he joined *Corsair* for a leisurely cruise in the Adriatic, returning to England for a weekend house party with the Harcourts at Nuneham Park that was honored by the presence of King Edward. They met again at Cowes for the annual regatta of the Royal Yacht Squadron, with *Corsair,* as always, staging some of the most hospitable entertainment.

Pierpont appeared remarkably unconcerned at rumors of a Wall Street slump, although irritated that one of his syndicates had failed to win support for a routine promotion of Lake Shore debentures. Others were also feeling the pinch. Westinghouse, General Electric's chief competitor, was struggling to keep afloat, Manhattan Elevated tumbled into receivership, and New York City's latest bond issue had misfired dramatically. The Treasury's lame attempt to rescue the hard-pressed rural banks with a paltry few million dollars confirmed Pierpont's low opinion of Roosevelt's financial expertise. On August 13, the day before sailing home from Southampton, he learned with dismay that Judge Landis of Chicago had fined Standard Oil nearly $30 million for extorting railroad rebates. It was thought that the Morgan-controlled International Harvester Co. would now be prosecuted for creating a monopoly, but the attorney general seemed nervous about an adverse verdict and backed off at the eleventh hour.

The Standard Oil suit depressed its stock as well as leading railroad shares, including Union Pacific and New York Central, but Pierpont remained sanguine. He chose to dismiss the various recent Wall Street casualties as a few hiccups from a surplus of undigested securities. However, he could not ignore persistent reports that the large well-established Knickerbocker Trust, in which his firm and Standard Oil had substantial interests, might be heading for serious trouble through overspeculation.

The trust, founded by an old schoolfriend of his, Fred Eldridge, had amassed enormous reserves from stockholders, supplemented by the savings deposited in its two downtown branches, but too much cash was tied up in long-term loans to companies building office buildings and costly electric plants. The president, Charles Tracy Barney, was sound though inclined to lord it over a tame board. Few of them knew about his dealings with two unscrupulous operators, Charles W. Morse and F. Augustus Heinze, a Brooklyn-born pirate of mixed Irish, German, and Jewish descent, who had blasted his way to a mining fortune in Montana. These two were recklessly attempting to corner the copper market with funds from Heinze's very suspect Mercantile

National Bank, and also had grandiose plans to create a monopoly of coastal shipping lines. Barney had pledged his trust's already vulnerable assets in support.

Morgan was disquieted by the rumblings but as yet unaware of the Knickerbocker's full involvement. He saw no reason to cancel his attendance at the Episcopal Triennial Convention that was scheduled to open in Richmond, Virginia, on October 1. As Anne was touring Europe with her mother, Louisa Satterlee would act as hostess in the house he had rented for a large number of friends and clerical guests, including the Bishop of London. No expense was spared for incidentals like recarpeting the stairs and installing an extra bathroom. His own car and a hired limousine were on hand to take the bishops and their wives back and forth, with Louis Sherry as always helping to keep bodies and souls together.

Pierpont's departure for Richmond helped to deflate the panicky rumors about Knickerbocker. Almost as reassuring was President Roosevelt's trip to hunt bear in Louisiana while Congress was in recess.

CHAPTER FOURTEEN

J. P. Morgan's dominant role in the 1907 crisis, when he virtually kept the Stock Exchange open and also saved New York City from bankruptcy, is embalmed in Wall Street's folklore. For a man of 70, almost ready to retire from active business life, it was a virtuoso display of physical stamina and leadership more remarkable than his organization of United States Steel or his handling of the gold crisis of 1895.

The events of that tense autumn have become familiar, but his methods and motivation will repay further analysis. Was he the patriotic hero, acclaimed by most contemporaries, or simply a power-drunk opportunist who cynically seized his chance of easy plunder? Sound arguments can be advanced for both views without quite clarifying one central teasing paradox. Even Theodore Dreiser and Upton Sinclair, adept at slaying financial gorgons, might have found it difficult to convince readers of a character who, while salvaging the trust system he had created, combined the opposing functions of arsonist and fire chief and did so with the apparent connivance of a president solemnly pledged to destroy "the malefactors of great wealth."

In Richmond, cossetting his bishops and soberly debating ecclesiastical affairs, he had been receiving reports from his partners who confirmed that the Knickerbocker was no longer the only trust in danger. Oakleigh Thorne's huge Trust Company of America looked almost as fragile. Equally disturbing, Augustus Heinze, after failing to corner the copper market, had resigned from Mercantile National when the New York Clearing House Association rejected his appeal for funds.

Morgan came back on Saturday, October 19, a day before the Episcopal convention formally ended. Throughout Sunday he held conferences in the Red Room of his library at the urgent request of several leading bank presidents headed by George Baker of First National and James Stillman of National City. The latter's presence implied support from the Rockefellers, but that link disqualified him from overlording an operation that might involve government help. Morgan automatically took command. Quite apart from his firm's resources and undoubted prestige, he could rely on Gary's cordial relationship with Roosevelt and Bob Bacon's potential as a go-between.

When not in conference, he spent weary hours updating himself on the various trusts and banks under threat. By midnight on the 19th he had worked out a provisional strategy that left no room for the weak. He had not hesitated to reject Charles Barney's desperate plea for an interview. On Monday morning, though suffering from a heavy cold, he disposed of a monster breakfast and lit the first of his Havanas. He then summoned Perkins and ordered him to assemble a suitable emergency squad to select the most deserving cases for immediate assistance. One of the firm's accountants and another from United Steel would be joined by Benjamin Strong of the Bankers Trust, together with Henry P. Davison, a lively young vice-president from the First National Bank.

Poor Barney had resigned from Knickerbocker, but the situation had become too helpless to keep it going under the proposed new management. Abnormally heavy withdrawals were by now threatening the Trust Company of America, together with many reputable banks and brokerage firms in practically every major city. Pierpont remained in his office until six every day, and then often had long conferences in the Red Room. Here he also received anxious visitors whose commitments and estimated resources had been carefully vetted by his corps of analysts.

By the small hours of Wednesday the 23rd he thought it

imperative to set up a salvage fund to which his own firm and the two leading Clearing House banks, First National and National City, would be the main contributors. As government aid might still prove essential, Treasury Secretary Cortelyou was alerted. He quickly arrived at the Manhattan Hotel where Perkins warned him that the Trust Company of America's failure might trigger off a general crash. Cortelyou looked grave but thought the bankers' plan for mutual aid would suffice. Pierpont became impatient. He hurried over to the Subtreasury and demanded more specific assurances before setting up a rescue group. Cortelyou hedged and repeated that individual corporations like Oakleigh Thorne's lay outside his jurisdiction. "The government," he pointed out, "can offer relief only through the national banks and private financial interests when they are united. If it can deal with the situation as a whole, the Treasury can and will help."

This did not go far enough, but Morgan accepted it as the broadest of hints that federal aid *would* be forthcoming once the various trust chiefs and bankers had formed a united front, with himself in overall command. Five years later, when Cortelyou was crossexamined on the Treasury's decision to place funds at the virtual disposal of a financial dictator, he replied, "By the consensus of opinion, he [Morgan] was regarded as the leading spirit among the businessmen who joined themselves together to meet the emergency. . . . He was generally looked to for guidance and leadership."

That consensus, in addition to New York's two key bankers, would include such disparate figures as the Rockefellers, Thomas F. Ryan, Frick, and even the maverick Harriman, but Morgan remained wary of certain other temporary allies. He rightly suspected the motives of James R. Keene, who never hesitated to sell anyone short in a crisis and had rather too eagerly volunteered his support. Instead of granting him an interview, Pierpont slipped out of a side door and did not return to his library until Keene gave up and went back to the Waldorf-Astoria.

Bernard Baruch had for years wistfully longed to establish closer links with J. P. Morgan & Co. He now planned to go to 23 Wall and personally offer the pool $1.5 million in hard cash. He spent a sleepless night worrying over the possibility of being snubbed by the old tyrant, either from anti-Jewish prejudice or his probable hostility to anyone associated with the Harriman-Schiff interests. Next morning he asked the Bank of Manhattan to make the contribution on his behalf without identifying its source.

The situation remained critical. Westinghouse was taken into receivership; the Pittsburgh Stock Exchange had suspended business, with New York likely to follow; and several trust companies looked certain to share the Knickerbocker's fate. On Wednesday, for once unable to face breakfast, Morgan swallowed a hasty cup of black coffee and, an unlit cigar in his mouth, sucked lozenges as he rode downtown. That morning Markoe had sprayed his throat and made him promise to cut down to only twenty cigars a day! From his carriage he saw an ominous queue of people in front of the offices of the Trust Company of America at Fifth Avenue and Thirty-eighth Street. Harry Davison and his aides had worked in the vaults right through the night counting securities as possible collateral.

At 11 A.M. Oakleigh Thorne burst into Pierpont's room and announced agitatedly that he would be drained of cash before three o'clock, the normal close of business, if the run went on. With boxes of securities arriving in bursts, Morgan hurriedly summoned Baker, Stillman, E. C. Converse, president of the Bankers Trust Company, and Edwin S. Marston of Farmers' Loan and Trust for an emergency meeting. A special line from Thorne's private office would be kept open for up-to-the-minute news of his cash position.

Pierpont assured his associates that the company's assets, roughly estimated at around $100 million, made it a safe risk for loans carrying interest at 10 percent. He repeated his confidence that federal support would follow. At 1:30 P.M., while bags and boxes of collateral continued pouring into 23 Wall Street, Thorne came on the line to announce hoarsely that his balance was now down to under a million dollars. With the lines outside still lengthening, he might have to close down in an hour at most.

Infuriated by whining pleas from his associates for more time, Morgan suddenly crashed his fist down on the desk and demanded an end to further evasion. He looked so menacing that drafts were hastily produced by the Farmers Loan and Trust Co. and the others who had been dragging their feet. Almost at zero hour, when Thorne's cash reserve had all but melted, Thorne learned that the pool had agreed to an immediate credit of $10 million. The bulk would come from various other trusts, supplemented by J. P. Morgan & Co. and the two Clearing House banks.

He went on working in his library throughout that evening. More than once he confided wearily to Satterlee how much he missed Jack, who was away in London but usefully keeping The Corner informed of the City's reaction to the crisis. Satterlee had selflessly taken indefinite leave of absence from his law practice to support his father-in-law. Belle Greene was another welcome asset. With her master spending so much time at the library over the past few days and nights, she had shelved her own routine duties to deal with his correspondence and, more important, defend his privacy from unwelcome visitors. For one so young she adapted remarkably well to pressures far different from anything she had met amid the Princeton bookshelves. Her girlish hero worship of Morgan tended to make her rather overprotective, but her firmness was tempered by an instinctive tact.

Henry Duveen arrived breathlessly one evening when the banker was dozing over his solitaire table after an exhausting spell in Wall Street. He apologized for calling without an appointment, but insisted on discussing an urgent problem that could not be left in limbo. Belle Greene had hesitated momentarily before admitting him to the presence. Back in June Pierpont had agreed to buy eleven paintings, among them Van der Weyden's magnificent *Annunciation* and three Memling portraits. He had asked for payment to be held over for his next year's budget. This was not unusual, but the recent financial scares had made Uncle Henry anxious for some reassurance that the deal would stand. Pierpont heard him out, touched his arm, and said almost gently, "I have pledged my word."

George S. Hellman, another expert and respected old friend, also managed to break into the fortress, although Belle had told him severely that her employer was far too busy to see anyone from the art world. She relented when he promised to stay only a few minutes. Morgan looked up irritably from his desk and snapped, "I'm buying nothing more at a time of national crisis."

The dealer bowed, calmly extracted a file from his valise and announced, "I'm not trying to sell anything. I'm giving something away. And when you've seen these Lincoln letters, you will agree they are a gift!"

Morgan glanced through the documents, some of them messages written during the Civil War to Andrew Jackson and Ulysses S. Grant. He grew even more excited on hearing they could be bought for under a thousand dollars. He lit another cigar and said, "All right, I'll take them," adding with a grunt, "but I won't pay for them for a year." He then turned back to the analysts' reports and statistics that had to be mastered before next morning's office conference.

Although the Trust Company of America and a few others were temporarily reprieved by the syndicate's dramatic last-minute intervention, the securities market was toppling, with railroads and steel among the major casualties. Investment remained at a standstill through lack of capital and confidence. Just before noon on Thursday, October 24, R. H. Thomas, president of the Stock Exchange, crossed the road to The Corner and warned that he would be forced to suspend business without an immediate injection of cash. Morgan, promising support, ordered him not to close a moment before three o'clock. He at once contacted the Treasury Secretary, then in conference with Perkins, and extracted a pledge for $25 million from government funds. Within a quarter of an hour he, Stillman, Baker, and the others had agreed to lend Thomas up to $27 million at 10 percent. The news was telephoned to the floor, which broke into pandemonium as brokers surged forward to place orders before closing time. Their cheering could be heard out in Broad Street. Without that whiff of oxygen, so Perkins recalled, "the Exchange and a hundred or more firms would have gone up. It was touch and go."

The outlook still remained dark for several trusts and smallish banks, three of which closed down that very afternoon. Morgan was cheered and slapped on the back when he left his offices, but he shrugged off all requests for interviews with the blunt advice, "If people will keep their money in the banks, everything will be all right." President Roosevelt, back at last from hunting bear, helpfully issued a statement praising "those influential and splendid businessmen . . . who have acted with such wisdom and public interest." It was flattering, but did not replenish the syndicate's drained coffers or pierce to the real core of the money crisis. The issue of Clearing House certificates had merely eased the currency shortage, due to a nervous hoarding of gold and bank-notes. It was still vital to unblock bullion, frozen solid in London, Paris, Berlin, and Amsterdam from the moment the New York Exchange had begun to stagnate.

On Saturday morning, the 26th, Morgan was heartened by a cable from Jack informing him that the London banks would be shipping $3 million in gold. Satterlee quickly informed the leading press agencies so as to encourage the Exchange when it opened for Monday business. He then departed to Highland Falls for a brief weekend break with his father-in-law, who was too exhausted to get up next morning for services at the Church of the Holy Innocents. He heard later that Archbishop J. M. Farley had held a special Mass for New York's business chieftains, while the Rev. John F. Carson of Brooklyn extolled "that magnificent and praiseworthy leader, J. P. Morgan."

In the evening he was back in the Red Room chairing yet another meeting. After a sound night's sleep—the first in a fren-zied fortnight—he strode into his office on the stroke of ten. The Stock Exchange looked firmer and the Trust Company of Amer-ica opened in fairish shape, but New York could not raise the cash to pay its schoolteachers. Alerted to the problem, Morgan at once directed his experts to make an assessment pending the arrival of Mayor McClellan. McClellan was shown into the Red Room at four o'clock and asked for a short-term emergency loan of $30 million to avert a collapse of all municipal services. Morgan again persuaded Stillman, Baker, and the others to issue Clearing House certificates, this time in exchange for the City's 6 percent bonds. He was confident that his firm would be able to shift them once the market regained its balance.

That seemed overoptimistic during the next few days when several trusts went down after failing to convince Morgan's realistic syndicate about their management structures and earn-ing potential. Others deserved to be rescued. Morgan was now certain that if the leading banks and trusts ran for cover to protect their own skins, leaving the smaller houses to their fate, they too would face disaster as the bank runs continued and forced a general market collapse. The only realistic solution was a return to liquidity. The two most immediate and interlocking problems persisted: how to release hoarded cash and arrest the flow of bullion overseas. A substantial intake of foreign gold was crucial to recovery, Morgan explained to Bob Bacon, who had come to New York to assess the deteriorating financial situation. He reported back to Secretary of State Root who urgently advised the president to reclassify cotton and grain as top-priority rail freight. Washington moved so fast that another $10 million in gold from Europe was soon being unloaded in the docks.

During these troubled days and nights Pierpont Morgan held one council of war after another, but never failed to slip away for an hour or so every afternoon. Armed with a bouquet of her favorite red roses, he visited Mrs. Rainsford, who was then recovering from a serious illness in Roosevelt Hospital.

There was nothing sentimental about his treatment of Moore & Schley, one of New York's most prominent firm of brokers, now terminally sick. If it failed it would rock the stock market and might bring down the Trust Company of America, still struggling to regain investor support.

By the first weekend of November J. P. Morgan was convinced that all his recent efforts could soon dissolve into a pile of shredded out-of-date securities. The time had passed for first aid. Major surgery looked essential if the Trust Company of America, the Lincoln, and many more were not to follow the Knickerbocker into the mortuary. Moore & Schley, which had recklessly overspeculated, would have to be the first on the operating table. By the end of October it could no longer meet several large short-term loans, but still possessed one valuable asset: a majority holding in T. C. & I. (the Tennessee Coal, Iron and Railroad Company) with large reserves of coal and iron ore in Alabama.

Morgan at once saw the chance of buying it out with U. S. Steel bonds, which would simultaneously remove one of the trust's most awkward competitors and save Moore & Schley. Since Grant B. Schley happened to be George Baker's brother-in-law, the First National Bank would no doubt support the plan, but the Stillman-Rockefeller interests might be reluctant to strengthen U. S. Steel. Morgan's attorney and yachting crony, Lewis Cass Ledyard, considered the move technically sound, but warned him that its success might hinge upon federal approval for what could be interpreted as a breach of the Sherman Act against monopolies.

Morgan remained unconvinced. On Saturday evening, November 2, he arranged two meetings in his Library. Benjamin Strong of the Bankers Trust, Edward King of Union Trust, and the heads of several other companies were summoned for a talk in the West Room. He announced gruffly that more cash would be needed at once, notably for the vulnerable Trust Company of America, and they were "invited" to contribute another $25 million. The threat that he would withdraw as leader if they failed to reach his target figure hovered plainly in the air.

In the smaller East Room he had assembled Baker, Stillman, and other bank presidents, who were soon joined by Frick and Judge Gary representing the finance committee of U. S. Steel. Without preamble he asked them to discuss his plan for buying the T. C. & I. stock. It would require a bridging loan of $18 million until the steel trust could formally complete the stock transfer. His firm would put up one-third, with the National City Bank and Baker's First National contributing the balance between them. He did not mince words. Moore & Schley would go down and precipitate a national banking crisis unless it could be rescued before the Exchange opened on Monday morning. He stressed his intention to discontinue further efforts to salvage the trust companies unless the T. C. & I. takeover was endorsed.

While the two groups debated their respective but allied problems, he secluded himself in Belle Greene's small north office and set up his card table. Agonizing over their dilemma, Strong and the others in the West Room had no time to admire a sixteenth-century Flemish tapestry by William van Pannemaker. It portrayed *The Triumph of Avarice,* one of a set illustrating the Seven Deadly Sins! At intervals one of them would cross over to Belle's office either to plead for more time to consult codirectors or usually to argue that the contributions demanded of them were excessive and impossible to raise at such short notice. Flabby, puffy-faced, their throats rasped by nervousness, brandy, and too many cigars, they moved heavily in a grotesque saraband while Belle Greene glided coolly back and forth with her master's scribbled notes. He would not shift from his figure of $25 million or withdraw his threat. As hour after hour passed he became if anything testier and more arrogant, often crumpling a message and tossing it into a wastepaper basket or slashing a thick red line through some elaborate evasion.

The bankers had left the building with the T. C. & I. problem still unresolved, but arranging to resume talks next day. The trust presidents were less fortunate. According to Ben Strong, they were literally prisoners. Wilting under the grinding pressure and desperate for sleep, Strong decided to leave around midnight only to discover that Morgan had locked the bronze front doors and pocketed the keys. He alone still looked fresh, thanks to several catnaps between spells of solitaire. By 4:45 A.M. his victims had caved in. He smiled cheerily on entering the airless, smoke-filled room with the "document of surrender." Each of the five trust chiefs signed and stumbled out at last to gulp the dawn air on Thirty-sixth Street.

Later that morning he received Stillman, Baker, and Grant Schley in the West Room. They were regaled with drinks while he almost offhandedly awaited their opening moves. Leaning back in his red plush armchair before a blazing log fire, he seemed perfectly composed when his lawyers, Charles Steele and Cass Ledyard, appeared with Perkins, who had briefed himself with fuller details of the proposed T. C. & I. stock transfer. Baker, anxious to save his brother-in-law, was eager to go ahead, although Stillman looked most reluctant to part with several million dollars for a project from which his bank and its principal depositors, the Rockefellers, obviously stood to gain far less than Morgan.

Stillman received welcome support from Henry Frick, who had arrived during the afternoon with Judge Gary. Frick also argued against a full-scale takeover and preferred making a direct loan to Moore & Schley, with the Tennessee Company's stock as collateral. Morgan shook his head but listened gravely to Gary's warning of a likely antitrust prosecution of U. S. Steel if they failed to consult with the White House.

The technical arguments continued for several hours, with Morgan pointedly looking up at the clock to remind them that time was running out for Moore & Schley. Stillman and Frick finally yielded, in the face of this very real threat, but they supported Gary's view, backed by Cass Ledyard, that no action should be taken without the government's approval. Whenever Roosevelt's name was mentioned, the old banker scowled at the prospect of kowtowing to a politician who had shattered Northern Securities and might still attack the steel trust to win liberal support. He brought the meeting to an end by reluctantly ordering Gary and Frick to catch the midnight train for Washington. They promised to telephone before the Exchange opened.

He was sitting bolt upright at his desk in the West Room when Ledyard and Perkins arrived at half-past eight next morning. He remarked cheerfully that he had slept well. He had no doubt that Gary would win over Roosevelt and Elihu Root at their early breakfast conference. The telephone rang at 9:55. It was from 23 Wall. The president had agreed not to take any action to oppose the purchase of the T. C. & I. stock by United States Steel. The news, relayed to the floor of the Exchange, at once revived the flagging market. For the first time in weeks, banks, trust companies, and brokers felt almost secure.

Morgan's ruthless exercise of centralized financial control had, in fact, done nothing to improve national production or tackle the basic causes of a depressed economy. The forced sale of T. C. & I. stock for around $50 million would ultimately enrich the steel trust tenfold, without comforting investors ruined by the failure of the Knickerbocker and several small banks. Unemployment continued soaring to over three million and men soon became desperate to work for thirty-five cents a day. The coming months also witnessed an alarming crime rate in the cities, while thousands of so-called vagrants would be brutally rounded up by the police in rural areas.

These social evils did not sour the euphoria of the stock market or public relief that the crisis had apparently ended with far less damage than many feared. Balanced judgment was suspended in near-hysteria over the dramatic reprieve from disaster. A hack on *Pearson's Magazine* acclaimed Morgan the Magnificent: "Plain Mr. Morgan, fresh from the dronings of a great Episcopal church convention at Richmond, was suddenly aroused by the peril of the financial situation to take command of the fierce, clashing money forces of Wall Street, gone crazy out of sheer fright . . . to become protagonist and hero."

Robert La Follette, the liberal Senator from Wisconsin, a fierce opponent of railroad monopolies and the money-grabbing franchises enjoyed by operators like Thomas Fortune Ryan, took a different view. He accused the banking moguls of having engineered the panic: "In their strife for more money, more power . . . government, society, and the individual are swallowed up." Others also refused to accept Pierpont Morgan as the country's savior and deplored Washington's passive consent to the cannibalization of Tennessee Coal and Iron. A section of Roosevelt's own party thought that he had either allowed himself to be outsmarted or had cynically shelved his trust-busting for political expediency.

Democrats sneered openly at the legendary cavalryman whom Morgan had exposed as a Don Quixote with a wooden sword and a lance of marzipan. Roosevelt always insisted that he had only taken action when confronted with "a panic and a situation where not merely 24 hours, but one hour, might cause widespread disaster to the public." But in yielding, even under such extreme pressure, to what was virtually an ultimatum, he may have been misled by smooth-talking Judge Gary. No record survives of their crucial breakfast palaver, but over the years Roosevelt would claim that he had moved to save "a certain business concern," ostensibly the Trust Company of America, whose disintegration might have toppled dozens of other houses with irreparable damage to the entire money market. If so, he had been naive in accepting Gary's résumé of the emergency without probing Moore & Schley's situation. But whether or not he suspected the hidden motives behind the salvage plan worked out in Pierpont Morgan's Red Room, he could hardly have taken any other course. The old Rough Rider was enough of a strategist to retreat in fairly good order against impossible odds.

Piqued by unrelenting criticism from Congress and the radical press, he now threatened to resume his antitrust program. This irritated his right-wingers and totally failed to pacify the Democrats, who clamored even more noisily for the prosecution of United States Steel. Roosevelt pulled no punches in his message to Congress on January 31, 1908, stressing that there was "no difference between gambling at cards and gambling in the stock market." His point was underlined by the suicide of Knickerbocker's hapless former president, Charles Barney.

Roosevelt's speech, urging "a moral regeneration of the business world," was interpreted as a warning to Standard Oil, the tobacco trust, and other prime targets. Although the autumn crisis had starkly exposed the limitations of his antimonopoly measures, it had nevertheless proved that only banking decentralization, with stricter and far more responsible federal control, offered any hope of lasting stability.

In the afterglow of his astonishing personal triumph, J. P. Morgan chose to disregard these signals. He seemed to have been born for this hour of destiny and now saw no reason to retire gracefully, although at three score and ten he stood at a lifetime peak of social and business eminence, with ample means to travel anywhere like a prince and add to his hoard of paintings, manuscripts, and bibelots from the world's treasure chests. He preferred to consolidate his position as the undisputed supremo of American finance.

The recent crisis had, after all, proved that he could impose his will on the most powerful banks and trusts, and if necessary on the federal government. The next logical step was to underpin his imperial base with the asset-rich life insurance corporations and such easy prey as the weakened Trust Company of America.

International Mercantile Marine, which still paid no dividends, might also be revived in a renewed thrust for the Atlantic freight and passenger traffic. It was no idle whim on his part to sail home in June 1908 aboard the *Mauretania*. It was the first time he had patronized Cunard in many years and he had to see for himself how the big liner shaped up against White Star's rather outdated fleet. He made careful notes of its performance and facilities before taking a special train to receive his honorary LL.D. from Yale.

No iceberg loomed on the fair horizon.

CHAPTER FIFTEEN

Maxine Elliott was not among Wall Street's many victims. The heroine of a thousand and one illicit nights made herself equally at home between the balance sheets. She had returned to New York after a shaky London season but invested heavily and with quite remarkable success through Tom Chadbourne and other discreet brokers. Even allowing for an undoubted flair, her profits were almost phenomenal in the precarious state of the market. In April 1908 she spent upwards of $100,000 for a fifty-fifty partnership with the Shuberts to buy a site in West Thirty-ninth Street on which Maxine Elliott's Theatre rose by the end of the year.

Her long-estranged husband, Nat Goodwin, commented in his sardonic memoirs, "We were very happy—at least I was—for a few months. I made the mistake of introducing her to a few conspicuous, powerful financiers who gave her tips on the stock market (and casual luncheons!). They also gave me tips. Mine lost invariably. Hers always won. How very strange!" The eight-year liaison with Morgan had become less close. Maxine spent more time in England and on long tours, but the two remained on such excellent terms that newspaper gossips always coupled their names, on the smallest pretext, whenever she arrived in New York. Pierpont Morgan, however, stoutly denied that he had figured as the kindly angel behind her new venture. He assured a reporter, "The only interest I have in Maxine Elliott's Theatre is that I'd like to get a free ticket on the opening night."

For weeks before the elegant 725-seater opened on December 30, rumors about his alleged gift multiplied, mostly inspired by Nat Goodwin, who was filing for divorce in order to commit matrimony for the fourth time. It was soon reported that J. P. Morgan would head a roll call of corespondents, including Alfred de Rothschild, debonair P. A. Widener, and a string of leading men, past and present.

This would have acutely embarrassed Morgan, the family man and devout churchgoer who had always insisted on his young executives living respectable lives. Goodwin suddenly decided on a quick undefended Reno suit for desertion, and it was freely whispered that his cronies had advised him not to confront the proud and vindictive magnate.

During the fall of 1908 Roosevelt stepped down in favor of "Big Bill" Taft, who handsomely defeated Bryan for the presidency. One of his last gestures, which surprised his inner circle, was to offer a government post to Herbert Satterlee who, like Bob Bacon and Judge Gary, had never allowed his loyalty to Jupiter to diminish his admiration for the legendary Rough Rider. His spell as Assistant Secretary of the Navy would only last until Taft's inauguration, but he had prudently asked his father-in-law's blessing before accepting.

Roosevelt's action has sometimes been scorned as a cynical attempt to mollify the mighty banker who could yet be useful to him, but it may also be considered a good-natured tribute to his inspired leadership in the recent crisis. It did not appease J. P. Morgan. Over foreign policy and such awkward problems as the anthracite miners' strike he had found it expedient to cooperate with the president, but he could neither forgive nor forget the antitrust campaign, still less a personal insult like "the malefactors of great wealth" speech.

After the election, Roosevelt embarked at Hoboken for a hunting trip to Africa. *Scribner's Magazine* was paying him a $50,000 fee to describe his experiences, and he stood majestically on the bridge of the S.S. *Hamburg,* wearing his colonel's greatcoat like a suit of chivalric armor. Morgan had of course absented himself from the throng of cheering well-wishers. Working at his desk in Wall Street he commented sourly, "I hope the first lion he meets does his duty." He had contributed a modest $30,000 to Taft's campaign, no doubt preferring to await the new president's policy on trusts while moving ahead to fortify his firm's growing hegemony.

The crisis of 1907 had surprisingly brought James Stillman of the National City Bank, his most reluctant associate, into a closer alliance. The tight-lipped and astute banker had been as much impressed by Morgan's patrician life-style and prestige as by his brilliant strategy. For years a Rockefeller satrap, he feared the consequences for himself if Taft made good his boast to shatter Standard Oil's monopoly, but he also felt outraged by the vulgar abuse to which the Rockefellers were being subjected despite their multimillion dollar (tax-exempt) Foundation "for the well-being of mankind." A vain and snobbish man, he squirmed when old John D. was denounced by Senator La Follette as "the greatest criminal of his age—he gives with two hands but robs with many more." But Morgan was still reveling in popular esteem, except from a few radicals, and had won approval for philanthropy inspired far more by personal sentiment than by any urge to nourish the bodies or minds of the underprivileged.

It cost him $800,000 to put up an art gallery of pink marble as an annex to the Wadsworth Atheneum "in loving memory of Junius Spencer Morgan, a native of Massachusetts, a merchant of Hartford . . . afterwards a merchant of London." He handed over another $100,000 in securities to found a Yale Chair in Assyriology and Babylonian Literature in the name of his old friend, William Laffan. His richer offerings to the Harvard Medical School gained him another honorary LL.D., although the ceremony had a sweet-sour flavor when Theodore Roosevelt was similarly capped and gowned.

Henry P. Davison, who had joined the firm as Perkins' potential successor, and Jack Morgan (by now on the board of U. S. Steel) both became directors of Stillman's bank, in which the firm had bought more and more stock. At Pierpont's direction, George Baker's First National Bank (a Morgan affiliate) also bought a majority holding in Chase National, but the richest plunder came from carving up Harriman's empire.

Unlike George Jay Gould (whose companies lost several million dollars in declining stock values and would forfeit Western Union to the Morgan-controlled American Telephone Company), Harriman had continued to invest heavily in the Equitable Life Assurance, despite opposition from the Morgan-Ryan interests and the Guaranty Trust Company in which his holdings exceeded Morgan's. His stake in American rolling stock, valued at $116 million by the Interstate Commerce Commission, had sharpened his appetite for a network dominating Europe, Russia, and the Far East, linked to an international shipping fleet that would dwarf Cunard, White Star, and all other rivals. These blueprints could only have been realized by someone with Morgan's genius for centralizing and applying massive banking power, the one weak spot in Harriman's make-up. He was further handicapped by his capacity for making powerful enemies. A sudden decline in health dealt him the final crippling blow.

In the late summer of 1909 he lay dying in his 150-room eyrie on West Mountain, near Arden, Orange County. He sent a pathetic message to Pierpont expressing a wish to talk over old times. Morgan at once commandeered a private car and engine from the Erie Railroad. Harriman, muffled like a mummy, was propped up on the porch, and there they chatted in private for an hour before warmly shaking hands. "We made our peace," Morgan remarked afterward, refusing to say more, even to Satterlee.

Harriman died within a few days, leaving a fortune estimated at $100 million.* Morgan was less interested in the 18,000 miles of railroad than the chance to snap up his holdings in Guaranty Trust and Equitable Life. Two of his partners, the swiftly rising Harry Davison and William H. Porter, went on the board of Guaranty, which soon absorbed several weaker companies. Aided by the phenomenal growth of the insurance business, the two huge corporations began amassing between them liquid assets exceeding $360 million before the end of Taft's term in office.

Nothing seemed to check Morgan's sweep to unchallengeable mastery. His well-tried strategy of forging a chain of voting directorships had brought substantial control of New York's two most flourishing banks, three trusts, and the leading insurance

---

*His son, Averell, now in his nineties, has enjoyed a distinguished career both in business and public affairs. He served three presidents, Franklin D. Roosevelt, Truman, and Kennedy, was ambassador to the U.S.S.R. in World War II, and governor of New York, 1955–58.

companies, with a solid capital infrastructure from 50,000 miles of railroads and such near-monopolies as United States Steel, General Electric, International Harvester, and the American Telephone Company.

The only two serious threats to total supremacy would come from a hostile administration and Pierpont Morgan's own spiraling *folie de grandeur.*

He had rightly laughed off Taft's solemn declaration that "Jews make the best Republicans" as a ludicrous attempt to catch the votes of New York's militant garment makers. He had also dismissed his forty-five antitrust prosecutions as of little importance until he moved against the Rockefellers. In November 1909 a court ordered the Standard Oil Company of New Jersey to be dissolved as a holding company. The Supreme Court upheld the judgment but made it subject to "undue" restraint of trade, a most elastic loophole for the defense lawyers. It took several months to dissolve the trust, which soon split up into over thirty separate companies with the Rockefellers continuing to own 25 percent of the shares in each corporation and still directing policy from 26 Broadway. At the dissolution, Standard Oil's stock was valued at over $660 million, which increased by $200 million within a few months. A year or two later the fortunate stockholders would be basking in a 60 percent dividend.

These makeshift prosecutions did not appease those who now demanded action against the Steel Trust. The American Federation of Labor alleged that it was being shielded by Attorney General George W. Wickersham, a very close friend of Judge Gary, Morgan's "steel viceroy," and had even demanded Wickersham's impeachment. The attorney general reacted by setting up a boneless investigating committee under a Kentucky congressman. Gary, as circumspect as one of his master's pet bishops, guardedly agreed with the committee that *some* cooperation *might* be possible under stricter federal supervision, but reminded them that an efficiently run trust was infinitely preferable to the wildcat speculation of the bad old days. Quizzed on banking autocracy, he pontificated vaguely: "I believe any man of Mr. Morgan's wealth and character and courage can do a great deal of harm in banking circles as well as a great deal of good. . . . That applies to the individual or the corporation and also applies to the Government." The committee subsided into impotence. Morgan had good cause to appreciate Gary's value as a lobbyist, past and present. He observed after a board meeting at 23 Wall Street, "I don't know what I'd do without him. The Judge can have anything within my power to give."

That faith was severely tested in the spring of 1909. During Morgan's absence on an overseas tour of Europe and Africa, the finance committee of U. S. Steel voted for wage cuts. Gary dissented, alarmed by mounting union discontent that would surely inflame Taft's antitrusters. He wired Aix-les-Bains for support. Jupiter was currently preoccupied with his mistress and his plans to endow an isolation wing at the local hospital, which would be commemorated by a street to be renamed Rue Pierpont Morgan. However, he could not ignore Gary's S.O.S. and cabled back, "My own views are in accordance with those of the financial committee in New York." However, Morgan promised to confer in Paris with Frick and Widener, then holidaying together in France, and stayed at the Embassy with Bob Bacon, whom Taft had recently appointed Ambassador Extraordinary, obviously preferring not to keep such an avowed supporter of Roosevelt and J. P. Morgan in his administration.

The meeting with Frick and Widener, both outspoken enemies of labor, must have seen vigorous discussion. Morgan, by this time, had been able to think the matter over and he managed to dissuade them from taking provocative action. The trio jointly signed a cable to Gary authorizing him to maintain the status quo with regard to wages.

It failed signally to appease the union chiefs whose members had expected a pay increase now that their fellow workers in the railroads and pits seemed to be winning one. A copy of Morgan's first cable to Gary was angrily produced for the Commission for Industrial Relations, whose members with the public relations instincts of true politicians came to the unilluminating conclusion that "the lives of millions of wage earners are subject to the dictation of a small number of men." More adverse publicity followed Morgan's merger of the New York, New Haven & Hartford system with the Boston & Maine. By neatly sidestepping the laws of Massachusetts, the merger also gave his firm a most lucrative streetcar franchise. A former state governor, Curtis Guild, promptly wrote an editorial in his *Boston Commercial Bulletin,* pilloring Morgan as a "beefy, thick-necked bully, drunk with wealth and power, who bawls his orders to stock markets, directors, courts, governments and nations." Coming from the very heart of New England, such abuse was hurtful, but he was gratified when his daughter Anne, whose liberal views had so often irritated him, angrily snubbed reporters who pursued her in the hope of eliciting indiscretions.

Her own record in social welfare work remained unimpeachable. She successfully founded and endowed a club and restaurant, with good, inexpensive food, at the Navy Yard in Brooklyn. She worked for a time as a volunteer sanitary inspector to check firsthand on factories. By 1910, defying police action, she was giving active support to the striking women garment workers, predominantly Jewish, in New York's foul sweatshops. Their cause was tragically vindicated by a fire in the Triangle Shirtwaist Factory that trapped 140 victims in the narrow blocked exits. The disaster strengthened her determination to improve conditions throughout industry, not excluding U. S. Steel. Almost singlehanded, she established a vacation fund to enable working girls in New York to enjoy an annual holiday.

In manner she remained an aristocrat, with more than a touch of the Morgan reserve and abruptness, but her crusades for the underdog were in a direct line of descent from those of her great-grandfather, the Rev. John Pierpont.

CHAPTER SIXTEEN

Anne Morgan's loyalty to her father did not blind her to his faults or lessen her disapproval of his opulent lifestyle and his lack of concern for the toiling masses. By contrast, his son-in-law eulogized his benefactions and business coups with an uncritical enthusiasm seldom matched by any other official biographer. Satterlee's hero worship even led him to ignore Pierpont's gross misjudgment over General Motors.

At the turn of the century, a limousine was almost as glittering a status symbol as the luxury yachts sailed by the Vanderbilts, Astors, and Rockefellers. Even Pierpont Morgan, who much preferred his carriage, had bought an electric car, although a sedan chair might have been more fitting for such a proud mandarin. At his Mack Avenue plant in Detroit, Ford was planning to turn out automobiles for "the average man" in the near future. By February 1908 he had produced his Model T, seven feet tall, eight feet four inches long, retailing at only $950, but like other pioneer manufacturers his cash flow had been drained by the recent share falls.

William Crapo Durant was no exception. The dapper former grocery clerk had made his first million by peddling cut-price insurance in Boston. He was a shrewd operator, if overly impatient of orthodox accountancy. But he had vision. Instead of Ford's popular market, he concentrated on the prospering middle class. Early in 1905 he had salvaged the decrepit Buick Company and tempted investors with an elixir of blarney and horse sense worthy of Gould in his heyday. Within two years his Buicks showed such good profits, heavily outselling the Ford, that he decided to absorb several struggling rival manufacturers into a combine roughly structured on Standard Oil and United States Steel. Unfortunately, this would require enormous capital at a time when dwindling profit margins and smaller sales were draining reserves, already strained by his heavy investment in plant and research.

Toward the end of 1908 he invited J. P. Morgan & Co. to underwrite one-third of an issue of $1.5 million for a group to be called the General Motors Corporation. It would have been almost a routine investment for the firm, but the Little Giant, as he was known in Wall Street, soon faced implacable opposition from Francis L. Stetson and George Perkins. Morgan's starchy attorney had some slight but unhappy experience of Durant and shared the Exchange's view of him as "the greatest living promoter outside of prison bars," while Perkins, the cold insurance expert and statistician, derided his boast to produce 500,000 cars a year when so far only one in fifty American families owned an automobile. Morgan needed but a few minutes with Durant to dismiss him as "an unstable visionary" and summarily reject his plea for financing. He showed even less interest in Henry Ford's rumored shortage of cash, preferring to inspect the Metropolitan Museum's latest dig in Egypt rather than summon the uncouth ex-farm boy for what might have been a most rewarding exchange of views.

Durant had no such inhibitions. He offered to buy out Ford, who was prepared to sell for $8 million cash, "and I'll throw in my lumbago," but Durant's backers did not think the Tin Lizzies worth support. The Little Giant had by now incorporated the General Motors Company of New Jersey with an authorized capital of $12 million, soon adding Oakland, Cadillac, and others to his Buicks. In little over a year he was paying his shareholders a divided of 150 percent, but he lacked Ford's genius for mass production and cutting profit margins.

In the summer of 1910 he turned desperately to the Seligmans of New York and Boston's Lee, Higginson for a large rescue loan at very high interest rates. He struggled on for a time but was soon ousted from the new board of General Motors, to the satisfaction of J. Pierpont Morgan, who preened himself, somewhat prematurely, on his intuitive wisdom.*

It had also failed him the previous year when he missed another coup by refusing exactly half a million dollars to a man he disliked. Bernard Baruch had been flattered when Charles Steele, a senior partner at 23 Wall, encouraged him to investigate and report on a sulphur dome near Brazonia, Texas, on the Gulf Coast. If satisfactory, Steele intimated that the firm would underwrite its development and give him 40 percent of the profits. With his team of surveyors Baruch spent several weeks on the site and returned in a state of euphoria. He assured Morgan that the odds in favor of satisfactory mining were at least fifty-fifty. The property could be bought outright, lock, stock, and barrel, for only $500,000. He was even confident enough to suggest "gambling" half that amount from his own funds.

Morgan puffed on his cigar and then said icily, "I never gamble," ending both the interview and his firm's interest in the proposition. Baruch was later told he would probably have succeeded by offering to "invest" instead of "gamble." He at once took his survey, together with details of a new process for smelting copper ore, to the Guggenheims and shared with them in a fat killing. Later he could console himself with the reflection that, had he closed the deal with Morgan and developed their association, he might never have become President Wilson's confidant or enjoyed the international prestige that came to him following the wartime boom years.

Morgan's decision may have been influenced by racial bias. If so, it must be set against his almost quixotic generosity, soon afterward, toward Henry Duveen, who had allegedly abused his position as consultant to the New York Customs by undervaluing the firm's own imports of art treasures, including a tapestry bought for George Jay Gould and a collection of rare Chinese

---

*Will Durant was resilient enough to stage a comeback with the help of a former Buick racing driver, Louis Chevrolet, with whom he started developing the six-cylinder engine model that would enable him to buy a majority holding in G.M. and return as its president.

porcelain. The authorities demanded forfeiture of the property in dispute, plus duty amounting to $1.4 million. Duveen was detained on disembarking from the *Lusitania* and then released on bail, but with the threat of a criminal charge. This could have led to imprisonment and incalculable damage to the firm that, characteristically, was too short of cash in hand to raise such a large sum at short notice.

Morgan was chairing a meeting in his private office on the top floor of the Bankers Trust Building when he first heard the news. He broke off to telephone Duveen's attorneys, Stanchfield and Levy of 120 Broadway, and growled, "We've got to get Uncle Henry off." Within minutes he had sent over a special messenger with a First National Bank check for the $1.4 million.

It was an act of extraordinary loyalty, rather more explicable after his long association with Duveen than his idiosyncratic kindness to a complete stranger at one of the Metropolitan's annual receptions. As always, he and Fanny formally shook hands with the guests, who were entertained by lavish refreshments after touring the galleries. Among the throng of people in full evening dress he noticed a shabby-looking young woman carrying a baby girl in her arms. She was the wife of a gallery attendant and about to be hustled out when he called her over with a pleasant smile and asked the child's name. The following day he signed a check for $1,000 entitling the infant to life membership, plus $500 to study art in Europe in later years if she so wished. (This was not taken up).

The gesture did not impress Roger Fry, who had recently suffered what he described to his friend Sir Charles Holmes as "a vile deed, villainously done with every kind of hypocritical slaver." This almost hysterical outburst resulted from Morgan's purchase of Fra Angelico's *Virgin and Child Enthroned* (formerly the property of King Leopold) at Kleinberger's gallery in London. He paid £110,000 for it, exactly the figure that Fry, intending to purchase it for the museum, had settled a few days earlier with a dealer in Paris. One must assume that the vendor thought the president of the Metropolitan was simply concluding the deal in that capacity and not as a collector.*

---

*The Fra Angelico remained in Morgan's private collection until his death, when his son sold it to the Swiss Baron Heinrich von-Thyssen-Bornemisza.

Fry saw himself as the victim of the banker's greed and duplicity and, refusing to admit any possible misunderstanding, at once wrote a most offensive letter of protest. Morgan, seething with anger, disdained to reply and had him dismissed by a unanimous vote of the trustees. It was rumored that one or two secretly sympathized with the rebel, but the museum had so long enjoyed Morgan's bounty and was currently benefiting so handsomely from his mounting passion for Egyptology that no one was about to fight for a headstrong English aesthete, even if they felt he would be missed.*

The Metropolitan, like other American museums, had at first limited its interest in Flinders Petrie's digs to a grudging subscription in exchange for some of his finds. President Morgan had queried even this meager outlay and made no personal contribution when the Metropolitan mounted its first expedition in 1907, excavating near the Pyramids of Lisht, thirty-five miles south of Cairo, following this by excavations at the Oasis of Khargeh in the Libyan Desert.

The banker's support was stimulated by Alfred de Rothschild, whose huge legacy to Almina, Countess of Carnarvon, would later help to finance the historic discovery of Tutankhamen's tomb by Howard Carter. At Alfred's table he sat beside Kitchener, the hero of Omdurman, and Sirdar of the Egyptian Army. Morgan did not go so far as Alfred, who showered his guest of honor with gifts, including a valuable parade set of ornate saddle steels originally made for Philip III of Spain, but he was enthralled when the imposing big-moustached general, normally as taciturn and reserved as himself, rhapsodized on the mysteries of Ancient Egypt. He felt an instinctive affinity with the military giant of whom Curzon had written not entirely in admiration: "He stands aloof and alone, a molten mass of devouring energy and burning ambition, without anybody to control or guide it in the right direction." Pierpont Morgan, now in virtual control of his country's cash and credit, would naturally admire a commander

---

*Fry's departure from the Metropolitan, which had long pooh-poohed his passion for modern French painters, helped to improve the face of Art. He soon broke new ground with his exhibition at London's Grafton Gallery of Post Impressionists like Gauguin, Van Gogh, and Cézanne, none of whose canvases would extract a red cent from J. P. Morgan's deep pocket.

whose personal magnetism had led vast armies to death or glory.

He was also influenced by Albert Lythgoe, the museum's supervisor of excavations, who, having already squeezed financial backing from Edward S. Harkness and others, would soon persuade the museum's president to advance the cash for a base at Luxor with comfortable two-bedroom quarters for the archeologists. After Morgan's first extended tour of inspection in March 1909—it was followed by regular annual visits—he helped to endow ten new galleries of Egyptian antiquities in the museum's north wing.

He had traveled with his sister, Mary Burns, his daughter Juliet and a large party of friends, among them Sir Hercules Read, Keeper of Antiquities at the British Museum, who acted as genial guide and lecturer. That first Nile cruise aboard Thomas Cook's finest private steamer was no hardship, thanks to a corps of chefs and attentive servants, but it was far less frivolous than the sightseeing trips of earlier days. Morgan studied every detail and listened to Read's lectures like a serious first-year college student. He bought many bas reliefs and other relics, almost all for presentation to the Metropolitan, but he invested these finds "clawed from the ancient earth of the Nile Valley" with a deeper significance than the far more valuable Old Masters, ceramics, statuary, and manuscripts that the world's dealers laid at his feet.

He was received with deference at the oasis village of Khargeh by the hereditary chief, elderly Sheik Mustafa Manad. Morgan, clothed as if for a Wall Street office meeting except for his panama and a fly swatter, sat on a couch beside the robed Omdeh and proferred his box of cigars. They smoked contentedly and exchanged civilities which Lythgoe interpreted. Morgan seemed to be savoring a tranquillity new in his experience.

On the sheltered deck of the Cook's side-wheeler, he would lapse into serene hour-long reveries. Lythgoe and Read were familiar with "expedition fever" but were unaware that Morgan had never quite discarded the case for reincarnation that the Rev. Pierpont always used to argue. His fascination with Egyptology was possibly rooted in some personal identification with the lonely majesty of the god-kings. More than once he passionately lauded the Pharoahs whose kingdoms had only achieved their full vigor from a wholly aristocratic structure.

His morning levées in the Red Room saw Morgan enthroned above the art dealers, the businessmen, and the fund raisers who craved his favor. Belle Greene, his devoted librarian and chatelaine, may have helped to nourish his fantasies. Her Renaissance gowns and matching jewelry blended with the sumptuous rooms to invoke memories of gracious Florentine and Venetian palazzi.

She was attractive to men but would never marry. One of her many suitors, a millionaire lumber king, cabled a frantic proposal with a prepaid reply. She had wired back, "All proposals will be considered alphabetically after my fiftieth birthday." She preferred the company of scholars, usually of mature years, like Sydney Cockerell, director of the Fitzwilliam Museum in Cambridge, England.

Traveling abroad as Morgan's representative, with wide authority to negotiate with bibliophiles and art dealers, she was courted and lavishly entertained but never became easy prey for charlatans. "If a person is a worm, you step on him," she once advised her secretary. She fully enjoyed her liberal expense allowance. She favored Claridge's in London and the Paris Ritz, whose staffs often found her even more exacting than her employer. She cantered in Rotten Row like a proud duchess and invariably demanded the best seats at Covent Garden. Back on East Thirty-sixth Street, however, though prepared if necessary to argue with Morgan, she treated him with unfailing respect and a sympathy that he valued during his occasional spells of melancholia.

He was now plainly assuming the role of elder statesman but with far more zest for cataloguing his treasures and for foreign travel than attending 23 Wall Street. From 1910 onward he preferred not to concern himself with projects involving less than five million dollars, although he still had to be consulted on major policy or senior staff appointments. And he would personally intervene at the White House level on any significant moves over railroad tariffs or foreign policy. He was gratified when Congress backed his syndicate to underwrite a $50 million Chinese loan for railroads and other concessions to counter the thrust by British, German, and French bankers into China, as well as increasing investment by Russia and Japan in Manchuria. It was one of his few amicable points of contact with Taft's lethargic and often unpredictable administration.

He continued to attend conventions of the Protestant Episcopal Church and never relaxed his grip on the Metropolitan Museum's affairs, but he had almost abandoned visiting his many clubs. The old friends with whom he used to share a drink or a game of whist were now entertained by him at home or on *Corsair*. The only exception was the Union Club where he sometimes dined in private with Charles Lanier or Chauncey Depew. It was also true that he hardly ever missed a meeting of the New England Society. The firm's distinguished lawyer, Joseph H. Choate, had succeeded him as president. He was not such a generous benefactor but his charm and wit appealed far more to members than Morgan's curt formality. At one of the society's pre-Christmas dinners he once assured the guests that he had most respect for the Pilgrim Mothers because they had not only suffered as pioneers but endured the Pilgrim Fathers!

Pierpont had drawn closer to his son and often visited his spacious three-story house and estate near Glen Cove on Long Island. Jack was moving smoothly into the succession with the advantage of excellent partners to whom he gladly delegated increased authority. He had the backing of a powerful legal staff, headed by Charles Steele and Stetson, with Harry Davison as the executive linchpin. Perkins had left the firm and been replaced by Thomas W. Lamont, Harvard '92, the tall and dignified blue-eyed son of a Methodist minister—almost ideal Morgan specifications. He had gone into banking after a spell of newspaper management and quickly showed an exceptional grasp of foreign affairs. He made himself particularly useful by developing closer contacts with the London branch, which, from New Year's Day 1910, formally adopted the title of Morgan, Grenfell & Co. The senior partner, Edward Grenfell (later, Lord St. Just), had joined Old Broad Street in 1904 and become a director of the Bank of England a year later.

With this strong team backing his heir, Pierpont had no anxiety over the firm, whose health and stability were now accepted by the world's money markets as the index of America's financial wellbeing. But at times Belle Greene sensed his innate pathos. He would often look old and vulnerable as he dozed in his red plush armchair, the cigar unlit in his mouth and the two solitaire decks scattered across the folding table, while Chun, his pekingese, snored wheezily on a red velvet cushion before the fire. His face was gaunter, the sunken cheeks and heavy white moustache emphasizing the florid bulbous nose.

Belle Greene noticed his taste for Nathaniel Hawthorne's allegorical tale, *The Birthmark,* which told of a young woman whose beauty was flawed by an indelible mark on her cheek. It vanished after she drank a potion prepared by her husband who was obsessed by the mark, but in that instant she died. Morgan often brooded over this macabre story, which he read and reread, possibly identifying his own affliction with the heroine's cruel disfigurement. His leanings toward reincarnation may well have inspired the hope that in some future existence he too would find release and emerge as a handsome clear-skinned Adonis, the symbol of masculinity he had so long envied and idolized.

He had need of such comforting fantasies for, in the harsh, everyday world, his nose continued to be cruelly caricatured. Even those who sympathized could not always escape embarrassment. Mrs. Dwight Morrow, whose husband would soon enter 23 Wall as a partner, once invited the great man to tea and suffered agonies of stage fright before he arrived. She was especially apprehensive that her small daughter, Anne (the future wife of Charles Lindbergh), might wreck the party. The tot, something of an *enfant terrible,* was sternly cautioned not to stare at the guest's nose or refer to its size and color. She kept her eyes dutifully averted, curtseyed to perfection, and departed with a polite, "Good afternoon, sir." Flushed with relief, Elizabeth Morrow stammered, "Do you like nose in your tea, Mr. Morgan?"

When restless or out of sorts, he would often turn to a favorite passage from Dickens or the Bible. His oculist had prescribed glasses for fine print, but he still complained of headaches and preferred to have Belle Greene read to him in her clear, caressing voice. He never seemed to tire of Jonah and the Whale. When she once asked if he really believed it, he replied earnestly, "If the time ever comes when I cannot believe every word in the Bible, then I could believe none of it."

Some afternoons, usually on Saturdays if not weekending at Cragston or Jack's estate on Long Island, he would slip out of the library and drive over to St. George's to kneel in prayer. He was always pleased when the organist offered to play for him. If the church happened to be empty, he would sing a hymn or two but had the doors closed during his visit.

Morgan's melancholia would lift the moment he arrived at the pier to embark on an Atlantic voyage. Only a few intimates like the Morton Patons, his chosen companions for the crossing in mid-February 1910, knew that, apart from a short Mediterranean cruise and the ritual stop-off in Aix-les-Bains, his program included two very special items.

He had arranged to study White Star's plans to build another liner, the *Titanic,* as sister ship to the *Olympic,* which was scheduled to sail on her maiden voyage in about a year. Between them they could be expected to restore the fortunes of International Mercantile Marine and check Cunard's domination. This was important but less so, in his view, than the wholesale removal of his collections from Europe. The operation, likely to take at least two years, had taken root some months before when Congress voted to exempt from import duty (previously some 20 percent of the declared value) all works of art over twenty years old. Until then it had been practical to keep his paintings, plate, statuary, and countless other treasures in England or on the Continent. Apart from those housed in Prince's Gate, the bulk were on loan or stored in museums, galleries, and vaults. The relief from American customs duty was tempting enough, but he could no longer hesitate once Britain's radical chancellor, Lloyd George, decided to impose death duties of 10 percent. One item alone, Raphael's Colonna Altarpiece, currently in the National ʿallery, would have reduced his estate by $425,000. The punitive effect on his heirs if he died suddenly, leaving a collection valued at around $50 million, had become too obvious to ignore.

In April, while cruising in the Mediterranean, he read of Lord Kitchener's American tour. The governor of California had greeted him as "the greatest general of the greatest army in the world." He was mobbed by the West Point cadets and, being an enthusiastic collector of rare china, he praised Morgan's superb Chinese porcelain in the Metropolitan.

The banker was in Paris buying antique watches when he heard on May 6 that King Edward had died. Next day he crossed the Channel. Apart from instructing museum officials on the shipment of his various collections, he remained quietly at Dover House. He also joined the quarter of a million people who filed sorrowfully past the catafalque in Westminster Hall where the king's body lay in State and he attended the funeral as one of President Taft's representatives, walking in step with Theodore Roosevelt.

One of his few social engagements was the Pilgrims' Society's dinner at the Savoy on June 10 to honor Commander Robert E. Peary for his expedition to the North Pole. The room was decorated to represent the Polar Sea with a model of the *Roosevelt,* locked in by icebergs, as its centerpiece. The waiters all wore white furs and parkas, and the Stars and Stripes was picked out in colored electric lights on each of the eighteen tables.

Morgan was gratified at being placed at Table One between Lord Chief Justice Alverstone and the Lord Bishop of Hereford. They faced the guest of honor and Captain Robert Falcon Scott, who would be sailing to Melbourne next month in the *Terra Nova* on the first leg of his ill-fated voyage to the Antarctic. The convivial dinner was slightly marred for Morgan, whose Christian name appeared as "Pierrepoint" on the table plan. One of his fellow guests jovially suggested that the guilty printer or typist must have subconsciously been thinking of Henry Pierrepoint, England's Official Executioner! Morgan smiled, but was not too amused.

The following year he was back for a longer European trip that included visits to London, Paris, and Rome and some weeks with the museum's archeologists in Egypt. Once again he rested at the Oasis of Khargeh, where the venerable Omdeh greeted him with baskets of local flowers and fruit. He reciprocated with a box of his strongest cigars, which the Sheikh politely sampled but had to put aside after a violent fit of coughing.

Morgan traveled to Belfast on May 31, 1911, for the launching of the *Titanic.* She would have a hundred more first-class cabins than the *Olympic,* which had sailed that day for New York on her maiden voyage. He approved the design and furnishings of his private suite. It would include a parlor, a reserved promenade deck, and every possible comfort—down to cigar holders in the bathrooms. The graceful vessel, 46,000 tons and almost 900 feet long, would boast a 50-telephone switchboard and a hospital equipped with a complete operating theater. First-class passengers would enjoy a gymnasium, a squash court (on which Jack Morgan was impatient to perform), a Turkish bath, and the first-ever swimming pool installed aboard ship.

That autumn he and Belle Greene, assisted by customs officials and experts from the Metropolitan Museum, were hammering out details for the shipment and storage of the scores of crates that would be leaving Europe during the coming months. Working out the complicated schedules had imposed a heavy strain on him after his recent trip. He was therefore even less inclined than usual to dwell on Washington reports that Taft, thwarted by Standard Oil, hoped to regain congressional support by a full-scale assault on U. S. Steel. Gary had not taken this too seriously until Attorney General George Wickersham assured him at a dinner party that prosecution was imminent.

On the night of October 27 Morgan had dined quietly with his son-in-law at his Madison Avenue home. He was savoring a final cigar with his coffee and brandy when a federal officer, ushered in by the butler, formally handed him a document. A glance at the cover confirmed the attorney general's threat to bring suit. Morgan seemed dazed. "Well, it has come to this!" he said hoarsely. He sat back, eyes half-closed, while Satterlee slowly read out the detailed indictment, charging the corporation and its subsidiaries as "unlawful monopolies." It would be several hours before he plodded upstairs for a sleepless night.

Morgan had overreacted, largely from hurt pride at the "treachery" of yet another Republican president. The suit, opening the following May in New Jersey before four circuit judges, drifted into a legal impasse that would lose all significance during the wartime boom in steel output. Almost a decade hence, long after Morgan had passed from the scene, a Supreme Court majority blandly decided that the trust represented "not monopoly, but concentration of efforts with resultant economies and benefits."

Its creator could hardly have improved on the wording.

Heavier clouds were gathering during his last years on earth. Theodore Roosevelt had become incensed by Taft's reminders to the electorate that he had personally disapproved of the suspect takeover of Tennessee Coal and Iron. Dripping with national and foreign honors, the Rough Rider now unfurled a new Progressive Party banner and charged forward with a salvo of imperialistic fancies and liberal reforms.

Morgan deplored this unseemly party infighting and refused to finance either of the rivals. He saw no possible chance of victory for the Democratic nominee, Woodrow Wilson, governor of New Jersey and a former Princeton professor. By all accounts he was a woolly, high-minded idealist, much less to be feared than a spellbinding demagogue like William Jennings Bryan, who had agreed to serve under him, if he were elected.

Sailing for England on December 30, 1911, Morgan was excitedly looking forward to the departure of the *Titanic* on her maiden voyage, although he intended to defer his own first crossing until later in the year. He had no taste for the photographers and reporters who would swarm aboard at Southampton. Meanwhile, he had planned another pleasant interlude in Egypt. This time his large party, including Mary Burns, the Lythgoes, and Bishop Lawrence and his wife, would cruise up the Nile in an all-steel luxury paddle-wheel steamer specially constructed for him by Cook's. It had been christened *Khargeh* at his command.

Before leaving New York he had also approved the final designs for a more compact modern structure to replace the old Drexel Building. Like his library, it would be built from marble. He would keep his glass-enclosed room on the main floor, but he and senior partners would have additional offices on the next floor for more privacy and for important interviews.

The new building would commemorate his long reign as the world's most powerful financial ruler and symbolize the firm's supreme confidence in its future. Rock-based on upward of seventy directorships ("one for each year of his life," a critic noted sourly), which he and his associates now held in corporations with aggregate resources of several billion dollars, the House of Morgan could ignore the noisy trumpetings of Taft or Roosevelt and, of course, of a donnish, would-be Joshua like Wilson, who had lately piped, "The great monopoly in this country is the money monopoly. A great industrial nation is controlled by its credit. Our system of credit is concentrated . . . in the hands of a few men . . . who chill and check and destroy economic freedom."

After the *Olympic* had put into Cherbourg, Morgan went on to Paris where he stayed a few days with Robert Bacon. His former partner and much-missed aide was giving up his post as ambassador to become a Fellow of Harvard at President Lowell's request. He was anxious to return home but generously agreed to stay on and smooth the takeover by his successor, banker Myron T. Herrick. With much reluctance he had therefore canceled his passage on the *Titanic*. Morgan was sympathetic and assured him that an office next to his own in the new building at 23 Wall Street would be permanently available to him whenever he needed to be in New York for business meetings.

Before cruising up the Nile, he asked all the ladies in his party to his suite in Shepheard's to admire the haul of bracelets, necklets, and gold coins bought that morning from a leading Cairo jeweler. "Help yourselves," he said jovially. At a dinner party given in his honor by the American ambassador, he met Lord Kitchener, who invited him to visit his new 500-acre estate, Broome Park near Canterbury, which would house his collection of paintings and china.

Morgan remained very cheerful during his tour of Luxor and such favorite haunts as the Oasis of Khargeh. He then headed back to Rome and Florence for a few days before arriving at Aix-les-Bains to take the waters and see his French lady (once Bishop Lawrence and his wife had left for England). He was celebrating his seventy-fifth birthday on April 17 when the tragic news broke that the *Titanic* had struck an iceberg about four days out of Southampton. One thousand five hundred and thirteen passengers lost their lives. Bruce Ismay and the luckless Captain E. J. Smith were among the survivors picked up by Cunard's *Carpathia*. Their rescue added to worldwide fury over the disclosure that lifeboats had been available for only half of those aboard. As head of International Mercantile Marine, Morgan was at once condemned by critics who claimed he had reduced safety standards to provide extra luxuries on "The Millionaires' Special." Pictures and drawings of his own staterooms were freely published, and it did not help when news leaked out that the fifth shipment of his objets d'art had been canceled because of last-minute holdups in crating.

The *Titanic* disaster was interpreted by many as a divine visitation on the evils of frivolity and extravagance that Justice Brandeis had denounced as "the curse of bigness." William Jennings Bryan, perhaps with half an eye on the Jewish vote, publicly mourned for elderly Mrs. Ruth Straus, who had insisted on going down with her husband rather than take her place in a lifeboat. The veteran tear-jerker poignantly reminded newspaper readers that another Ruth had said, "Entreat me not to leave thee."

Although White Star would eventually revive, the loss of its "unsinkable" flagship was a shattering blow in the competition with its principal rival, Cunard. Morgan felt even more bruised by the personal abuse which did not diminish even after an official inquiry by the British Board of Trade had dismissed the wild accusations of negligence. He refused to be drawn into technical arguments and turned for relief to the drugs of travel and treasure hunting. Regardless of expense he pounced on prized letters, the Sackville-West tapestries at Knole, and Old Masters from the Duke of Alba's palace to add to the already bursting basements in the Metropolitan Museum.

His collections would eventually fill 351 huge crates, after being checked for age, authenticity, and market valuation by a U. S. Treasury inspector, whose travel and living expenses he had willingly underwritten. His own expert, Jacques Seligman, had worked for a year in a vault at the Victoria and Albert Museum in London, packing each of the priceless and often fragile pieces. The jewels, porcelain, and ivories alone filled forty showcases. Among them were such masterpieces as a green jade cup decorated in gold and enamel from the Empress Frederick of Prussia's castle, an amber cup belonging at one time to the Farnese Cardinals, miniature carvings in boxwood and rock crystal of sacred objects fashioned at the peak of fifteenth century

Flemish craftsmanship, gold medallions dating from medieval days, and the unique Golden Cross of Honor, fashioned from thirty pieces of scroll decorated with enamels. Buried with Christian II of Saxony and later removed from his tomb, it was put up for sale in Dresden and afterward sold by Guttman of Berlin to Pierpont Morgan.

One of Dr. G. C. Williamson's most ornate catalogues was devoted entirely to his antique watches. Some of the silver gilt in the vaults of Prince's Gate included finds like a Charles II twelve-piece toilet service, as well as gold and onyx snuffboxes and the beautiful Holbein miniatures, which Queen Alexandra and her sister, the Dowager Empress of Russia, particularly admired when they visited the house for tea and a tour of inspection. Several pictures, among them Gainsborough's *Duchess of Devonshire* and the exquisite Fragonard panels, currently on exhibit at the Guildhall, had to be carefully handled to avoid any damage in transit.

The comprehensive removal of such a cornucopia did not pass without comment or recrimination. Morgan, seldom disposed to defend his actions, was stung into issuing a press statement: "I make the transfer with great reluctance, deeply appreciating the constant kindness and courtesies received by me and the appreciation shown by everyone in England. But, being an American citizen, there was no other way for me to avoid double duties by both the American and the British authorities." He was still smarting when Elbert Gary visited him at Dover House. They walked together in the garden for a while, the judge updating him on disturbing changes at home.

Wilson had been duly nominated at the Democratic Convention in Baltimore, where William Jennings Bryan took a swipe at both Taft and Roosevelt, urging the country to oppose "the nomination of any candidate for president who is the representative of, or under obligations to, J. Pierpont Morgan, Thomas F. Ryan, August Belmont, or any other member of the privilege-hunting or favor-seeking class." Morgan pooh-poohed "Cross of Gold" Bryan's now-familiar tactics, nor did he take too seriously Gary's news that the Senate had appointed a committee under Moses E. Clapp of Minnesota to probe Big Business contributions to Republican campaign funds from the 1904 presidential election onward. He assured Gary that he had nothing to hide from an investigation that Taft had obviously welcomed to discredit Roosevelt, whose Bull Moose Party was rapidly gaining support. He seemed rather more disturbed by the prospect of Wilson's driving a wedge between his two Republican opponents, and sweeping into the White House on an anti-Wall Street ticket.

He became more despondent after Gary's departure. While browsing in the library at Dover House he came across several bound volumes of his letters to his father, dating back to the early years with Duncan, Sherman & Co. Some were very sentimental, others referred to confidential business matters that might embarrass the firm and its clients, past and present, if exposed to unfriendly scrutiny. He decided impulsively to burn them all.

At the end of July 1912 he returned home and learned that he would have to appear before the Clapp Committee in October. This was depressing but not so irritating as the dilatoriness of the Metropolitan's trustees who, though overjoyed at receiving the most generous art donation of all time, had neither insured the priceless collection nor taken even preliminary steps to provide the special wing he had taken for granted. The museum's charter apparently precluded the allocation of such funds without vote by New York's civic authorities. The City Fathers, sensing an election swing against the Republican Party, showed little enthusiasm to glorify the name and memory of J. Pierpont Morgan and one section argued that a multimillionaire yachtsman, who had not hesitated to endow a luxurious Lying-in Hospital and who allegedly built a theater for Maxine Elliott, could well afford to house his own plunder.

On October 3 he went to Washington with Herbert Satterlee and calmly assured the Clapp Committee that his firm had indeed contributed $150,000 toward the Republican Party's campaign in 1904 but without exerting any pressure for "favors" from the candidate, Theodore Roosevelt, who had *not* telephoned him from the White House, as some of the press suggested. He agreed that he had sent a check for $30,000 in 1908 to help Taft, which somewhat aborted the latter's transparent attempt to discredit the Bull Moose candidate. Roosevelt was equally emphatic: "I knew that Mr. Morgan had felt very much aggrieved over the bringing of the Northern Securities suit, and I understood—though I cannot say that I knew it—I understood that he had expressed himself in very strong terms over the action which I took during the anthracite coal strike; and I had not known—I had supposed he was hostile to me—I had not known that he contributed to my campaign fund."

Morgan had dismissed this hearing as a nit-picking exercise by some publicity-hungry busybodies. He continued to sulk at the holdups in funding his new gallery for which he held the museum's trustees mainly responsible. His temper was not improved by the election of Woodrow Wilson, with Roosevelt edging Taft into third place.

He was abnormally gloomy at the family's Thanksgiving dinner. A few days later he summoned Edward Robinson, the Metropolitan's director, and brusquely intimated that he would not be bequeathing his collections as he had previously intended. He stated that his estate could not spare an estimated $50 million in assets, but his icy tone underlined the true reason. Robinson was dismayed but still did not take the threat too seriously, as Morgan had so far made no move of any kind to remove his numerous crates from storage. It was a fatal misjudgment of his character. By the time the City Fathers had agreed to fund a Morgan wing at the museum and the trustees had hastened to stage an exhibition in a temporary gallery, he had already taken steps to deprive the Metropolitan of the bulk of his collections.

Even this nagging problem receded before an attack on the firm's policy and his own probity. The Pujo Committee was appointed by the House of Representatives to investigate the events leading up to the 1907 crisis and the remarkable "community of interest" subsequently developed between 23 Wall Street and the country's most influential banks, trusts, and insurance concerns. With the president-elect's approval the committee would determine whether this constituted a "Money Trust" that had allegedly ignored the national interest for selfish motives of gain.

Harriman and Standard Oil's H. H. Rogers were now both dead; Stillman, a sick man and semiretired in Europe, would not be available; and William Rockefeller, also ailing and highly nervous of crossexamination, would make every excuse to avoid attendance. It left J. P. Morgan as the prime target.

The country was agog for his appearance as a witness. It had an added piquancy. Samuel Untermyer, chief counsel for the Committee, had made his reputation as a relentless prosecutor in exposing the Equitable Life Assurance Company's irregularities, the Standard Oil monopoly, and several other suits for violation of antitrust laws. As a lifelong champion of organized labor and his fellow Jews, he was expected to strip the proud old bigot of all his epaulets and decorations in what promised to be a Dreyfus trial in reverse. As it turned out, there was no vulgar attempt at character assassination, Untermyer's courtesy fully matching the dignity of his opponent.

Morgan arrived in Washington on December 17, 1912, attended by an eight-man team of lawyers, led by Choate and Stetson, who tried to calm him after he had exasperatedly flipped through the newspapers, almost all antagonistic, and snorted, "I'll go to jail rather than discuss my private affairs." At 11:30 next morning, he stalked unsmilingly into the committee room through a crowd of spectators and photographers. He was wearing his familiar velvet-collared topcoat with a silk hat and leaned heavily on his gold-knobbed stick. He bowed stiffly to Chairman Pujo and the five other members as if about to open a routine board meeting of one of his many railroad companies. However, he managed a polite request to sit in a swivel chair at the end of the long table occupied by his judges, explaining that his hearing was none too sound. Although rather pale, he gave no outward sign of strain or infirmity. Throughout the next two days he answered most questions with rarely a glance at the bulky sheaf of notes prepared by his lawyers. When at a loss for a figure, he casually told the committee that he would have it looked up and produced "in due course." He remained dignified and at times almost offhand in manner. He agreed with one of the committee who insisted that he had preferred combination above all else, adding with a half-smile, "But I *do* like a little competition." His audience enjoyed the touch of irony.

Untermyer had opened by asking formally, "Does your New York house function as a general banking house?"

"We try to, sir" he replied equably. Counsel led him through a maze of transactions designed to show that a gigantic syndicate, dominated by the witness, had clearly ruled the market. Morgan countered by stressing that, whatever some critics thought of the mammoth trusts, he had consistently checked abuses to preserve the nation's financial stability.

He seldom lost his poise yet, almost imperceptibly, found himself put on the defensive by the cumulative pressure of so many probing questions. Irritated by the hint that his whole strategy had been inspired by a lust for money and power, he replied sharply, "If it is good business for the interests of the country to do it, I do it."

"But, Mr. Morgan," prodded Untermyer, "does not a man quite subconsciously imagine that things are for the interest of the country when they are good business?"

"No, sir."

"You think you are able to judge and impartially to differentiate where your own interests are concerned, just as clearly as though you had no interest at stake, do you?"

"Exactly, sir." A titter of disbelief from the gallery encouraged Untermyer to press his advantage. He turned abruptly to the purchase of Equitable stock from Thomas F. Ryan and Harriman's executors.

"You may explain—if you care to—why you bought $51,000 par value of stock, that paid only $3,710 a year, for approximately $3 million?"

"Because I thought it was good business."

"Where is the good business, then, in buying a security that pays only one-ninth of one percent?"

"Because I thought it was better there than it was where it was. That is all." It sounded woolly. His lawyers looked even more uneasy when he added hastily, "The only reason I did it, on which I am willing to stand up before the community, is that I thought it was the thing to do."

"This is a little nebulous, is it not?" commented Untermyer.

"You may call it so," Morgan snapped huffily, "but I do not look at it in that light." From that moment he stood revealed as an arrogant self-satisfied financier, who seemed to have taken as his text, *"Call upon me in the day of trouble and I will deliver thee and thou shalt glorify me."*

On the second day of the hearing it became plain that Untermyer was on top. Even without fully establishing the existence of
an arbitrary Money Trust, his incisive cross-examination added
layer upon layer to that central thesis, until suspicion dovetailed
into near-certainty. At one stage he quizzed the banker on the
Southern Railway, which his firm and the First National Bank
had together controled through a voting trust. "You think that
where you name a board of directors that is to remain in existence
only for a year, and you have the power to name another board the
next year, that this board . . . is in an independent position to deal
with your banking house as would a board named by the stockholders themselves?"

"I think it would be better."

"More independent?" persisted the attorney.

"Better."

"Will you tell us why?"

"Simply because we select the best people that we can find for
the position."

Slightly nettled, Untermyer then asked, "Do you not realize
that a board thus selected is under the domination of the people
who name it?"

"My experience is quite otherwise, sir." Morgan then observed,
in parenthesis, that he had always disapproved of short selling
and reckless speculation. Counsel let that pass, but he did not
have to remind the committee of Morgan's past dealings with
characters like Gates and Thomas Fortune Ryan or the Steel
Trust's brutal rape of Tennessee Coal and Iron. He preferred to
make the witness admit that profit was the mainspring of his
system.

"No, sir" Morgan objected emphatically. "The first thing is
character."

"Before money or property?"

"Before money or anything else. . . . A man I do not trust could
not get money from me on all the bonds in Christendom. . . . I have
known a man come into my office and I have given him a check for
a million dollars and I knew that they [obviously, he meant the
applicant's firm] had not a cent in the world."

"There were not many of them?" gibed Untermyer.

"Yes, a good many."

The exchange won him applause and some rose in respect as he

stepped down. He shook hands with each member of the committee and also grasped the hand of a policeman, who had saluted as
he left the building with his son and Louisa.

He looked drained after returning to New York and became
more dispirited after reading the newspaper reports. Several,
including a number from overseas, approved his insistence on
"character before credit," but the majority professed shock over
the "billions of capital" at his autocratic command. All anticipated an adverse report by the Pujo Committee. None doubted,
least of all Morgan himself, that the incoming president would
soon introduce legislation to control the money-center banks and
remove their authority to act as stockbrokers. Washington would
also be empowered to issue legal tender backed by assets other
than government bonds.

The plans for a Federal Reserve had already been drafted.
Under the new system each of the nation's dozen Reserve banks,
to whose capital stock the 28,000 national, state, and private
banks would have to subscribe, would hold a gold reserve of 40
percent against federal bonds. Once the enabling act came into
force, the "Fed" would automatically become "a lender of last
resort," favorably placed to bail out banks or trusts menaced by
panic runs and crises, like that of 1907, instead of having to rely
upon the intervention of an individual financial dictator.

The complex details of this revolutionary measure owed much
to a team of experts headed by Paul Warburg of Kuhn, Loeb, the
firm that had so often aligned itself in the past with Harriman
and others opposed to Morgan's proud fiefdom. Even more ironically, the new Federal Reserve Act would almost coincide with
the completion of his splendid marble power base at 23 Wall
Street.

It has long been accepted that his life was shortened by the
humiliation of being publicly cross-examined, but he had already
suffered painfully from the Steel Trust suit, the personal abuse
directed at him after the loss of the *Titanic,* and the infuriating
quibbles over housing his collections. Before sailing for Europe
early in 1913 on the advice of his physician, George Dixon, who
had strongly recommended rest, sunshine, and Mediterranean
warmth, he summoned Cass Ledyard to revise his will, in partic-

ular the disposal of his treasures. Apart from his bequests to the Wadsworth Atheneum, in Hartford, Connecticut, which remained untouched, the Metropolitan would have received all the rest. He now stipulated that, unless the collections were transferred in his lifetime, they would pass to his son with full discretion to make "a permanent disposition of them or of such portions of them as he may determine."

He spent his last days in the Red Room, playing solitaire and seeing only Davison, Tom Lamont, and a few close friends. Crouched by the fire, he rummaged gloomily through old papers, many of which he destroyed. He brightened only when Colonel George Harvey, editor of *Harper's Weekly,* arrived to wish him bon voyage. Harvey, a lifelong supporter of the Democratic Party, tactfully commiserated with him on his recent ordeal in Washington. "I hated going," Morgan said sadly, "but am glad I went. Perhaps people know me better now." He then amazed Harvey by remarking very earnestly that, if called upon, he would happily place "any influence or resources" at Wilson's disposal in the national interest.

One can only surmise that, like a veteran actor reluctant to leave the boards, he still dreamed of making a triumphant farewell performance by upstaging the new president, like Cleveland, McKinley, and Theodore Roosevelt before him. If so, he was pathetically blinkering himself—not for the first time—to the hard facts of political reality. Had Wilson taken the unlikely step of restoring some of his lost prestige, it would have outraged liberal and trade-union opinion, now solidly united to destroy all that the name of Morgan symbolized. Without waiting for either Pujo's report or the Federal Reserve Act, the radical press was already dipping its pens in venom. Pierpont was particularly incensed by one cartoon depicting him as a vulture preying upon the entrails of the New Haven Railroad.

After George Harvey's departure, he received Judge Gary, who said in a choked voice, "Come back to us well and strong, Mr. Morgan."

He replied quietly, "I don't know. I may never come back." The previous day he had driven over to St. George's and handed a sealed envelope to Dr. Karl Reiland, the new rector, with instructions for his funeral service. It was to be simple, with no address or eulogy. He requested the choir to sing three of his favorite hymns and wished the service to end with Harry Burleigh, the great black baritone, giving "Calvary" as a solo.

His family noted sadly that he lacked the exuberance that had always preceded his trips overseas. This time, while fidgeting to be off, he shuffled around and absent-mindedly repeated trivial last instructions. He also decided against the ritual send-off party in his stateroom and embraced his wife, Jack, and the grandchildren at home before driving to the pier with Louisa.

The White Star liner *Adriatic* was comfortable, but he slept badly, ate little, and played continuous solitaire in his sitting room rather than face the cold and fog on deck. Stopping off at Monte Carlo, he went down to Naples and listlessly toured Pompeii. He became a little more animated at his impending Nile cruise in the *Khargeh,* but frowned angrily over newspaper excerpts from the Pujo Report. One passage confirmed that 23 Wall had marketed corporation securities worth close on two billion dollars during the past decade, exclusive of those privately issued. On the Morgan-Baker-Stillman coalition the committee noted bitingly, "The acts of this inner group have been more destructive of competition than anything accomplished by the trusts, for they strike at the very vitals of potential competition in every industry under their protection . . ." It was the clearest possible endorsement of Woodrow Wilson's new Federal Reserve system and his repeated pledge to check monopolistic stock holdings.

Morgan became testier. He picked fault with everything on the *Khargeh,* from the sluggish engines to the food. He ignored the most tempting dishes and nibbled at an egg, an onion, and a crust of dry bread, which aggravated his dyspepsia. Cook's hastily brought in a new chef and replaced several stewards. They also engaged Dr. Tribe, a cheerful American physician, who prescribed a more sensible menu and optimistically forbade cigars.

At Luxor he revived slightly but was still plagued by insomnia and indigestion. Tribe called in a local English doctor, who made a thorough examination but discovered nothing to cause alarm. Morgan continued to weaken, sapped by nervous exhaustion and an inability to assimilate enough food, but even more by his deepening melancholia. He yielded at last to his daughter's anxious pleas to cable Satterlee and Dr. Dixon to join them. He had reluctantly decided against inviting Jack, whose sudden departure from Wall Street might have confirmed rumors about his father's health and damaged the stock market.

Their arrival was a temporary tonic. He at once organized various excursions, including a trip to the Pyramids, but found it difficult to walk any distance. He studied reports of Wilson's inauguration on March 4 and scowled at his list of cabinet members, with William Jennings Bryan as secretary of state. He soon lapsed into gloom. A specialist, summoned from Italy, confirmed that his blood pressure was far too high and thought he might benefit from a change of scene. Morgan agreed to spend a few days in Rome before returning home for a long period of rest, strict diet, and careful nursing.

The party settled into a luxury suite of two parlors and eight bedrooms in the Grand Hotel. The usual horde of Italian art dealers and touts converged, reinforced by newspapermen hungry for the latest medical bulletins. He was soon impatient to get back to New York but abhorred the prospect of gawking fellow passengers and reporters. He cabled Jack to send over the *Corsair* with a supply of fresh butter, cream, fruit, and vegetables from Cragston. Excited at crossing the Atlantic in his yacht, he chatted almost genially and even pretended to enjoy his barley soup and chopped meat.

On Easter Sunday he attended the American Protestant Church with the Satterlees and walked unaided to a reserved pew, but he had to be helped out during the service. For some days he was fed intravenously. He rallied a little and curtly arranged for a special train to take him to Calais before crossing to England, where he planned to stay awhile at Dover House. But before long he had lost the power of speech and fell into a coma from which he emerged only fitfully. According to Herbert Satterlee, he mumbled about his schooldays in Connecticut and Vevey. During the night of March 31, 1913, he died peacefully in his sleep.

The coffin was sent by special train to Le Havre, where the local garrison turned out to salute a Commander of the Legion of Honor. He crossed the Atlantic for the last time aboard the steamship *France* and rested in a cabin converted into a mortuary

311

chapel. He lay in state in his library on East Thirty-sixth Street until the funeral. His embalmed face was waxen and relaxed, the hideous nose at last mercifully unblemished. Across the corridor Belle Greene sat alone in her room for hour after hour. She wrote brokenly to a friend, "He was almost a father to me. . . . His never-failing sympathy, his understanding, and his great confidence and trust in me bridged all the difference in age, wealth, and position."

The New York Stock Exchange closed for a day after solemnly declaring, "In the development of our country he contributed more than any man in our day. . . . The whole world has lost a wise counsellor and a helpful friend." Kitchener and the kaiser, whose armies would soon be slaughtering each other, sent wreaths, as did the kings of England and Italy and Leopold II's successor. A vast crowd thronged St. George's for the funeral service. The coffin was covered with red roses, Pierpont's favorite flower. The honorary pallbearers included old friends like Robert Bacon, George Bowdoin, Joseph Choate, Elbert Gary, and Elihu Root. After the short service, the coffin was taken by special train for burial in the family mausoleum on Cedar Hill. Hartford's fire bell rang out seventy-five times to mark each year of his life. It also tolled the passing of an era. His firm would grow far richer in the First World War and during the seven fat years before the Wall Street crash, but no private banker would ever again govern America's cash and credit as, for good or ill, he had for over a quarter of a century.

Pope Pius mourned the loss of "a great and good man." Theodore Roosevelt declared warmly that "any kind of meanness and smallness was wholly alien to his nature." More unexpectedly, Untermyer expressed admiration for "a man of rare breadth and public usefulness . . . who was animated by high purpose and never knowingly abused his almost incredible power." No doubt he was sincere, but it made a quaint footnote to the Pujo Committee's report.

Pulitzer's *New York World,* so often harshly critical of J. P. Morgan's business philosophy, came nearest perhaps to anticipating the verdict of history: "No man clothed with irresponsible, autocratic power could be expected to wield it more honorably or ably or patriotically than he."

POSTSCRIPT

J. P. Morgan's estate was valued for taxes at $68 million, but he had previously transferred substantial blocks of securities to his family. The art collections were underinsured at around $28 million. The Duveens were probably not too far off the mark in their estimate of $50 million. It was a comfortable fortune, if relatively modest compared with the Vanderbilts, Astors, Rockefellers, and Carnegie.

His widow, who survived until 1924, inherited an annuity of $100,000, together with the income from a million-dollar trust fund and the life use of 219 Madison Avenue and Cragston. The three daughters were each bequeathed a $3 million trust fund, with a separate million apiece for Herbert Satterlee and William Pierson Hamilton. St. George's benefited from the income of a half-million dollar fund, Dr. Markoe's Lying-in Hospital continued to receive its $100,000 per annum, and another $100,000 would endow a House of Rest for Consumptives, to be known as the Amelia Sturges Morgan Memorial.

Jack inherited an outright sum of $3 million, plus the residual estate, including the yacht, the London mansions in Prince's Gate and Dover House, Roehampton, and all the valuable books, manuscripts, and prints at 33 East Thirty-sixth where, in accordance with Morgan's wishes, Belle Greene was to continue indefinitely as librarian.

The Metropolitan had hoped to receive the entire collection of paintings, miniatures, ivories, porcelain, gems, and sculptures that were displayed in a temporary gallery before being removed permanently to the Pierpont Morgan Wing, but Jack soon made his intentions plain by declining to succeed his father as president. During the next few years he handed over about two-fifths of the treasures. It was still a munificent bequest of nearly 7,000 rare objects, but he was severely criticized for hastily disposing of so much of the heritage. Frick paid $1.2 million for five of the Fragonard murals originally bought by Pierpont for only $310,000. The Vermeer went to the sugar magnate, H. O. Havemeyer. Peter Widener secured the superb Mazarin tapestry and other rich Morgan prizes. Many pieces were sold in Europe but would find their way back to American connoisseurs like Bache and Andrew Mellon.

Jack always claimed that he had faithfully executed his father's intentions. He also needed cash to meet taxes and the very handsome legacies when the firm faced a period of uncertainty as a result of the new administration's policies. The Clayton Act had been rushed through to check monopolies and arbitrary price fixing. It also made it illegal for anyone to serve on the boards of two competing companies or on more than one bank whose capital reserves and undivided profits exceeded $5 million.

Jack and his partners resigned from nearly thirty directorships, including the National City Bank, the National Bank of Commerce, and various railroads and insurance companies, but they would retain seats on U. S. Steel and certain other key concerns. Their gloom and despondency lifted dramatically as soon as the hard-pressed Allies turned to leading American investment houses for loans to buy munitions and other essential supplies. The London office of Morgan Grenfell & Co. quickly emerged as the natural Anglo-American liaison base for the British Treasury and the Bank of England. The New York firm, supported by its Paris branch, was also uniquely placed to become the chief purchasing agent for England, France and, to a lesser extent, Russia. It would organize syndicates to handle some $2 billion in bonds during the war years.

The first enormous Anglo-French loan of a half-billion dollars for munitions was floated by J. P. Morgan & Co., which generously declined any handling fee. The leading banks, trusts, and investment houses in New York City distributed the bonds, which were underwritten at 96 and offered to the public at two points higher. They carried interest at 5 percent to mature in five years. The issue was oversubscribed in two days.

Lord Moulton, head of the British Munitions Board, would later acknowledge gratefully, "The British and French armies couldn't have held out through 1915 except for the efforts of three American concerns—Morgan & Co. in purchasing munitions, Du Pont in supplying powder, and Bethlehem Steel in making guns and shells." At 23 Wall Street, where the staff worked around the clock in eight-hour shifts, the turnover often exceeded $10 million *a day*. The commission was enormous even with rates kept lower than those extorted by many profiteers, but there were pleasant fringe benefits. The stagnant International Mercantile Marine cartel had soon shed its mothballs, and U. S. Steel, which had paid no dividends in 1914, showed a profit of $48 a share within two years.

The isolationist Midwest, backed by many citizens of German origin across the country, singled out the Morgan firm as a puppet of British imperialism. But President Wilson and his powerful neutral bloc were severely jolted in May 1915 when a U-boat torpedoed the unarmed British liner *Lusitania* with a hundred Americans aboard. A few weeks later Jack Morgan literally came under fire for his uncompromising Anglophile stance. One weekend he entertained the British Ambassador, Sir Cecil Spring-Rice, and his wife at Glen Cove. Over breakfast they were planning a pleasant day's sailing in *Corsair* when a tall skinny man, named Dr. Erich Muenter (also known as Holt), a former teacher at Cornell, drove up to the house and demanded to see the owner. He then took out two revolvers (a stick of dynamite was later found in his pocket) and forced his way into the library. The butler shouted a warning. Jack rushed in and grappled with the intruder, who shot him twice, one bullet entering close to the spine. With the help of the butler and his own 220 pound bulk, he managed to floor his attacker, who committed suicide in prison before coming to trial.

Jack made a quick recovery. Aided by a superb team of specialists, including Davison, Lamont, Dwight Morrow, and Edward

315

Stettinius, who had taken charge of the firm's new Export Department, he redoubled his efforts to counterbalance Wilson's isolationism. That autumn he crossed the Atlantic and, at the urgent request of Lloyd George, Minister of Munitions, agreed to organize five equal credits of $300 million a month to tide England over a sticky period. Before sailing back he visited Dover House, which had been converted into a convalescent home for disabled British officers.

He returned to find Wilson engaged in his successful reelection campaign as "the man who kept us out of the war." On January 22, still clutching neutrality like a lifebelt while the U-boats continued to sink practically everything within periscope view, he dedicated himself anew to winning "Peace Without Victory." By early April, however, he had to ask Congress to help him make the world "safe for democracy" by declaring war on Germany and her allies. In the same breath he welcomed Kerensky's provisional government, which had taken over in Russia after the Tsar's abdication. His faith was not shared by Jack Morgan, whose warm sympathy for the doomed Romanovs offended many of Washington's liberals and discouraged the president from accepting his offer to serve as a dollar-a-year man.

He had already placed *Corsair* at the navy's disposal for convoy and antisubmarine patrols. His older son, Junius, who had entered 23 Wall straight from Harvard, joined the Naval Coast Defense Reserve less than a month after America went to war. Anne Morgan, Pierpont's spinster daughter, founded the American Friends of France and won the Croix de Guerre for several risky missions to help wounded fighting men and evacuate civilian refugees. She contributed large sums to provide food, clothing, and desperately needed medical supplies.

Her exploits only added to Jack's resentment of Washington's cold rejection. He had to stand by while his partners were given official duties but seldom with any reference to their association with J. P. Morgan & Co. Lamont traveled back and forth as a financial roving ambassador, Davison headed the American Red Cross, and Stettinius was appointed secretary of state. Jack had congratulated Bob Bacon on being seconded from Pershing's staff to become chief of the American Military Mission at Haig's headquarters, but the elevation of certain others, whom he and his father had long despised, was almost intolerable. Schwab had been invited to reorganize the rundown aircraft manufacturing industry, while Bernard Baruch became chairman of the powerful War Industries Board and would later act as Wilson's economic adviser at Versailles.

Jack"s irritation was exacerbated by a series of death threats from pro-Germans and radicals enraged by his outspoken comments on the Bolshevik Revolution. He took out a policy for half a million dollars, then a record sum for life insurance, and reluctantly submitted to police protection.

The end of the war brought no respite. On May Day 1919 he received a bomb by post. He denounced it as the work of liberals and trade union agitators, whom he lumped together as "anarchists" indistinguishable from those who had butchered the Tsar and his family. He seemed far more annoyed by yet another slight from Capitol Hill. In a burst of generosity he had offered his mansion in Prince's Gate rent free to the American embassy, in London, which occupied Dorchester House on a £12,000 a year lease. Congress only accepted with reluctance several months later.

In September 1920, while he was on holiday in England, a bomb exploded in front of the Assay Office facing the Morgan building. It wrecked part of the handsome interior and blew out many windows. The firm's chief clerk was among the thirty killed. Hundreds more were injured in the streets. Jack's son, Junius, was cut by flying glass while sitting at his desk, but after treatment calmly went off to keep a luncheon engagement. "Bolshevik" enemies of the firm's reactionary policies were held responsible for the outrage, but the culprits were never identified. For several years the windows at 23 Wall would be screened by steel wire and security heavily reinforced.

The firm absorbed this shock as smoothly as the upheavals and national disenchantment following victory in Europe. The country was racked by steel and railroad strikes, the cost of living soared, unemployment shot up to 12 percent, and America found itself in the grip of its sharpest depression in many years. Wholesale price levels dropped by an alarming 40 percent in nine months, and the Fed had a struggle to tighten the money supply.

With its massive capital reserves J. P. Morgan & Co. not only rode out the storm but was poised to take advantage of an era of

317

unprecedented prosperity and "open market operations" once the crippled, disillusioned Wilson had left the scene. Squalid Warren Harding presented no more threat to bullish Wall Street in the freewheeling twenties than his successors, Coolidge and Hoover. At the height of the 1920 crisis, the firm corrected one of Pierpont's historic blunders. With General Motors shares slumping, Durant needed to be rescued from yet another cash crisis. J. P. Morgan & Co. preferred to link up with Pierre du Pont and oust Durant by buying a majority holding. For a one-year loan of only $4 million at 8 percent the firm secured the bluest of chips, one that would improve still more after G.M. combined with Standard Oil to manufacture and market ethyl gasoline. A similar onslaught on the Ford Motor Company, which had laid off thousands of its workers and owed millions in taxes and overdue loans, was less successful. A Morgan vice-president, bulging briefcase in hand, had confidently hurried off to Detroit with the offer of a huge loan to refinance. He was shown the door by Henry Ford, who thought the conditions oppressive. Within a few months the Lizzies were back in full production.

This was the firm's only setback in the postwar decade, aside from having to cut its losses and withdraw from the now doomed international shipping cartel. Foreign government loans were issued to Italy (Lamont went to Rome and arranged a $100 million bond issue for Mussolini in 1925, yielding the firm nearly five million in profits and commission), to Cuba, the Argentine, Japan, and Australia. Through various affiliates it also acquired valuable oil rights in Mexico, a stake in Chilean nitrates, and, with the Guggenheims, a footing in world copper concessions.

On the domestic front it lent almost unlimited cash, understandably ignoring the Federal Reserve Board, whose erratic policies of first reducing interest rates and then appealing to the private banks to lend less for speculation, failed to check the Stock Exchange's almost delirious buoyancy. Sitting at their rolltop desks, Jack and his associates had no need to employ the vulgar tactics of one huckster who reminded a nervous client, "Remember that Christ Himself took a chance."

Throughout the twenties they sold more securities than anyone else in America. Jack became chairman of U. S. Steel after

Judge Gary's death in 1927, and the firm also had extensive holdings in General Electric, International Harvester, and the Radio Corporation of America, which soared to $549 a share before the crash. On New Year's Eve 1928, each of the partners drew a bonus of a million dollars over and above their handsome salaries. Next day the firm formed the United Corporation with gigantic interests in hydroelectric plants and the supply of public utilities to many cities. In June, after promoting the Allegheny Corporation's mighty railroad issues, it merged Fleishmann, Royal Baking, and other retail food concerns into Standard Brands Inc., generously issuing stock at below market prices to certain private subscribers after disposing of its own option warrants for a profit of over $8 million. Among those favored were Calvin Coolidge, Pershing, Lindbergh, and Alfred P. Sloan of General Motors. The beneficiaries, described loftily by Jack Morgan as "men of affairs and position," also included Bernard M. Baruch, who picked up a useful wad of 4,000 shares.

As chairman, Jack lacked Pierpont's dominant personality and his unique flair for innovating and executing bold financial moves. He was also far readier to delegate authority. Although easygoing, if at times peppery and arrogantly disdainful of criticism, he was no mere figurehead and had revealed good business sense at several important conferences on reparations. Nevertheless, in Wall Street and the money centers of Europe he was generally considered a second-rater who had inherited little more than a proud name, a tidy fortune, and a remarkable physical resemblance to his celebrated parent.

The death of his wife in 1926 from sleeping sickness was a cruel blow. He had been a devoted husband and never indulged in liaisons. Like his father, he was a regular churchgoer, but took no part in Episcopal conventions. He once bought a Tintoretto and he paid a Berlin dealer nearly $2 million for a cache of antique watches, but could not be regarded as a serious collector. He showed little interest in old Bibles, illuminated manuscripts, or rare first editions. His literary taste was largely restricted to the latest detective stories, which he devoured during his frequent cruises in *Corsair* after becoming commodore of the New York

Yacht Club. In February 1924 he incorporated and endowed the Pierpont Morgan Library "as a memorial to my father and for the use of scholars," later adding an annex on the site of 219 Madison Avenue after that house was demolished. Belle Greene remained an active director until her retirement almost a quarter of a century later.

A few years after his mother's death Jack sold Cragston, which became a yacht and country club until it was destroyed by fire. He had long preferred his fifty-six-room house at Glen Cove, Long Island. He seldom missed visiting England for several months each summer. He enjoyed dukes far more than bishops. He bought himself a Mayfair mansion in Grosvenor Square and also Wall End, a delightful country house standing in some four hundred acres between Watford and Radlett. At his lodge in Angus he entertained society, often with a royal sprinkling, for lavish grouse shooting parties. Among the regular guns were two aristocratic new recruits to the London office, which had moved to more spacious premises at 23 Great Winchester Street, his nephew, Lord Harcourt, and Lord Charles Cavendish, the son of his close friend, the Duke of Devonshire.

When the stock market first started to crack in the fall of '29, he saw no reason to cancel his order to build *Corsair IV* at a cost of $2.5 million. Forty-one feet longer than her predecessor (which he planned to present to the government), she would be the largest and most luxurious private yacht afloat; 3,083 tons, with 6,000 horsepower electroturbine engines and a steaming radius of 25,000 miles. He was visiting England while she was being built on the Kennebec River, Maine, and did not return until November.

On Black Thursday, October 24, 1929, Tom Lamont called a meeting in Jack's office with Charles Mitchell, new chairman of the National City Bank, Albert Wiggin of Chase National, William Potter of Guaranty Trust, and George F. Baker, Jr., of First National. They were rumored to have put together a multimillion dollar "rescue" pool. The actual figure was probably under $50 million. It failed to shore up the market and had no more lasting effect than a groin hastily erected to protect a private beach while a tidal wave engulfs its neighbors. If Wall Street, recalling the historic meeting in Pierpont Morgan's Library, expected a Second Coming, it was sadly disappointed. Sixteen and a half million shares were unloaded in a single day of panic selling. After a brief lull, thanks to oversanguine reports of the bankers' consortium, the market slipped again, at least $25 billion being written off paper values.

Jack returned to the States to hysterical accusations that the firm was immunized by its past profits. One cartoon depicted him buying a rag doll from a pushcart hawker: it was captioned, "Helping to turn the tide." The *New Yorker* commented ironically, "Thousands of minor clerks and small tradespeople, hearing faint noises of railroads they had never seen, mines they had never worked, steel they had never tempered, fled before the terror of the dark. Then came the voices. Two hundred and five for twenty-five thousand Steel, said Morgan, gritting his teeth."

In fact, the firm was itself among the walking wounded, although the partners would never be observed in the long lines of hungry unemployed. Its net worth, assessed at $118 million in the fall of '29, declined to less than half within the next three years. Over that same bleak period, U. S. Steel stock would drop from a buoyant 261 to 21; and G.E.C. slumped from close on 400 to under 70. The slide was paralleled by a collapse in foreign securities, with several Latin American governments defaulting. Once again the finger was pointed at unbridled banking power.

Jack's sumptuous new yacht inevitably encouraged adverse publicity. His appearance before the Senate's Subcommittee on Banking and Currency did not improve his image. "We have made many mistakes (who has not during the past five years?), but our mistakes have been errors of judgment and not of principle," he recited from a handwritten sheet. But in the prevailing climate of agony and disillusionment his offhand superior manner made an unfortunate impression. He had to admit with obvious impatience that he had "no idea" how many directorships he and his partners held. Counsel drily informed him that the figure was 167 in corporations representing aggregate assets of some twenty billion dollars.

"What assurance has a depositor of the solvency of Morgan & Co.?" he was asked.

"Faith." It failed to register with anything like his father's dignified insistence on "Character" in replying to Samuel Untermyer.

"Has any public statement ever been made . . . since the Elder Morgan testified before the Pujo Committee twenty years ago?"

"No," he retorted stiffly. "That was the only public statement we have ever made about anything."

The firm was soon jolted by Franklin D. Roosevelt's new legislation prohibiting commercial banks from owning common stock or underwriting and selling corporate bonds to their customers. All security issues would have to be registered with the federal government and full accountability enforced by heavy penalties. With the virtual outlawing of holding companies, J. P. Morgan & Co. was now faced with the stark choice between private deposit banking and its considerable turnover in underwriting securities.

It elected to continue exclusively as a commercial deposit bank. Jack's older son would remain on the board with his father, Lamont, and other senior partners. His younger brother, Henry, departed with two directors to start up in investment banking in the original tradition of Peabody and Junius Morgan. It was the friendliest of partings. The new firm of Morgan Stanley was capitalized at a modest $7.5 million and at once started offering a lucrative series of utility and telephone company issues. (Over almost half a century it has become a force in corporate finance, real estate, and brokerage, with a deserved reputation for advising clients on mergers, long-term planning, and overseas markets.)

Jack soon stepped down from the parent firm in favor of Tom Lamont. He laid up *Corsair IV* for reasons of economy and also sold many of his father's miniatures and a number of paintings, including the Fra Angelico that had led to Roger Fry's departure from the museum. He was still a man of enormous personal wealth but could no longer ignore a heavy increase in surtax and death duties, which impelled him to settle much of his fortune on his children, with the lion's share going to his two sons.

In 1940 J. P. Morgan & Co. Inc. offered stock to the public for the first time in its long history. It then held an estimated $600 million in deposits. Two years later it was admitted to membership in the Federal Reserve system. The incorporation of the New York firm had made it necessary for the London house of Morgan Grenfell to become a limited liability company itself, with 23 Wall retaining only a minority shareholding.

Soon after the outbreak of World War II, *Corsair* was presented to the Royal Navy for service as a patrol vessel. In March 1940, Anne Morgan, then in her late sixties, sailed to France with a corps of women volunteers to join the headquarters of the American Friends of France. She helped in the evacuation of thousands of French and Belgian refugees and led an ambulance unit under heavy artillery fire. After her death in 1952, a plaque was dedicated to her memory in Les Invalides. Her brother, Junius, returned to the U.S. for naval service and became a destroyer captain.

Jack, who had been ailing for some years, died in 1943. His net estate was appraised at $4,642,791. In 1949 the Glen Cove mansion was taken over for a while by the Soviet Delegation to the U.N. It was sold two years later. His house at Madison Avenue and Thirty-seventh was acquired by the United Lutheran Church in America.

Junius, a quiet-spoken man who puffed thoughtfully at his pipe and preferred sailing and duck-shooting to the Anglo-American social circus, remained a vice-president in the firm, under H. P. Davison. His younger brother, Henry, continued as treasurer and then advisory partner of Morgan Stanley, but he gave up most of his leisure to his duties as commodore of the New York Yacht Club and a very active chairmanship of the Pierpont Morgan Library's board of trustees.

In 1959, following a sharp reduction of the Federal Reserve market, the Morgan Guaranty Trust Company of New York was formed by the merger of the Trust with the holding company of J. P. Morgan & Co. Inc. The main office is still located at 23 Wall with a connecting thirty-eight-story building at 15 Broad Street. Firmly established among the five most powerful American banks, its offices and subsidiaries in all the world's money centers also handle large-scale foreign exchange, Eurobond underwriting, project finance, and trust services. It has over 12,000 employees. The latest available figures disclose assets exceeding $53 billion.

The bank is a daily reminder of the Wall Street giant. Many New Yorkers still pause before the great library or admire his treasures in the Metropolitan Museum. But romantics will search in vain for Maxine Elliott's enchanting theater on Thirty-ninth Street. It was reduced to rubble after serving Columbia Broadcasting as a television studio.

The City of London also carries echoes of the still-potent legend. A few hundred yards from the main offices of Morgan Grenfell, now one of the world's premier merchant banks, an imposing new building in Lombard Street houses the headquarters of the Morgan Guaranty Trust Company in the United Kingdom. By a happy geographical coincidence, the foreground is favored by the fine statue of George Peabody, who formally appointed Pierpont's father as his partner on that fateful first day of October, 1854.

The Morgan family is no longer a financial dynasty. For many years the bank's affairs have been directed by others, rightly proud of a celebrated name and tradition, but with far more regard for significant social and political change than J. P. Morgan, so often to his cost, was ever willing to accept.

BIBLIOGRAPHY

Apart from contemporary newspaper files, court records and miscellaneous material from many varied quarters, including Morgan Grenfell & Co., whose excellent short history of the firm was privately printed in 1959, special acknowledgment is due to Herbert L. Satterlee's Official Life, *J. Pierpont Morgan* (Macmillan, 1939). Other biographical sources are *The House of Morgan* by Lewis Corey (G. Howard Watt, 1930); *The Life Story of J. Pierpont Morgan* by Carl Hovey (Heinemann, 1913); *The Great Pierpont Morgan* by F. L. Allen (Harper, 1949); *Morgan the Magnificent* by John K. Winkler (Knopf, 1931); *The House of Morgan* by E. P. Hoyt (Dodd, Mead, 1966); *The Incredible Pierpont Morgan* by Cass Canfield (Hamish Hamilton, 1974); and *Corsair* by Andrew Sinclair (Weidenfeld & Nicolson, 1981). Two reference works of special value were *Maxine* by Diana Forbes-Robertson (Hamish Hamilton, 1964) and *The Letters of Roger Fry*, edited by D. Sutton (Chatto & Windus, 1972).

Other works consulted or quoted include:

Adams, James T. *Founding of New England,* 1923.
Adler, Cyrus. *Jacob Schiff: His Life and Letters,* 1928.
Agnew, Geoffrey (Ed.). *Agnew's 1817–1967,* 1967.
Anderson, Roy, *White Star,* 1964.
Baruch, Bernard. *My Own Story,* 1958.
Beard, Charles and Mary. *The Rise of American Civilization,* 1927.

325

Beebe, Lucius. *The Big Spenders,* 1966.

Beer, Thomas. *The Mauve Decade,* 1926.

Behrman, S. N. *Duveen,* 1952.

Birmingham, Stephen. *Our Crowd,* 1967.

Bishop, J. B. *Theodore Roosevelt and His Times,* 1920.

Boorstin, Daniel J. *The Americans,* Vol. I, 1958.

Brough, James. *The Ford Dynasty,* 1978.

Clews, Henry. *50 Years in Wall Street,* 1908.

Cortesi, Salvatore. *My 30 Years of Friendships,* 1927.

Crewe, Quentin. *The Frontiers of Privilege,* 1961.

Curry, J. L. M. *George Peabody,* 1898.

Depew, Chauncey. *My Memories of Eighty Years,* 1922.

Duveen, J. H. *Collections and Recollections,* 1936.

Emden, Paul. *Money Powers of Europe,* 1937.

Emerson, Barbara. *Leopold II of the Belgians,* 1979.

Goodwin, Nat C. *Nat Goodwin's Book,* 1914.

Gunther, John. *Inside U.S.A.,* 1947.

Hoyt, E. P. *The Vanderbilts and their Fortunes,* 1962.

Hutchinson, T. *History of the Colony and Province of Massachu-setts Bay,* 1936.

Jackson, Stanley. *The Savoy,* 1964.

———. *Inside Monte Carlo,* 1975.

Josephson, Matthew. *The Robber Barons,* 1934.

———. *Edison, 1959.*

Lichtervelde, Louis de. *Leopold of the Belgians,* 1929.

Lundberg, F. *America's Sixty Families,* 1937.

Mayer, Martin. *The Bankers,* 1974.

Morris, Richard B. *Encyclopaedia of American History,* 1953.

Myers, Gustavus. *History of the Great American Fortunes,* 1936.

Nicolson, Harold. *Dwight Morrow,* 1935.

Parker, George F. *Recollections of Grover Cleveland,* 1909.

Pringle, Henry F. *Theodore Roosevelt,* 1931.

Rainsford, William S. *The Story of a Varied Life,* 1922.

Roth, Cecil. *The Magnificent Rothschilds,* 1939.

Scott, James B. *Robert Bacon—Life and Letters,* 1924.

Scroggs, Oscar. *Filibusters and Financiers,* 1916.

Steichen, E. *A Life in Photography,* 1963.

Tarbell, Ida M. *Elbert H. Gary,* 1933.

Thomas, G. and Morgan-Witts, M. *The Day the Bubble Burst,* 1979.

Tomkins, Calvin. *Merchants and Masterpieces,* 1970.

Tully, Andrew. *Era of Elegance,* 1947.

Wade, Wyn Craig. *The Titanic,* 1980.

Wasson, R. G. *The Hall Carbine Affair,* 1948.

Weeden, William B. *Economic & Social History of New England,* 1891.

Winkler, John K. *The First Billion,* 1934.

Woolf, Virginia. *Roger Fry,* 1940.

The assistance of the Pierpont Morgan Library is gratefully acknowledged for permission to reproduce illustrations as well as for much helpful information.

INDEX

Agnew's, 110, 209-10, 249-50
Aetna Insurance Co., 29, 32
Ascoli Cope, 241, 252
Astor, Caroline, 109, 120, 129, 164
Astor, John Jacob, 27, 40

Bacon, Robert, 172-80, 182, 193,
    199, 212 *seq.*, 240, 255, 272, 280,
    284, 300, 312, 316
Baker, George F., 216, 233, 245, 266
    seq.
Baring Brothers, 36, 42, 49, 76, 101,
    156-57
Baruch, Bernard, 105, 173-74, 221,
    267-68, 289, 317, 319
Belmont, August, 76, 96, 99, 121-23,
    129, 166, 171-80, 184, 302
Bennett, James Gordon, 126, 169
Bethlehem Steel, 222, 228-29, 237
Bowdoin, George S., 53, 58, 62, 131,
    136, 143-44, 312
Bryan, William J., 167, 172, 179,
    181-87, 209, 220, 280, 299,
    301-2, 311
Burns, Walter Hayes, 78, 110-12,
    115, 138, 159, 219, 225

Canterbury, Archbishop of (Randall
    Davidson), 241-42

Carnegie, Andrew, 83-87, 104-5,
    125, 147, 167-68, 191 *seq.,* 236
Castellane, Boni de, 163
Choate, Joseph P., 93, 136-37, 158,
    294, 305, 312
Clarke, Sir Purdon, 245-46
Cleveland, Grover, 136-37, 147, 164
    seq.
Cooke, Jay, 65-66, 95-96, 98-103
Corbin, Abel, 91
Corsair IV, 320-23
Cortesi, Salvatore, 252-53
Coster, Charles, 108, 112, 139,
    143-44, 199, 219
Crédit Mobilier, scandal of, 84-85,
    99, 137

Dabney, Charles H., 53, 55, 60, 70,
    75 *seq.*
Dabney, C. W., 43
Dabney, Morgan & Co., 75-97
Davison, Henry P., 266-68, 281-82,
    309, 315-16
Depew, Chauncey, 82-83, 85-87,
    115-22, 136, 138-42, 147-49,
    160, 164, 189, 196, 256
Devonshire, Duchess of
    (Gainsborough's), 110, 209-10
Drew, Daniel, 31, 37, 59, 73, 83, 103f

Drexel & Co., 66, 95-97
Drexel, Morgan & Co., 97-171
Du Pont, Pierre, 318
Durant, William C., 105, 287-89, 318
Duveen, Henry, 128, 226, 248-50, 269, 289-90
Duveen, Joseph (Lord), 249-50

Edison, Thomas A., 83, 92, 125-30, 150-51, 158-59
Edward VII, King, 155, 170, 197, 214-15, 223, 227 *seq.*, 261-62, 297
Elliott, Maxine, 195-97, 228, 235, 279-80, 324

Fabbri, E. P., 108, 112, 125, 143
Federal Reserve, 308-9, 314 *seq.*
Field, Cyrus W., 122, 137
Fisk, Jim, 59, 65, 83, 88-91, 99
Ford, Henry, 287-88, 318
Franco-Prussian War Loan, 94-95
Frick, Henry C., 167-68, 200, 206, 246-47, 273-75, 284, 314
Fry, Roger, 245-47, 290-91, 322

Gary, Judge Elbert, 192 *seq.*, 266 *seq.*, 274 *seq.*, 283-84, 302-3, 309, 319
Gates, John W., 191 *seq.*, 307
Goodwin, Jim, 38, 42, 45, 52-53, 58, 68-70, 75, 81, 87, 97
Goodwin, Nat, 195-96, 279-80
Gould, George Jay, 149, 163, 186, 281, 289
Gould, Jay, 59, 73, 83-91, 102-3, 122, 125, 135, 137, 142-44, 149, 162-63
Grant, Ulysses S., 86, 91, 96, 101, 112
Green, Judge Ashbel, 140-42
Greene, Belle, 259-60, 269, 273, 293-96, 312, 320
Guggenheims, the, 41, 253, 289

Hall, Mayor Oakey, 83
Hankey, Thomson, 41, 49, 56-57
Hanna, Mark, 187-88, 190, 203, 216, 230, 237-38

Harcourt, Lewis (Viscount), 225, 262
Harriman, E. H., 91-92, 103-5, 124, 148, 166, 180, 185-87, 199, 208, 255-57, 267, 282
Havemeyer, Henry O., 182, 314
Heinze, F. A., 263, 266
Herter, Christian, 127-28
Hill, James J., 180-82, 208 *seq.*
Huntington, Collis P., 40, 76, 96, 149

Insull, Samuel, 130, 151, 159f
Ismay, Bruce, 210, 227, 300

Keene, James R., 103, 207, 213, 221, 267
Ketchum, Edward, 54, 58, 68, 70, 73-76, 92
Ketchum, Morris, 31-32, 54, 62, 75
Kitchener, Lord, 210, 291-92, 296-97, 300, 312
Kuhn Loeb & Co., 41, 86, 99, 123-24, 161, 180, 185, 308

Lamont, Thomas W., 233, 294, 309, 315-16, 318, 320-22
Lanier, Charles, 136-37, 157, 294
Ledyard, Lewis Cass, 136, 272-75, 308
Leopold II, King, 170, 253-55, 312

McKim, Charles F., 202, 258
McKinley, William B., 187 *seq.*, 216
McLeod, Archibald, 161
Mann, Col. W., 235-36
Markoe, Dr. James, 164-66, 182, 188, 194-95, 268, 313
Metropolitan Museum of Art, 93, 146, 301 *seq.*
Mills, Darius O., 129, 151, 159, 162
Moore, William H., 192, 200
Morgan, Amelia Sturges (Mimi), 54-55, 58-62, 66-70, 77, 175, 313
Morgan, Anne, 107, 136, 145, 163, 223, 237, 285-86, 313, 316, 323
Morgan, Frances Tracy (Fanny), 72-73, 77 *seq.*
Morgan, Henry Sturgis, 217, 322-23
Morgan, J. Pierpont, Jr. (Jack), 77, 82, 115, 121, 127, 136, 138, 142,

152, 160-61, 175, 186, 189,
223-26, 260, 269, 271, 284, 294,
298, 311 *seq.*
Morgan, J. Pierpont, Sr.
First years, 35-43
Early travels, 43-45
Education (Europe), 47-52
Business apprenticeship, 53-62
Hall Carbine affair, 67-68
Gold, "a corner" in, 73-75
First marriage, 68-70
Second marriage, 77 *seq.*
Albany & Susquehanna Rail
coup, 88-90
Buys "Cragston," Highland
Falls, 98 *seq.*
First govt. bond promotion, 101-2
First visit to Karnak, 111
Womanizing, 113 *seq.*
Sells Vanderbilt New York
Central stock, 116-22
Edison Electric Light Co., 125-26
Moves into 219 Madison Avenue,
127 *seq.*
Corsair I, 131 *seq.*
Corsair II, 153 *seq.*
Corsair III, 190 *seq.*
Railroads, "Gentlemen's
Agreement," 148-50
Death of father, 152-53
Panama Canal Co., 157-58
Silver-gold crisis, 170-80
J. P. Morgan & Co. created, 171
seq.
Union Pacific Railroad, 185-86
Buys Cape Uncas estate, 188-89
United States Steel, 198 *seq.*
Maxine Elliott liaison, 195-97,
279-80
Theodore Roosevelt, relations
with, (*see* Roosevelt)
Shipping cartel, 206, 210, 216, 227
seq., 258, 277, 315, 318
Gainsborough's Duchess of
Devonshire, buys, 209-10
Northern Pacific Railroad deal,
208 *seq.*
Northern Securities, 214-16, 220
seq., 235, 238, 240, 304
Anthracite mining strike, 228-32

Pierpont Morgan Library, 202,
258-60, 313, 320, 323-24
Metropolitan Museum, 93, 242
seq.
Panama Canal syndicate, 239-40
Collector and connoisseur, 245
seq.
Crisis of 1907, 265-77
Tennessee C. I. & R. coup,
272-75
Egyptologist, 291 *seq.*
General Motors, 287-89
Titanic, 296-98, 300-1
Pujo Committee investigation,
304-8
Last illness and death, 310-12
Estate, 313-14
Morgan, Joseph, 27-37
Morgan, Juliet (Hamilton), 47, 94,
97, 160, 189, 210, 292
Morgan, Juliet Pierpont, 31 *seq.*
Morgan, Junius Spencer, 27, 30-153
Morgan, Junius Spencer II, 37,
42-43, 47, 57
Morgan, Junius Spencer III, 160,
217, 316-17, 322-23
Morgan, Louisa (Satterlee), 77, 82,
145, 203 *seq.*
Morgan, Mary (Burns), 37, 78, 110,
225-26, 292
Morgan, Miles, 22-27, 47
Morgan Grenfell & Co., 294 *seq.*,
323-24
Morgan Guaranty Trust Co.,
323-24
Morgan Stanley & Co., 322-23
Morrow, Dwight, 233, 295, 315
Morton, Levi J., 42, 86, 101-2, 115,
147, 187

Peabody, George, 36-37, 41-46, 52,
56-57, 61, 66, 71-72, 76, 93, 324
Peary, Cdr. Robert, 297
Perkins, George W., 199-200,
221-22, 233-34, 241, 256-57,
267, 270, 275, 281, 288
Pierpont, Rev. John, 30-34, 39, 48,
63, 78, 285
Pinkertons, 110, 168, 209
Pius X, Pope, 253, 260, 312

Pujo Committee, 304-8
Pulitzer, Joseph, 172, 184, 209, 240, 312
Pynchon, William, 24, 26

Rainsford, Dr. William S., 131-34, 146, 237
Ramsey, Joseph H., 88-90
Roberts, George H., 137-41, 149, 161
Rockefeller, John D., 83, 87-88, 125, 136, 168, 184, 214
Rockefeller, William, 125, 136, 164, 184, 196, 214, 304-5
Rogers, H. H., 193, 211, 262, 304
Roosevelt, Theodore, 174, 190, 203, 216, 218 *seq.*
Rothschild, Alfred de, 155-56, 186, 196, 210, 215, 225, 280, 291
Rothschild, N. M. & Co., 37, 41, 47, 94-95, 115, 155, 157
Russell, Lillian, 195
Ryan, Thomas F., 258, 267, 276, 302, 306-7

Sage, Russell, 103, 122, 137
Satterlee, Herbert L., 63, 74, 203, 280, 298 *seq.*
Schiff, Jacob H., 123-24, 161, 185-88, 212 *seq.*, 258
Schwab, Charles M., 167-68, 200 *seq.*, 316-17
Seligman, Jacques, 250, 301
Seligman, Jesse, 157-58
Seligman, Joseph, 41, 86, 115
Sherry, Louis, 160, 164, 216, 220, 242, 264
Sloan, Samuel, 82, 89

Spencer, Samuel, 149
Standard Oil Corp. *see* Rockefellers
Stanford, Leland, 40, 85
Steele, Charles, 136, 212, 233, 241, 289
Steichen, Edward, 234-35
Stetson, Francis L., 172, 288, 305
Stewart, Alexander T., 109
Stillman, James A., 150, 184, 186, 266 *seq.*, 304

Taft, William Howard, 280 *seq.*
Thorne, Oakleigh, 266-69
Titanic, 296-301
Twain, Mark, 246, 255f

U. S. Steel Trust, 198 *seq.*
Untermyer, Samuel, 261, 305 *seq.*

Vanderbilt, Commodore C., 22, 28, 31, 40, 46, 58-59, 65, 71 *seq.*, 88-91, 103, 112
Vanderbilt, William B., 73, 85, 112, 114-27, 137-42
Vanderbilt, "Willie K.," 112, 120, 142, 153, 162-63
Villard, Henry, 126, 136-37, 150-51, 159

Widener, Peter, 207, 211, 233, 280, 284, 314
Wilhelm II, Emperor, 220, 228, 233, 312
Wilson, Woodrow, 299-304, 309, 316-18
Winthrop, Governor John, 21-25
Worth's of Paris, 97, 202